AF539196

Legal Safeguards for Defence Personnel

Legal Safeguards for Defence Personnel

A Comprehensive Treatise on the Legal Safeguards and Privileges for Defence Personnel

Air Cmde Ranvir Kumar, AVSM
Former Judge Advocate General (Air)

Manas Publications
New Delhi-110002 (INDIA)

MANAS PUBLICATIONS
(We convert Fighters into Writers)
(Publishers, Distributors, Importers & Exporters)
4402/5-A, Ansari Road (Opp. HDFC Bank)
Darya Ganj, New Delhi-110 002 (India)
Off. 23260783, 23265523, Res. 23842660
Fax: 011-23272766
E-mail: manaspublications@gmail.com
manaspublications@yahoo.com

2nd Impression 2014 (FP - 2007)

ISBN 978-81-7049-277-7
₹ 495/-

Designed at
Manas Publications

Printed in India at
HS Offset, Delhi and published by Mrs Suman Lata for
Manas Publications, 4402/5-A, Ansari Road,
(Opp. HDFC Bank),
Darya Ganj, New Delhi-110 002 (INDIA)

Acknowledgements

It is good grace to acknowledge the gratitude where rightfully due. Therefore, my sincere thanks to:

Air Force Association, Race Course, New Delhi, Directorate General of Rehabilitation and Resettlement, Wg. Cdr. Ajay Bhalla, Advocate Supreme Court and Shri D.R. Ratra for rendering help and assistance to get the relevant material and for meticulously keyboarding the manuscript and the endless corrections thereafter.

And last but not the least, to TANYA and SOHAM, my grandchildren, who gave me company and cheers at all odd times, thus rejuvenating me to see this book through.

Air Cmde R.V. Kumar

AVSM (Retd)

Preface

My close association with the Armed Forces for over three decades brought out one stark realty. That is, these members are highly disciplined, efficient, brave and dedicated but when it comes to their personal matters, they are totally casual & indifferent. Particularly, their knowledge about the law and the legal procedures were highly insufficient. A mere mention about the courts or even a notice, or summon far less a warrant was sufficient to send shiver down their spine making them rush to the nearest office of the J.A.G. or any of his deputies or even less trained legally qualified officers. The situation about the superior was no better. They were not only ignorant but they also did not realize the importance of the courts. One commander when I mentioned to him about the irregularity in the composition of a court martial and told him that immediately the courts will strike it down as illegal. He flared-up retarded, as how was that possible, as courts have nothing to do with us because we were members of the Armed Forces.

On the part of the legal professions, their knowledge about the Armed Forces, their procedures, terminology, customs etc. were equally poor and insufficient. It, thus occured to me, if after retirement I could write something to bridge this gap, it would be a great service to the members of the Armed Forces as well as the bar. As I went along, I found a lot of relevant things like law of litigations, limitations arrest, choice of court, succession, pension, houses, rent, customs and other duties etc. apart from the host of Monetary Awards and other privileges granted by the Central government as well as State governments. The addition of case law at the end of each chapter was also found to be rewarding.

It is hoped that this will serve the purpose (or purposes as has been intended), I will find it highly rewarding, if it will be found useful to the members of the Armed Forces as well as legal profession. Any mistake or omission in work of this nature is bound to creep in advertently or inadvertently. Any suggestion or correction in this regard will be highly valued and acknowledged.

Air Cmde Ranvir Kumar

Contents

1

Privileges in Matters of Litigation

The Indian Soldiers (Litigation) Act, 1925, the rules and notifications made and issued under the Act, deal exclusively with safeguarding the interests of serving soldiers in matters of litigation in Civil Courts.

The term soldier for the purpose of this Act, means any person subject to the Army Act, 1950 or the Air Force Act 1950 or the Navy Act, 1957. It may be noted that the word soldier does not signify soldier or airman as it is commonly understood in the services, but means all persons subject to these Acts including officers and for all such persons who are subject to the Army Act/the Navy Act/the Air Force Act. By looking in the said Act, it would be seen that even persons who are not members of the regular Forces, but belong to some other categories like Reserve Forces, Territorial Army, Regular Air force Reserve, Air Defence Reserve, Auxiliary Air Force, Indian Naval Reserve Force and even certain classes of civilians on active service, are also subject to these Acts under certain circumstances. Placed under those circumstances, these personnel would also be eligible for priviledges under the Indian Soldiers (Litigation) Act, 1925.

The Act confers three important priviledges in matters of civil litigation on the members of the armed forces. These are:-

(a) Suspension of proceedings;

(b) Postponement of proceedings;

(c) Setting aside the decrees, orders, judgments, in cases where such decrees, orders or judgments were passed when the soldier was serving under special conditions".

Suspension of Proceedings

Section 6 of the Indian Soldiers (Litigations) Act, 1925 impose a duty on all Courts that where any proceedings are pending before them and they have reasons to believe that the soldier who is a party to the proceedings, is unable to appear therein, and is not represented by any person duly authorized to appear, plead or act on his behalf, they shall suspend the proceedings. Thereafter they are to give notice to the prescribed authority c/o the G.O.C-in-C of the Command, or the area in which the Court is situated, to enquire whether the soldier is serving; under special conditions and whether postponement of the proceedings is necessary in the interests of justice. In case of persons subject to the Air Force Act, 1950, the notice is to be given to the prescribed authority care of the Air Officer (Personnel), Air Headquarters, New Delhi. The term "Party to any proceeding" appears to mean a person who is actually impleaded in the proceedings as defendant, or respondent, as the case may be. The prescribed authority means the authority competent to sanction leave of absence to the soldier.

The prescribed authority on receipt of such notice, is to send a reply to the Court within two months, if the soldier is resident of the District in which the Court is situated, and in any other case within three months from the date of the issue of such notice. Although, the Act does not lay down the stage at which the notice should be issued by the Court, but it is submitted that it will be appropriate to issue the notice only after the summons have been served. In this way the soldier will get prior intimation about the suit, and if he so chooses, he will be in a position to take steps to get himself adequately represented in the suit, thus avoiding any unnecessary delay consequent on the issue of the notice.

The Collector of the District in which the soldier ordinarily resides or has property, has also been empowered by Section 5 of the Indian Soldiers (Litigation) Act, 1925 to certify to the Court that he has reasons to believe that the soldier who is a party to the proceedings, is unable to appear therein, and if not represented, the Court should make a reference to the prescribed authority of the soldier, as required by Section 6 of the Indian Soldiers (Litigation) Act, 1925.

It would thus be seen, that in case a soldier is unable to appear in the proceedings, and is not represented by anybody on his behalf, the Court has to suspend the proceedings, the only over-riding condition being that the Court must have reasons to believe that the soldier is unable to appear therein. Therefore, in order to enable the Court to have such belief, it is advisable for an individual that, when he receives a notice, summons or any other process from the Court or intimation about a suit having been instituted against him in a Court, and if he has not authorized any person to represent him, he should forthwith address a communication to the Court stating that he is unable to appear in the Court and request that the Court may give a notice to the prescribed authority under Section 6 of the Indian Soldiers (Litigation) Act, 1925. If this is done, the Court shall suspend the proceedings. Therefore, in case the soldier so desires, the privilege of getting the proceedings suspended is achieved.

In this connection, it is also useful to note that the Indian Soldiers (Litigation) Act, 1925 vide Section 4 has cast a duty on every party presenting any *plaint,* application or appeal before any Court, against a soldier, that where he has reason to believe that such solider is a soldier serving under special conditions, he must state this fact in the plaint, application or appeal.

It would be noticed that the suspension of proceedings is irrespective of the fact whether the soldier is or is not serving under special conditions at the time of the institution of the suit or other proceedings is basically to protect the interests of an absent soldier, when he is unable to appear in the proceedings and is not represented by any person authorized to appear, plead or act on his behalf.

The importance of this privilege can be visualized, when the position of a soldier is compared less with that of his civilian counter-part in whose case, if after due notice, he does not appear before the Court, the case can be decided ex-parte.

Prior to 1970, for the purposes of this Act, the" Court" meant Civil or Revenue Court. Since neither the word 'Civil Court nor 'Revenue Court had been defined in the Act, nor it had been defined in the General Clauses Act. Difficulties arose in certain cases, in determining whether a particular Court or Tribunal would come within the meaning of the term Civil or Revenue Court or not, as to attract the application of the Act. Further the definition was restricted, and that restricted the nature of Tribunals where these priviledges could be claimed. In order to enlarge its scope, the definition of the word 'Court' has been amended vide The Indian Soldiers (Litigation) Amendment Act, 1970. section 2(1) (a) of the Amending Act (Act 23 of 1970), the term 'Court' has been defined to mean "a Court other than criminal Court" and includes any such Tribunal or other authority as may be specified by the Central Government by notification in the official gazette, being a tribunal or authority which is empowered by law to receive evidence on any matter pending before it and on the basis of such evidence to determine after bearing the parties before it, the rights and obligations of the parties in relation to such matter. By virtue of the amendment, therefore, the definition has been enlarged to include all Court other than criminal Court. Also Central Government by notification can specify any tribunal or authority to be a Court for the purpose of this Act, though strictly speaking it may not be a Court in the technical sense.

In Sub Section (2) of Section of the Act, there is also a provision of far-reaching importance so far as suspension of proceedings is concerned. According to this provision, even if a soldier is not himself a party to the proceedings, but is materially concerned in the outcome of the same, and the Court thinks that his interests are likely to be prejudiced by his inability to attend, then also the Court may suspend the proceedings and give notice thereof in the prescribed manner, to the prescribed authority.

From the definition of the word 'Court' it will be seen that the priviledges under the Act are not available in proceedings before criminal Courts. They are also not available in suit filed by a soldier with the object of enforcing a right of pre-emption. In a case where the interest of the soldier merely is of the formal nature or is identical with that of any other party to the proceedings and which is adequately represented by such other party, then the requirement of notice by the Court is not mandatory. However, it submitted that even though the requirement of notice is not mandatory in such case, it is desirable that discretion should be exercised by suspending the proceedings and issuing notice rather than exercising the discretion the other way. In many cases it may be very difficult to say whether the interest is merely of a formal nature. It may be quite material from a different angle, which at the preliminary stage may not be well appreciated, particularly when no chance has been afforded to the soldier to explain his point of view. Similarly, whether the interest of the soldier is identical with that of any other party and further, whether it is adequately represented is again a subjective assessment and is likely to cause hardship in some genuine cases, as the interest of the solider will be left at the mercy of some other party, and for whose default, the solider may suffer. The object of the legislature being to protect the interest of the absent soldier, it is submitted that the Courts even in such case, should exercise the discretion in favour of the soldier as that is not only permissible, but also is not likely to cause any injustice or hardship.

Disposal of Proceedings

As stated earlier, the Court, after giving notice to the prescribed authority and suspending the proceedings, has to wait for the reply as to whether or not the soldier is serving under special conditions and whether the postponements of the proceedings is necessary in the interests of justice. The form in which the notice is to be given by the Court to the prescribed authority, is as under:-

Notice under section 6 of the Indian soldiers (Litigation) Act, 1925

In re...No.....................................

of...

Versus

....

To

The Prescribed Authority

Care of the General Officer Commanding-in-Chief.................. Command or The Air Officer(Personnel), Air Headquarters, New Delhi

Please take notice that (upon the certificate of Collector.............. Under Section 5 of the Indian Soldiers (Litigation) Act, 1925)

(having had reason to believe) that..........son of...................................an Indian Soldier, who is a party in the above mentioned proceedings now pending in this Court and is not represented by any person duly authorized to appear, plead or act on his behalf, is; unable to appear therein, this Court has, under Section 6 of the said Act, suspended the proceedings. If, within the period prescribed in Section 8 of the said Act, no certificate is received from; *you* under Section 7 thereof, the Court will, if it thinks fit, continue the proceedings.

Given under my hand and the seal of the Court, this the...........day of

................19..........

Presiding officer of the Court
Registrar

Notes:

Strike out, whichever is not applicable.

1. The prescribed authority is the authority competent to Sanction leave of absence to an Indian Soldier. On receipt of the notice from the Court, the General Officer Commanding-in-Chief/Air Officer (Personnel) (as the case may be) shall cause the notice to be forwarded as soon as possible to the authority competent to sanction leave of absence to the Indian Soldier concerned. The time limit within which the prescribed authority's certificate should reach the Court is two months in the case a soldier resident of the district in which the Court is situated and three months in other cases (Section 8 of the Indian Soldiers (Litigation) Act, 1925, refers).
2. The service number, Rank, full name and unit of the Indian Soldier or such full service particulars as are known to the court should be stated on receipt of notice there can be two situations:-
   (a) The soldier is not serving under special conditions, and he can be spared for the proceedings in which that case, it would be desirable that the proceedings are finalized expeditiously;

   or

   (b) The soldier is serving under special conditions and the soldier cannot be spared and therefore the proceedings should be postponed.

Expeditious Disposal of Proceedings

In case where the soldier is not serving under special conditions and he can be spared for the proceedings, it would be desirable that the proceedings should be finalized expeditiously. The soldier should although his Commanding Officer, take action to move the Court for speedy disposal of the case under Section 32 of the Army/Air Force Act, 1950, Section 24 of the Navy Act, 1957.

These sections enjoin a statutory duty on all Courts whether Civil or Revenue that when they are moved under these provisions of law they should arrange as may be possible, for the hearing and the final disposal of the case within the period of the leave of the soldier/airman.

If the Court is unable for one reason or the other, to arrange for such hearing or disposal, it is under statutory obligation to record the reasons in writing for its inability to do so. Further, the soldier/airman is entitled to ask and get a copy of such reasons in writing, without payment of any Court fee either for his application or for the copy of the order. The reasons for non-disposal of the case, within the time asked for are also to be intimated by the Court to the commanding officer of the soldier concerned.

For moving the Court under these Sections all that the soldier has to do, is, to obtain a certificate from the Commanding Officer that he has been granted leave or that he has applied for leave, for the purpose of prosecuting or defending such suit or proceedings, stating the exact dates of leave granted or applied for, and present the certificate to the Court. Also for presenting the certificate before the Court, the soldier/airman is not required to pay any Court fee. The form of certificate to be given by the Commanding Officer is as follows:-

Certificate of priority of hearing

Certificate to enable the person herein named, being subject to the Army Act/Air Force Act to obtain priority Act 46 of 1950) of hearing for his case in accordance with Section 32 of the Army Act, 1950). Section 32 of the Air Force Act, 1950 (Act 46 of 1950), Section 32 of the Air

Force Act, 21950 (Act 45 of 1950) and Section 24 of the Navy Act, 1957.

I certify that No....................Rank..........................Name.... ....

Regiment/Unit....................been granted/applied for leave from...................

to................for the purpose of prosecuting/defending a suit/proceedings brought by/against him...

for........................on account of.. in the Court

of..

1. Should the Court be unable to arrange for the final disposal of the case within the above dates, I request the favour of being informed upto what date it will be nefcessary to extend the man's leave.

Station......... Commanding Officer

Date................... ....Regiment/Unit

Instructions

The soldier should hand this certificate to the Court on presenting himself. Should the Court be unable to arrange for the final disposal of the case within the above period, it should record its reasons, vide Section 32 of the Army Act, 1950, Section 32 of the Air Force Act, 1950 and Section 24 of the Navy Act, 1957.

The soldier/airman should apply for a copy of these reasons to which he is entitled free of charge, and should forward or bring them to the Commanding Officer.

It would be noticed that the provisions regarding speedy disposal of the case are applicable not only when the soldier has been granted leave but also when he has merely applied for leave, with the intention of prosecuting or defending the suit.

So far as the persons subject to the Navy Act, 1957 are concerned, more or less identical provisions have been made in this regard, under Section 24 and 25 of the Navy Act, 1957. According to Section 24 (1 to 4), the aforesaid priviledges are available in respect of litigation Civil and Revenue Courts. Vide Section 24(5), a duty has been case on all the criminal Courts to expeditiously dispose of all cases pending against persons subject to Naval Law, in the respective Courts. Vide Section 25 of the Navy Act, the Chief of Naval Staff or ;the officer Commanding of the accused, is also entitled to obtain a copy of the judgment or final orders in respect of cases against Naval personnel, without payment of any fees and without delay. Further, according to the departmental regulations for the army and the air force when the suit or proceedings cannot be disposed of with in the period of leave granted; the civil officer concerned, i.e. the Court, can extend the leave of the soldier/airman for such period, as will admit the receipt of a reply to an application to the Commanding Officer for necessary extension of leave. In such a case, however the civil officer has to report to the Commanding Officer any extension any extension of leave sanctioned by him.

Postponement of Proceedings

Where the soldier is serving under special conditions and cannot be spared and therefore postponement of the proceedings is necessary in the interest of justice, the prescribed authority should act under Section 7 of the Indian Soldiers (Litigation) Act, 1925. Under this section the prescribed authority should send the prescribed certificate to the Court within the time laid down i.e. two months when the Court is situated within the district in which the soldier is residing, and within three months in any other case, from the date of issue of the notice. The certificate is to be in the following form:-

Certificate under section 7 of the Indian soldiers (Litigation) Act, 1925

From...

To

"..

...."

No.................of.................................19

Versus

....

No...........................dated....................

Sir,

I have the honour to acknowledge receipt of your notice, dated............under Section 6 of the Indian Soldiers (Litigation) Act, 1925

(4 of 1925), in the above mentioned proceedings, and to certify under Section 7 of the said Act that................................son of.......................in respect of whom the above mentioned notice has been given, is serving under special conditions and that a postponement of the proceedings in respect of the soldier is necessary in the interests of justice.

Yours faithfully,

(Prescribed Authority)

Notes:-

(i) This certificate should be sent by post in a registered cover, or by hand, and an acknowledgement be obtained for it.

(ii) It should be addressed in the case of High Court to the Registrar of the Court, in the case of a board of Revenue to the Secretary of such Board, or in the case of Financial Commissioner to the Clerk of the Court, or in other cases, to the Presiding Officer of the Court. Once the Court receives such certificate, it is under obligation to postpone the proceedings. It has been further laid down by rule 7 of the Indian Soldiers (Litigation) Rules, that the proceedings shall remain postponed till another certificate is received from the prescribed authority to the effect, that the soldier is no longer serving under special conditions or further postponement is not necessary or till the time the soldier concerned is represented by some person duly authorized to appear, plead or act on his behalf. The certificate to be given by the prescribed authority in such a case would be as under:-

"Certificate under rule 6 of the Indian Soldiers Litigation Rule, 1938"

From

....

....

To

....

....

In re..............No...............of....19......

Versus

....

No...........................Dated..................

Sir,

I have the honour to invite a reference to my letter No..............

dated.....................and to certify under rule 6 of the Indian Soldiers (Litigation) Rules, 1938 that circumstances no longer exist for the postponement of the above mentioned (enter suit, appeal, application or other proceedings), now pending in (enter name of Court), wherein...............son of..............................an Indian Soldier, is a party.

Yours faithfully
Prescribed Authority

Notes:-

(i) The certificate should be sent by post in a registered cover, or by hand, and an acknowledgement should be obtained for it.

(ii) It should be addressed, in the case of High Court to the Registrar of the Court, or in the case of a Board of Revenue to the Secretary of such Board, or in the case of a Financial Commissioner, to the Clerk of the Court, or in other cases to the Presiding Officer of the Court.

At times, it may also happen that the soldier concerned is not actually serving under special conditions, but is on leave of absence, on termination of which, he has to start or resume service under special conditions. Even in such a case postponement of the proceedings is provided for, under Section 6 of the Indian Soldiers (Litigation) Act. For the benefit under this section a certificate from the Commanding Officer of the soldier is necessary. The commanding officer is to certify that the soldier is on leave for a period not exceeding two months and on the expiry of his leave, is to proceed on service under special conditions, or on sick leave for a period not exceeding three months, and on the expiry of his leave is to rejoin his unit with a view to proceed on service, under special conditions. Once this certificate is presented to the Court, the Court has to postpone the proceedings under Section 7 of the Soldiers (Litigation) Act.

Service under special conditions

For the purposes of this Act, the service under special conditions has been defined in Section 3, which states:-

"For the purposes of this Act, an Indian Soldier shall be deemed to be or, as the case may be, to have been serving:-

(a) Under special conditions - when he is or has been serving under war conditions, or overseas, or at any place beyond India or at any such place within India as may be specified by the Central Government by notification in the official gazette.

(b) Under war conditions - when he is or has been, at any time during the continuance of any hostilities declared by the Central Government by notification in the official gazette to constitute state of war for the purposes of this Act, or any time during a period of six months thereafter -

 (i) Serving out of India,

 (ii) Under orders to proceed on field service,

 (iii) Serving with any unit which is for the time being mobilized, or

 (iv) Serving under conditions which, in the opinion of the prescribed authority, preclude him from obtaining leave of absence to enable him to attend a Court as a party to any proceeding, or when he is or has been at any other time serving under conditional service under which he has been declared by the Central Government by notification in the official gazette to be service under war conditions and

(c) Overseas - when he is or has been serving in any place outside India (other than Sri Lanka) the; journey between that place and India is ordinarily undertaken wholly or in part by sea."

(Explanation - For the purpose of this section and with effect from the 3rd day of September, 1939, a soldier who is or has been a prisoner of war shall be deemed to be or to have been serving under war conditions).

In November 1962, in consequence of the hostilities following the Chinese aggression, the Central government vide S.R.O. (3E) dated 5th November, 1962, issued a notification in; pursuance of Section 3(b) of the Act, declaring the service of soldiers during the military operations against external aggression in relation to which the proclamation of emergency was issued on 26th October, 1962, as service under war conditions of the purposes of the Indian Soldiers (Litigation) Act, 1925.

Similarly, in consequence of Indo-Pak conflict in December, 1971, the Central Government under the powers vested in by Section 3 of the Indian Soldiers (Litigation) Act specified service in a number of places as service under special conditions vide S.R.O. 437 dated 23rd November, 1971, which read as follows:-

"S.R.O. 437 dated the 23rd November, 1971 - In pursuance of clause (a) of Section 3 of the Indian Soldiers (Litigation) Act, 1925 (4 of 1925), the Central Government hereby specified the following places within India as the places where an Indian soldier shall be deemed to be or, as the case may be, to have been serving under special conditions for the purposes of the said Act, namely:-

(a) any place in the state of Assam, including Meghalaya;

(b) any place in the district of Banaskanatha and Kuch in the State of Gujarat;

(c) any place in the district of Kinnaur, Lahaul and Spiti in the State of Himachal Pradesh;

(d) any place in the state of Jammu and Kashmir;

(e) any place in the state of Nagaland;

(f) any place in the state of Punjab

(g) any place in the district of Barmer, Bikaner, Ganganagar, Jaisalmer, Jalor and Jodhpur in the state of Rajastahan.

(h) any place in the district of Chamoli, Pithoragarh and Uttarkashi in the State of Uttar Pradesh;

(i) any place the state of West Bengal;

(j) any place in the Union territory of Manipur;

(k) any place in the Union territory of Tripura;

(l) any place in the North East Frontier Agency

To make the notification more exhaustive and to cover all soldiers at all places during the military operations; this notification was superseded by S.R.O. 467 dated 8th December, 1971. The said notification is reproduced below:-

"In pursuance of clause (b) of Section 3 of Indian Soldiers (Litigation) Act, 1925, (4 of 1925) and in suppression of the notification of the Government of India in the Ministry of Defence No. S.R.O. 437 dated the 23rd November 1971, the Central Government hereby declares that service of soldiers during the military operations against external aggression in relation to which a proclamation of emergency has been issued on the 3rd December, 1971, shall be deemed to be service under war conditions for the purposes of the said Act".

After the cessation of military operations of 1971, in order to cover the soldiers deployed in certain states like J&K, Manipur, Mizoram, Nagaland and others, a notification vide S.R.O. 17-(E) was issued on the 5th September, 1977. The said notification is reproduced below:-

"S.R.O. 17(E) - In exercise of the powers conferred by Section 9 of the Army Act, 1950, (46 of 1950) and in super session of the notification of the Government of India in the Ministry of Defence, No. S.R.O. 6-E, dated the 28th November, 1962, the Central Government hereby declares that all persons subject to that Act who are not on active service under clause (i) of Section 3 thereof shall, while serving in the areas specified below, be deemed to be on active service within the meaning of the Act for the purpose of the said Act and of any other law for the time being in force:

1. The States of -
   - (a) Jammu & Kashmir
   - (b) Manipur
   - (c) Nagaland
   - (d) Tripura
   - (e) Sikkim
2. The Union Territories of -
   - (a) The Andaman and Nicobar Islands
   - (b) Arunachal Pradesh
   - (c) Mizoram

The Districts of -

- (a) Uttarkashi, Chamoli and Pithoragarh in the State of Uttar Pradesh
- (b) Lahaul and Spiti, Kinnaur and Kulu in the State of Himachal Paradesh."

Further to cover the troops employed in peace-keeping operations in Sri Lanka, serving in operation Rhino, operations Bajrang and Rakshak, Lakshadweep, notification vide S.R.O. 20(E), 6(E), 1(E) and 78, were issued on 9th November, 1991, 17th January, 1992 and 19th February, 1992 respectively. These notifications are reproduced below:-

"S.R.O. 20(e) - In exercise of the powers conferred by Section 9 of the Army Act, 1950, (46 of 1950), the Central Government hereby declares that all persons subject to that Act who are not on active service under clause (i) of Section 3 thereof shall, while serving with the Indian Peace Keeping Force in Sri Lanka, be deemed to be on active service within the meaning of the Act for the purpose of the aforesaid Act and of any other law for the time being in force."

"S.R.O. 6(E) a- In exercise of the powers conferred by Section 9 of the Army Act, 1950, (46 of 1950), the Central Government hereby declares that all persons subject to that Act who are not on active service under clause (i) of Section 3 thereof shall, while serving with the Army Formations and Units deployed on Operation Rhino be deemed to be on active service within the meaning of the Act for the purpose of the aforesaid Act and of any other law for the time being in force."

"S.R.O. 1(E) - In exercise of the powers conferred by Section 9 of the Army Act, 1950, (46 of 1950), the Central Government hereby declares that all persons subject to that Act who are not on active service under clause (i) of Section 3 thereof shall, while serving with the Army Formations and Units deployed on Operation Bajrang be deemed to be on active service within the meaning of the Act for the purpose of the aforesaid Act and of any other law for the time being in force."

"S.R.O. 1 (E) - In exercise of the powers conferred by Section 9 of the Army Act, 1950, (46 of 1950), the Central Government hereby declares that all persons subject to that Act who are not on active service under clause (i) of Section 3 thereof shall, while serving with the Army Formations and Units deployed on operation Rakshak in the States of Punjab, Jammu and Kashmir, Rajasthan, Gujarat and the Union Territories be deemed to be on active service within the meaning of the Act for the purpose of the aforesaid Act and of any other law for the time being in force."

"S.R.O. 78 - In exercise of the powers conferred by Section 9 of the Army Act, 1950, (46 of 1950), the Central Government hereby declares that all persons subject to that Act who are not on active service under clause (i) of Section 3 thereof shall, while serving in the Union Territories of Lakshadweep, be deemed to be on active service within the meaning of the Act for the purpose of the aforesaid Act and of any other law for the time being in force."

Setting aside Decrees and orders passed against soldiers when they were serving under special conditions or war conditions.

In addition to the foregoing provisions, the Indian Soldiers (Litigation) Act, 1925 has provided for yet another important priviledge. The priviledge is, the provision to move the Court for setting aside the decree or the order passed at the time when the soldier was serving under special conditions or war conditions.

The provision of setting aside decrees etc., it is provided in Section 10 of the Indian Soldiers (Litigation) Act, 1925 and is primarily intended to safeguard the interests of a soldier, when he is serving under special conditions, so that he may be able to devote his complete and undivided attention to the duties on which he is employed at such times. Instances have happen when despite the provisions of postponement, an adverse decree or order may be passed against a soldier, when he was serving under special conditions. If there was no provision like the one contained in Section 10 of the Act, at times it may result in great injustice or suffering to the concerned soldier and may even indirectly act to the prejudice of good morale of the forces.

Section 10 lays down that in any proceeding before a Court, in which a decree or order is passed against a soldier, whilst he was serving under special conditions, the soldier (or if he is dead his legal representative) may apply to the Court, which passed decree or order for an order to set aside the same, and if the Court after giving an opportunity to the opposite party of being heard, is satisfied that the interests of justice require that the decree or order should be set aside as against the soldier, the Court shall, subject to such conditions, as it thinks fit to impose, make an order accordingly.

When the decree or order in respect of which an application is made is of such a nature that it cannot be set aside as against all or any of the parties against whom it has been made.

When the Court sets aside a decree or order in pursuance of the above provision, it shall appoint a fresh date for proceeding with the suit, appeal or application as the case may be.

It would be noticed that the only requirement for availing this priviledge is that the soldier should be serving under special conditions, at the time when such decree or order was passed, whereas for postponement of proceedings under Section 7 various other conditions are to be fulfilled. For postponement, the notice is issued only when the Court has reason to believe that the soldier is unable to appear and is not represented by any person duly authorized to appear, plead or act on his behalf. A certificate is also required from the prescribed authority that the soldier is serving under special conditions, and that the postponement of proceedings is necessary in the interests of justice.

For the purposes of this Act who is to decide whether the soldier is serving under special conditions or not? Regarding this question it would be observed that under Section 7, the Court on receipt of the certificate is required to act and postpone the proceedings. Thus; it appears that it is the prescribed authority, who has to decide whether the soldier is or is not serving under special conditions for the purposes of Section 7 of the Act. For the purposes of Section 10, it has, however, been laid down by Section 12 that if the Court has any doubt as to whether, the solider is or was at any particular time serving under special conditions, the Court may refer the point for the decision of the prescribed authority. The prescribed authority for this purpose is the GOC-in-C of the Command in which the Court is situated in case of army personnel or the Air Officer (Personnel) for air force personnel as the case may be. Law has further laid down that the decision of the said authority and certificate of that authority shall be conclusive evidence on the point. This means that no further evidence can be allowed to be led in disproof thereof. Though in this Section the word "may" has been used, yet it is submitted that since the point involved is purely of military nature of which the military authorities are the best judges, the Court should normally refer the point to the military authorities concerned.

Since the entire scheme of the Act is to protect the interests of soldiers in matters of litigation, when they are serving under special conditions and wide powers have been given to the Courts under Section 10 for setting aside the decree etc. It is felt that a provision under the Section should be liberally construed in favour of the soldiers serving under special conditions.

Section 14 of the Act has authorized the Central Government and the State Governments in respect of State Public Services, to apply the provisions of this Act by notification in the official gazette to any other class of persons in the service of the Government.

Under these provisions the Central Government by orders dated 25th September, 1943 and 3rd February, 1945 had extended the provisions of the Act to persons subject to the Navy Act and persons attached to or employed by the Indian Navy, in the manner as they applied to the Indian Soldiers. The Indian Seamen Litigation Rules, 1944, were also made under section 13 of the Act for the Naval personnel and were more or less on the same lines as the Indian Soldiers Litigation Rules, 1938. However, vide amendment to Section 2(b) of the Indian Soldiers (Litigation) Act, 1925 by Section 2(ii) of the Amendment Act (Act 23 of the 70), the Soldiers Litigation Act, 1925 has been made applicable to Naval personnel also, as it applies to the army or the air force personnel thereby now these notifications and rules have become redundant.

Gist of Decided Cases

For the benefit of the keen reader and the actual Litigant or those who may otherwise need, a gist of the Decided Cases on various provisions of the Indian Soldiers (Litigation) Act, 1925 has been given below:-

(i) The object of the Act and the Amending Ordinance is to protect Soldiers who are involved in litigation or whose interests are affected by litigation, (Interests of soldier not involved in litigation or whose interests are affected by litigation, (Interest of soldier not involved in litigation - Obligation to pay money existing for 12 years before War - Obligation not of soldier but of his mother - Soldier's plea in affidavit being one admiseri cordiam - Held, Sec 6 or Sec 7 did not apply).

AIR 1945 Mad 354 (355)

(ii) Act is applicable to Civil and Revenue Proceedings only and not to Criminal Proceedings. Act does not apply to proceeding to enforce an order for maintenance under S.488 Criminal Procedure Code.

AIR 1944 Pesh 48 (48)

46 Cri LJ 185

Section 2(b)

(i) Indian in employ of military department - presumption arises that He is Indian Soldier.

AIR 1944 Lah 351 (352) (DB) Section 3

(i) Person serving in Indian Army - His period of service synchronizing with A portion of period of last World War - person can be regarded as serving under War Conditions.

AIR 1952 All 1974 (976)

Where the plaintiff claims exemption from limitation on the ground

that he was serving under War Conditions as specified in S.3 (b) (iii) i.e. serving with a unit; which for the time being was mobilized, the question is one of the fact which has to be provided by the plaintiff - A certificate of discharge from Army on account of de-mobilization is not sufficient to prove it. De-mobilization in the context only means discharge from the Army.

AIR 1958 Ker 228 (229) (DB)

(iii) The existence of special and/or war conditions in the country is not a justifiable matter. Once a certificate is issued by the prescribed authority, as contemplated by Section 7, the Court has no option but to stay the proceedings. May be, if malafides or ulterior motive is alleged on the part of the prescribed authority, the Court can go into it. The Court is not even justified in requiring the solder's Counsel to provide the Court with information about the place of his posting. That seems to be a reason why a certificate under section 7 of the Act has been made conclusive. If Court were to enquire into places of postings of soldiers or of existence of non-existence of special and/or war conditions, there is likelihood of serious threat to the defence of the country. Sometimes, the absence of judicial review in subjective field may cause even serious jeopardy to the rights of the subjects, but such like statutes have to be construed having regard to the circumstances in which they are intended to operate.

AIR 1968 Punj 26 (28)

= (1966) 68 Punj LR (D) 225

(iv) A person on active front can get his house vacated if he produces a certificate of serving under special conditions from the prescribed authority.

1968 Cri LJ 536 (540) 70 Punj LR 672

Section 4

(i) Section 4 does not provide a penalty for ommission to mention the fact and as such ommission to mention that adverse party is Indian soldier does not deprive person concerned of benefit of S. 11.

AIR 1962 All 577 (581) =ILR (1962) 2 All 85

(ii) Section 4 only lays down certain rules of guidance which a plaintiff in his plaint or an applicant; in his application has to dobserve, the object merely being of apprising the Court on the one hand and warning the opposite party on the other of the true nature of the claim made, as well as the background in which it was made.

AIR 1952 All 974

(iii) Soldiers Litigation Act, 1925 Ss. 4, 11-Ommission to mention that adverse party is Indian Soldier does not deprive person concerned of benefit of S.11

Ss 6,11 - S.II is not controlled by S.6 - Benefit of S.11 is available if one of Persons who is party to the proceedings is serving under special conditions irrespective of the fact whether other parties can or cannot represent the interest of soldier party.

Limitation Act, 1908, Article 182(5) - Final order is the order which brings Execution to end.

AIR 1952 ALL 974 (Reversed)

AIR 1962 ALL 577

Section 5

(i) On getting information from the Collector under S.5 or on obtaining Information from some other source himself the presiding officer of the Court has first to see whether (i) the soldier is unable to appear in the case, and (ii) the soldier is not represented by any person duly authorized to appear, plead or act on his behalf.

AIR 1945 Pesh 37 (38)

AIR 1968 Punj 26 (27)

= 1966 (68) Punj LR(D) 225

(ii) Power of Collector under it can be exercised by him only where soldier is party to pending proceeding.

AIR 1966 Cal 625 (628)

(iii) Soldiers Litigation Act, 1925 S.5 - Decree holder joining Army after decree - Section does not extend time for doing act ordered by decree within the time fixed therefore.

AIR 1922 Oudh 131

Section 6

(i) Before acting under Section 6 the Court has to see whether (i) the soldier is unable to appear, and (ii) the solider is not represented by any person duly authorized to appear, plead or act on his behalf. If these two conditions are fulfilled, there is a *prima-facie* case for acting under S6. The court has, however, still to find out whether (a) the suit is one for pre-emption or (b) the interests of soldier are identical with and adequately represented by some other party, or (c) the interest of the soldier is of a formal nature. If any of these questions is answered in affirmative, the Court would refrain from acting under S.6 but if all the questions are answered in negative the Court shall issue a notice. Section 6 and 7 apply where there is no authorized agent or male member of family of prisoner of war on whom the service is to be effected.

AIR 1945 Pesh 37 (38)

AIR 1944 Lah 351(352)

AIR 1943 Lah 327 (329)(DB)

AIR 1968 Bom 206 (207)=69 Bom LR 875

AIR 1968 Ker 230 (231)=68 Lab IC 1055

AIR 1968 Punj 26(28) = (1966) 68 Punj LR(D) 225

(ii) Section 6 applies to a pending proceeding by or against a person who is soldier either not represented or unable to plead before the Court. To this extent the rule contained in S.11 remains unaffected in the sense that while that rule is one of exclusion the rule in S 6 is one of suspension of a pending proceeding and the two may hardly be imagined and indicating the same conception.

AIR 1952 All 974 (977)

(iii) If a soldier is unavoidably absent personally but is represented by a pleader authorized to appear on his behalf the Court is under no obligation to give notice in the prescribed manner to the prescribed authority and can proceed with the case.

AIR 1923 All 185 (185)

(iv) Decree against A and B members of joint family, A being manager -sale of family property in execution - B serving in Army overseas applying to set aside sale - sale held should not be set aside.

AIR 1946 Mad 460 (460) (461) (DB)

(v) Court before issuing notice to prescribed authority must find out that Indian soldier is materially concerned in outcome of proceedings and that his interest will be prejudiced by his inability to attend.

AIR 1944 Pesh 14 (14,15)

(vi) Where the interests of the absent defendant in the proceeding are "merely of a formal nature" within the meaning of the second part of proviso (b) to S.6, the Court may not suspend the proceedings while the ex parte order is in force.

AIR 1945 Sind 98 (100)

(vii) Under S. 6(2), the powers of the Court are limited to suspending the proceedings after which it must give notice in the prescribed manner to the prescribed authority and then proceed under S.7.

AIR 1945 Mad 264 (264)

(viii) Sub-section (1) deals with the case where the soldier is himself a party to the pending proceeding. In such a case it is obligatory upon the Court to suspend the proceeding unless of course the proviso is attracted. Now, the circumstances under which the Court shall suspend a proceeding under sub-section (1) are either that a certificate under section 5 issued by a Collector has been received by the Court or that the Court thinks it reasonable that the soldier unable to appear therein and is not represented by any person duly authorized to appear to plead or act on his behalf. But sub-section (1) clearly has no application where the soldier is not a party to the proceeding. Sub-section (2) of course, applies even though the solider is not a party to the proceeding, but the discretionary power of the Court to suspend the proceeding has to be governed by two conditions. These conditions are (a) that the soldier is materially concerned in the outcome of the proceeding and (b) that his interests are likely to be prejudiced by his inability to attend. These two conditions are cumulative and not alternative. The concluding portion of sub-section (2) namely, that the Court shall give notice thereof in the prescribed manner to the prescribed authority, comes into play only where the Court exercises its discretionary power to suspend a proceeding on being satisfied on the two points mentioned above.

AIR 1966 Cal 625 (628)** (1966) 1LJ 286 (287)

(ix) Dy. Commissioner may take the initiative and give a certificate under S.5 but the Court has still to satisfy itself under S.6 and then give notice to the prescribed authority under that Section. The trial Judge is consequently wrong in postponing the case merely because he received a certificate under S.5 of the Act based on a letter issued by the liaison officer of the instance of the father of the soldier.

AIR 1944 Pesh 44 (14, 15)

(x) Section 11 is not controlled by S.6 -benefit of Section 11 is available if one of the persons who is party to proceedings is serving under special conditions irrespective of fact whether other parties can or cannot represent interest of soldier party.

AIR 1962 All 577 (581)= LR (1962) 2 All 85(DB)

AIR 1952 All 974b (Reserved

(xi) Where a revenue Court stays a suit under S.6 with the result that the procedure prescribed by law, i.e. S.7 and 8 of the Act, is not followed, there is a material irregularity in the exercise of jurisdiction such as t o justify interference in revision.

AIR 1950 All W.R. 692 (693)

(xii) Soldiers (Litigation) Act, 1925 - Sections 2(d) 6 and 7 - combined effect of - Soldiers (Litigation) Rules, Rule 7 and form (d) - Suspension of proceedings. The combined effect of the above provisions is that if a soldier litigant satisfied the conditions of Section 6, the Court is required to suspend the proceedings and give notice thereof to the prescribed authority. Where the prescribed authority certifies that the soldier litigant is serving under special conditions and that the postponement of the proceedings in respect of such soldier litigant is necessary, in the interests of justice the Court is required to postpone the proceeding; until the certificate is revoked in form D by the prescribed authority or until the soldier is represented in the proceedings by some person duly authorized to appear, plead or act on his behalf. The expression "proceedings has a particular meaning given to it in Section

2 (d) of the Act as including suit, appeal and an application It is not necessary for the trial court to seek any clarification from the prescribed authority as regards the period for which the postponement should be operative in consequence of the certificate issued by such authority under Section 7.

S.C. Dogra vs Inder Raj

AIR 1977 J & K 25

(xiii) Soldiers (Litigation) Act, 1925 S.5 - Power of collector under - it can be exercised by him only where soldier is party to pending suit.

S.6 (1) (2) - Scope and applicability.

AIR 1966 CAL 625

(xiv) Soldiers (Litigation) Act, 1925, Ss. 3, 5, 6 and 7 - Certificate issued by the prescribed authority under S.7 of the Act - Conclusion - Court has no option but to stay the proceedings - Court not justified in requiring the soldier's counsel to provide him with information about the place of his posting - However, if malafide or ulterior motive is alleged on the part of the prescribed authority, the Court can go into it.

AIR 1968 Punj 26

(xv) Soldiers (Litigation) Act, 1925, S.10 -al construction must be put - case under S.10 held not made out - The terms of S.10 are to be liberally construed in favour of the soldier serving under the special conditions contemplated by the Section.

S.6 - Ex-parte order not set aside - Suspension under S.6 cannot succeed.

AIR 1945 (Sind) 98

Section 7

(i) A certificate under S.7 as amended, has no validity unless the soldier to whom the certificate is issued is, in fact, interested in the proceedings.

AIR 1945 Mad. 354 (355)

(ii) Under S.7, it is necessary before ordering a stay to find that the soldier is serving under special conditions, and that a postponement is necessary in the interests of justice. Suit was stayed against soldier as other defendants having identical interests had lost the same and were not properly guarding interest of soldier.

AIR 1945 Mad 264 (264)

AIR 1944 Pesh 1 (2) = 46 Cri LJ 585 (DB)

(iii) All that the prescribed authority has to do in response to the notice is to issue a certificate under the section and on receipt of the certificate the Court has to stay the suit.

AIR 1944 Pesh 14 (14,15)

AIR 1968 Punj 26(27)=(1966)
68 Punj LR(D) 225

(iv) Stay of proceedings does not automatically follow merely on receipt of a notice from the Collector under S.6(i).

AIR 1945 Mad 264 (264)

(v) A Court acts with material irregularity in staying proceedings without complying first with the provisions of Ss 7 and 8.

AIR 1950 all WR 692 9693)

(vi) Suspension of proceedings to which soldier is a party can be done as provided in Section 6.

AIR 1968 Bom 206 (207)

= 69 Bom LR 875

(vii) Where a suit was instituted by a soldier along with others and he actually appointed a pleader to act for him and the certificate produced showed the soldier was on leave then and nothing more, it cannot be held that such suit is to be stayed or postponed under Section 7 or Section 9 of the Act.

1952 ALJ (Rev) 271

= 1952 AWR (Rev) 252

Section 9

Intimation from Commanding Officer -No indication therein that soldier was to proceed on expiration of leave on service under special conditions - suit or appeal cannot be postponed.

1952 All J(Rev) 271= 1952 All WR (Rev) 252

Section 10

(i) The terms of the section are wide and should be liberally construed in favour of the soldier serving under the special conditions contemplated by the section.

AIR 1945 Sind 98(99)

(ii) Decree against persons serving out of India under war conditions - decree can be set aside either under order 47, or under section 10.

AIR 1921 Cal 393 (395) (DB) also see
AIR 1918 (Lah) 41 (1) (41
= 1917 Punj Re No, 94(DB)

(iii) person serving under war conditions - Court not giving notice to prescribed authority - defendant can set aside decree within 3 months after cessation of service.

1017 Punj Rev No. 94 (DB)

(iv) Where a decree passed against a soldier is of such a nature that it cannot be set aside against such soldier only, it may be Set aside as against all or any of the parties against whom it is made.

AIR 1921 Cal 393 (395) (DB)
AIR 1918 Lah 41 (41) (DB)
AIR 1917 Punj Rev No. 94 (DB)

(v) Apart from provision (a) to S.10, Adjutant General's certificate that applicant was serving under war conditions is sufficient ground for admitting application for review after period of limitation.

AIR Cal 393 (394) (DB)

(vi) Where an order of sale is made the proper course for the judgment debtor is to apply under S.10 to have the order set aside within 90 days of the order or of his gaining knowledge concerning it, and once time has begun to run against him in relation to that order it cannot be a arrested notwithstanding that he was a serving soldier.

AIR 1948 Lah 205 (207)

(vii) Decree against A&B members of joint family, A being Manager -sale of family property in execution - B serving in Army overseas applying to set aside sale - sale held should not be set aside.

AIR 1946 Mad 460 (460, 461) (DB)

(viii) An order made by the executing Court under Section 10 Indian Soldiers (Litigation) Act cannot be regarded as an order falling under S.47 Civil P.C. and therefore an appeal is incompetent. The High Court can however be treated an appeal as a revision under S.115 C.P.C and has power under that Section to correct the order made by the subordinate Courts on the basis that there has been material irregularity in the exercise of the jurisdiction.

AIR 1948 Lah 205 (206)

Section 11

For case law on the subject also see Chapter 2.

Section 12

(i) Under S.12 of the Soldiers Litigation Act, reference can be made to the prescribed authority for the decision of any one or more of the following points (i) whether the soldier was at any particular time serving under special conditions; (ii) (whether) the soldier was serving under special conditions at the time of his death (iii) the death of the soldier and (iv) the date on which official intimation on the death of the soldier was sent to his next of kin by the authorities in India.

AIR 1951 Punj 235 (237)

(ii) The certificate of the prescribed authority must necessarily be accepted as correct even though there may be glaring proof of the incorrectness thereof. If the certificate recites that the soldier was serving under special conditions at the time of his death, the recital of the fact in the certificate shall be conclusive evidence on the point.

AIR 1951 Punj (Simla) 235 (237)

(iii) When the Court is in doubt as to whether a party can be said to be serving under war conditions or not it ought to refer the matter to the prescribed authority and act on the certificate even by such authority. If in such a case the Court fails to notice the provisions of S. 12 it acts with material irregularity in the exercise of its jurisdiction and the case falls under S. 115 of C.P.C.

AIR 1951 Punj (Simla) 235 (237)

(iv) Although the power under S.12 is couched in permissive terms, the words 'may' is used not to give a discretion, but to confer the power. The intention of the Section is that when there is a doubt in the mind of Court as to whether or not the party before it is entitled to the priviledges conferred by the Act it is incumbent upon the Court to exercise the power conferred i.e. it must make a reference to the prescribed authority which will produce the necessary certificate. The intention of the section is that where there is doubt concerning the point, whether the parities have led evidence in the case or not such doubt shall be resolved not by a decision of the court by the certificate of the prescribed authority. Failure to do so is a material irregularity in the exercise of jurisdiction which attracts the revisional powers under S.115 of C.P.C.

AIR 1948 Lah 205 (206, 207)

2

Privileges in Matters of the Law of Limitation

The Limitation Act, 1963 lays down time limits within which various suits, applications and appeals can be filed in the Courts and if a party files an application, suit or appeal after the expiry of the time limit, they are not entertained. For the members of the armed forces however, in certain cases period of limitation has been extended. Further, in their case certain periods are also allowed to be excluded whilst calculating period for the purpose of the law of limitation.

Extension of

Section 11 of the Indian Soldiers (Litigation) Act, 1925 provides that the period during which a soldier has been serving under special conditions shall be excluded and if the soldier has died whilst so serving, then in addition, the period from the date of his death to the date on which official intimation thereof was sent to his next of kin, shall also be excluded. Service under special conditions has been defined in Section 3 of the Indian Soldiers (Litigation) Act, 1925 and has been explained in the preceding chapter.

An important point to note in this connection is, that this exclusion of period is applicable not only in cases where the application is made to set aside a decree or order under section 10 of the Indian Soldiers (Litigation) Act, 1925 but also for any other suit or application for which the period of limitation has been laid down under the Limitation Act, 1963 or under any other law for the time being in force. Similarly, this priviledge is also available in all Courts in which priviledge of suspension and postponement of proceedings is claimed under the Indian Soldiers (Litigation) Act, 1925.

Vide Section 12 of the Indian Soldiers (Litigation) Act, 1925, if the Court has any doubt as to whether the soldier was or was not serving under special conditions, or that he died whilst serving under special conditions or about the date of his death or about the date which such death was officially intimated to the next of kin, the Court is to refer such a question for determination to the GOC-in-C of the Area in which the Court is situated, and in case of Air Force personnel to the Air Officer (Personnel), Air Headquarters New Delhi. The decision of the said authorities is final and binding. A certificate issued by the said authority in this regard, is conclusive proof of the facts stated therein.

The period of limitation for an application under Section 10 of the Indian Soldiers (Litigation) Act, 1925 for setting aside a decree or order of the Court is 90 days from the date of decree or order, in case where the summons or notice was duly served on the soldier and in cases where the summons or notice was not duly served on the soldier, the period of limitation is 90 days from the date on which the applicant had knowledge of the decree or order.

In addition, to the provisions of Section 11, in all cases where the solider can satisfy the Court that he had sufficient cause for not making the application suit or appeal within the prescribed period, the Court can extend the period of limitation under Section 5 of the Limitation Act, 1963.

Section 5 of the Limitation Act states "Any appeal or any application, other than an application under any of the provision, of Order XXI of the Code of Civil Procedure, 1908 may be admitted after the prescribed period if the appellant or applicant satisfied the Court that he had sufficient cause for not preferring the appeal or making the application within such period."

The question of the existence of sufficient cause is one of fact, and is to be determined from the circumstances of each particular case. Under this section, the Courts have wide powers, which of course are to be exercised based on judicial principles. If the Court is satisfied that the applicant had sufficient cause for not preferring the application within the time limit laid down, it can be admitted even if the time limit has expired. For example, in a case before the Assam High Court where the party against whom judgment had been given, was away on military duty, and was not present when judgment was given and he came to know of the judgment only when he came on casual leave, and thereafter applied for to obtaind the copy of the judgment and preferred the appeal, it was held that there was a sufficient justification to condone the delay and admit the appeal.

Gist of case law

1. Apart from proviso (a) to Section 10, Adjutant General's Certificate that the applicant was serving under war conditions is sufficient ground for admitting application for review after period of limitation.

   AIR 1921 Cal 393 (394) (DB)

2. Section 11 is applicable only to plaintiff who is Indian Soldier at the time of his suit.

   AIR 1926 Lah 187 (187)

3. Plaintiff ceasing to be soldier at the date of the suit – Section 11 does not apply.

   AIR 1923 Lah 655 (656) (DB)

4. The period during which a soldier is serving under war conditions commences when he is ordered on field service.

AIR 1923 Lah 465 (466)

5. Decree holder joining Army after discretion sec. 11 does not extend time for doing act ordered by decree within the time fixed therefore as the section is applicable to cases where the period is not fixed by any law but by the decree itself.

AIR 1922 Oudh 131 (132)

6. The legislature has every right to have statutes construed in a reasonable manner and it is, clear that the object of the Soldiers (Litigation) Act is to give any one who has served in the Army on the war time conditions the benefit of this period of service in any litigation on which he wishes to embark and also to any party having a claim against a soldier. The legislature never intended that any plaintiff who himself never served in the Army could, by leading an Ex-soldier as proforma defendant extend the time of limitation of his suit claiming the benefit of the military service of such a defendant.

AIR 1957 Punj 69 (71)

7. Where the plaintiff is in military service and as such obtains an extended period of limitation, the privilege being a personel one his brother cannot take advantage of it.

AIR 1954 SC 269 (269)

8. Where the Court has chosen to regard the absent party as duly represented by those who are present or regards the interests of the latter and the former as absolutely identical, the Court is empowered not to issue the notice as required by Section 6.

AIR 1952 All 974 (977)

9. The words 'the time during which the soldier has any special conditions' in Section 11 of the Soldiers (Litigation) Act must not be construed in a literal sense. In computing

the period of Limitation for an application to set aside an order of dismissal of a suit for default only the period the plaintiff was in service under war conditions after the order of dismissal can be excluded. There is no justification for excluding the period he was in service prior to the order of dismissal. During this period the plaintiff was not and indeed could not be prevented from making the application by reason of his service.

AIR 1950 Cal 411 (411,412) (DB)

10. Where the plaintiff claims exemption from Limitation under Sec. 11 on the ground that he was serving under war conditions the question is one of fact which has to be proved by the plaintiff.

AIR 1958 Ker 228 (229)(DB)

11. Section 11 is not controlled by S.6 – benefit of Section 11 is available if one of the persons who is party to proceedings is serving under special conditions irrespective of fact whether other parties can or cannot represent interest of soldier party.

AIR 1962 ALL 577 (581)=L (1962) 2 All 85 (DB) AIR 1952 All 974, (Rev)

12. Ommission to mention that adverse party is Indian soldier does not deprive person concerned of benefit of Section 11.

AIR 1962 All 577 (581)=LR (1962) 2 All 85 (DB), AIR 1952 All 974, (Rev)

13. Sec.11 provides that an Indian soldier is entitled to the exclusion of only that period when he was serving under special conditions and that too in cases where a claim was not barred before his enrolment, as this section does not revive a barred suit.

1952 All LJ (Rev) 271 = 1952

3

Privileges under the Code of Civil Procedure, 1908

Execution of Power of Attorney

According to the Civil Procedure Code, whenever a person is to file or defend any suit in a civil Court or is to make any application or plaint in the Court he has to appear in the Court. According to Order No. III Rule 1, however, a party may appear in the Court in person or by his recognized agent or by a pleader appearing, pleadings or acting on his behalf, unless the Court directs that the party must appear in person.

The recognized agent means the person holding a power of attorney from party to the suit authorizing him to appear, plead or act for the said party. Such a power of attorney is required to be stamped with the stamp duty, attested by a magistrate, or a notary public etc. and is to be filed in the Court. The procedure of executing such power of attorney is at times quite inconvenient and expensive.

For the benefit of the persons in the armed forces and to save them to the inconvenience of getting the power of attorney executed and attested in this manner, the Code of

Civil Procedure Order No. XXVIII Rule 1 has granted a valuable priviledge. According to this order when an officer, soldier, sailor or airman, who is a party to a suit or wishes to institute a suit, and cannot obtain leave of absence for defending or prosecuting the suit in person, he may authorize any person to sue or defend him on his behalf. Such authority should be in writing and should be signed by the individual concerned in the presence of his Commanding Officer. When the soldier serving in any staff appointment, it can be executed before the head or other superior officer of the individual. If the Commanding Officer himself is to execute the power of attorney he can execute the same in the presence of his immediate subordinate officer. Such Commanding Office or other superior officer should counter-sign the power of attorney. According to the said order when such power of attorney is signed and filed in the Court it shall be sufficient proof of the fact that the power of attorney was duly executed and the individual concerned could not obtain leave of absence for prosecuting or defending the suit.

Though no specific form of such Power of Attorney has been laid down by law, yet to meet the legal requirements, and to ensure uniformity, a form has been devised for such power of attorney. The form so devised is as under:

Whereas I (Name.....................) inhabitant of village................. Pargana....................................in the district of....................son of..................of the caste of.....................
Stationed at.................................having occasion to institute (or defend) an action for (nature and object of suit and name of adverse party), do hereby nominate and appoint (name, residence, caste and relationship, if any) to be my attorney and I bind myself to abide by whatever he, the said attorney, may do on my behalf in the prosecution (or defence) the suit in person, or will appoint one or more of the authorized vakil of the Court to prosecute (or defend), the same under the instructions of the said attorney, as he may think proper. In the event of an appeal being preferred from the judgment

passed in the suit, the said attorney is hereby empowered to act for me in the appeal in a like manner as in the original suit.

Signature........................
Signed in my presence
....
(Commanding)
Officer

Such Power of Attorney is exempted from payment of Court fee Act and Notification No. 6 dated 12th Sept. 1931 issued under section 9 of the Indian Stamp Act, 1899. Thus the law has given the soldier a priviledge of executing a Power of Attorney in a simple and inexpensive manner.

Service of Summons

In order to enable the Commanding Officer to know when a suit etc. has been filed against a soldier serving under him, so as to enable him to effectively intervene to protect his interests, the Civil Procedure Code, Order V Rule 28, has laid down that when the defendant is a soldier, sailor or airman, the Court will serve the summons on the said soldier, sailor or airman through his Commanding Officer. The Commanding Officer on receipt of the summons, (which will be in duplicate) will obtain the signatures of the soldier on one copy and return the same under his signatures to the Court from where the summons were received. In case the Commanding Officer cannot serve the summons the summons should be returned to the Court with a full statement of reasons as to why the service was impossible, and what steps had been taken to procure the service. It will be seen that this provision is applicable only in the case of soldiers, sailors and airmen and not to officers. In case of officers, the summons are to be served directly, and not through the Commanding Officer.

Exemption of Properties from Sale and Attachment

Regarding properties liable for attachment and sale in execution of a decree, section 60 of the Civil Procedure Code provides that generally speaking all saleable property (whether) moveable or immovable belonging to the judgment debtor over which or the profits of which he has disposing power, which he may exercise for his benefit, are liable to attachment and sale in execution of a decree, vide sub-sections (i) and (j) of Section 60 however, the pay and allowances of persons to whom the Air Force Act, 1950, or the Army Act, 1950 or the Navy Act, 1957 applies, are not liable for such attachment or sale. For immunity from attachment of pay and allowances and personal items reference should also be made to Section 28 of the Army Act/Air Force Act, 1950 and Section 20 of the Navy Act, 1957. In this connection, it is also useful to note that under Section 11 of the Pensions Act, 1871 all government pensions including military pensions are protected from attachment in the execution of decrees of Civil Courts.

Notice for Suits etc.

Whilst discussing the privileges of the armed forces personnel under the Civil Procedure Code, it is also useful to note the provisions of Section 80, 81 and 82 of the Code. Though the privileges and protections given by these Sections are not exclusively meant for the personnel of the armed forces and are meant for all public officers in respect of acts done by them in their official capacity, yet they are of great use to the officers of the armed forces, as they also constitute public officers.

According to Section 80, no suit can be instituted against the government, or against a public officer for any act purporting to be done by him in his official capacity unless a written notice of intention thereof is given at least two months in advance. The intention of this Section is that in case such a suit is being filed by any party, the public officer may get sufficient notice so that he may prepare for the case or redress the complaint if he considers such a course to be proper and may also obtain adequate departmental or legal assistance. For the action to be taken on receipt of notice, the departmental assistance available in such cases and also in criminal proceedings, reference should be made to Chapter 5.

Section 81 of the Civil Procedure Code provides that when a suit is instituted against a public officer in his official capacity, such public officer is not liable for arrest or attachment of his property as a result of such suit. Also when the Court is satisfied that the public officer cannot absent himself from his duty without detriment to public service, the Court shall exempt him from appearing in person.

Section 82 makes provision for the time lag for issuing the execution process of a decree, passed against the Government or a public officer in his official capacity. When a decree is passed, normally a time limit is to be specified in the decree itself within which the decree should be satisfied. According to Section 82, if no time limit is specified it shall be three months from the date of the decree. If the decree is not satisfied within this period, the Court will not immediately issue execution process, but will report the case for the orders of the State government. Execution process will be issued only when the decree remains unsatisfied after the expiry of three months, computed from the date of such report to the State Government.

Gist of case law

For the benefit of keen reader, gist of some of the cases decided on Order V Rule 28 of the Civil Procedure Code are given below:

1. Section 80 in effect provides that an advance copy of the plaint should be served on; the defendant and no suit

should be instituted in Court until the expiry of two months after such service. Section 80 does not define the right of parties or confer any rights on the parties. It only provides a mode of procedure for getting the relief in respect of a cause of action.

(1881) 50 L.J. Ex.55

2. The legislative intention behind this section is that public money and time should not be wasted on unnecessary litigation and the government and public officers should be given a reasonable opportunity to examine the claim made against them lest they should be drawn into avoidable litigations. The purpose of law is advancement of justice. The provisions in Section 80 CPC are not intended to be sued as booby-trap against ignorant and illiterate persons.

AIR 1969 SC 674

1969 All L.J. 570

3. In the plaint the main relief claimed was a declaration that the order of discharge or removal of the respondent was illegal and arbitrary. Therefore, there was no substantial difference between the two and the notice under Section 80 CPC could not be held to be invalid on the ground urged on behalf of the appellant.

AIR 1958 SC 905

4. When a summon is sent to a C.O. for service on a soldier under him, he is bound to cause the summons to be served upon him. He cannot refuse to have the same served, on the ground that under Section 144 of the Army Act of 1881 (44 & 45) Vict, (Ch 58) the soldier was entitled to protection.

(1881) II Mad 475 (477) (DB)

(1887) IO Mad 319 (322)(DB)

5. A mechanic serving in the Indian Marine is subject exactly to the same rules as every other person under the Code as regards service.

AIR 1914 Cal 845 (845, 846)

42 Cal 67 (DB)

4

Privileges under Criminal Procedure Code

The Code of Criminal Procedure, inter alia, contains provisions for procedure and powers of arrest, investigation of offences, constitution of Criminal Courts, their jurisdiction and procedure for trials etc. There are certain provisions in the Code which are of great importance to the members of the armed forces, and confer on them valuable privileges in these matters. They, along with the allied provisions, can be discussed conveniently by grouping them in the following groups:

(a) Privileges in matters of arrest.

(b) Privileges of protection from vexatious prosecutions.

(c) Privileges in the matters of choice of Courts.

Privileges in Matters of Arrest

The Code of Criminal Procedure, 1973 which has repealed the Code of Criminal Procedure, 1898 and has come into force with effects from 1st April 1974, has vide Section 45, incorporated a new provision of far reaching significance for the members of the armed forces, in so far as their arrest by civil police is concerned. According to this Section, no member of the armed forces of the union can be arrested by civil police for anything done or purported to be done by him in discharge of his official duties, except after obtaining the consent of the Central Government. The reason for this provision appears to be that when a member of the armed forces is deputed for the protection of public property or other such purposes, in discharge of his duties he may be called upon to take some action which may expose him to the possibility of being arrested and prosecuted by the civil police. Prior sanction of the Central Government has been made mandatory before any such arrest can be made. It is worthwhile noticing that the prior consent of the Central Government is required for the arrest of a member of the armed forces for anything done or even purported to be done by him in discharge of his official duties. However, the nature of the official duties has neither been specified nor restricted in any sense. Thus the terms of the Section are fairly wide and confer a very valuable safeguard.

In so far as the arrest by the civil police, on other occasions is concerned, there has been a misconception in the minds of considerable number of personnel in the armed forces, that the civil police has no power of arrest over them. A study of the relevant provisions of the Code of Criminal Procedure both of 1898 and of 1973 would reveal, that in matters of arrest in ordinary circumstances the Code does not make any distinction between the ordinary citizens and members of the armed forces. According to Section 41 of the Code of Criminal Procedure, 1973 (Section 54 of Code of Criminal Procedure, 1898) a police officer can arrest without any order from a Magistrate or without a warrant, any person who has been concerned in any cognizable offence or against whom a reasonable complaint has been made or credible information has been received of his having been so concerned. This provision does not make any distinction between the arrest of ordinary citizen and the members of the armed forces.

The Army, Navy and Air Force Acts, which are applicable to Military, Naval or Air Force personnel, also do not restrict the power of arrest of the civil police over persons subject to these Acts. The wordings of Section 475 of the Code of Criminal Procedure, 1973 (Section 549 of the Code of Criminal Procedure, 1898) also indicate that it only deals with the procedure for trial of military personnel, and does not restrict the powers of police to arrest a member of the armed forces or to investigate cognizable offences against them. Legal position therefore, appears to be that in matters of arrest for alleged offences, which are neither done nor purported to be done in performance of the official duties, the civil police has the same powers over the members of the armed forces as it has over the ordinary citizens. In such cases, the difference in procedure or the preferential treatment starts only when the police bring a member of the armed forces before a Magistrate for trial and the Magistrate has to give notice to the Commanding Officer before proceeding with the trial. Those provisions have been discussed separately subsequently.

Although the civil police has the same powers of arrest over the members of the armed forces in the above mentioned case, yet by the direction of the Government of India, they are required to report such arrest to the Commanding Officer of the person arrested for appropriate action. (Government of India, vide Home Department letter No. 11-1001 dated 6th Aug 1874 and Home Department letter No. F.709/29/Judl dated 13th Aug 1929) addressed to all the State Governments, has directed that immediately on the arrest of the military personnel, the report of the arrest should be sent by the police, to the Officer Commanding of the Unit/Regiment to which such person(s) belong(s) and to maintain close cooperation in such matters between the military and civil authorities. The same has been reiterated in Ministry of Home Affairs letter No. 31/49/Judl dated 27th Jan 49 and 50/54/Judl dated 14th Jul 54. It has been again stressed in Ministry of Home Affairs letter No. F. 9/7/60-Judl II dated 14th Jul 60 that the report should be sent immediately, as it would enable the Officer Commanding to take such timely measures as may be necessary in the circumstances of the case, whilst the delay would not only cause administrative inconvenience both to military and civil authorities but also would affect the morale and confidence of the defence personnel.

In addition, there are also certain special provisions in the Code of Criminal Procedure 1973 and the Army, Navy, Air Force Acts, concerning arrest of service personnel by civil authorities. Sub-Section 2 of Section 475 of Code of Criminal Procedure, 1973 (Sub-Section 2 of Section 549 of Code of Criminal Procedure, 1998) has cast a duty on all Magistrates, that when they receive a written application from the Commanding Officer that person, subject to military law, is accused of an offence, for which he is liable to be tried either by Criminal Court or by a Court Martial, and that such person should be arrested, Magistrate is to use his utmost endeavor to apprehend and secure the offender. Provisions of Section 105 of the Air Force Act, 1950 (Section 104 of the Army Act) are more comprehensive and enjoin a duty on all Magistrates and police officers that they are to aid in apprehension of a person subject to these Acts, who is accused of an offence under these Acts if he is within their jurisdiction and deliver him to military custody, when they receive a written application to that effect, signed by the Commanding Officer of such person.

In view of the foregoing, it is felt that when military authorities desire to take over the custody of a person subject to the Army/Air Force/Navy Acts, who is the accused of an offence under the said Acts, which includes civil offences, and he is in civil custody, the Commanding Officer should make an application to the effect to the Magistrate or police officer within whose jurisdiction such person is situated; and it is submitted that on receipt of the application, in view of the foregoing, the police officer or the magistrate is to hand over the custody to service authorities. A specimen of the letter, by the commanding officer, for taking over custody is produced below:-

Confidential

Ref No............ ....(Unit)

..............(Dated)

Orders Under Section 124 AFA

Whereas (Service No)...........(Rank)............(Name)...........Air Force Act, 1950 (45 of 1950) as a person enrolled under Act, who is serving under my command, is in civil custody for having committed some civil offences(s) in respect of which a criminal Court and Court-martial have each jurisdiction.

And Whereas proceedings for the trial of the said offence(s) have not so far been instituted before any Court.

Now therefore, in exercise of the powers vested in me under Section 124 of the Air Force Act, 1950, (45 of 1950), I decide that the proceedings in respect of the aforesaid offences against the said (rank)...............(name)...............shall be instituted before a Court-martial. And Further I direct that the said (rank)................(name)..... Shall be detained in Air Force custody. Signed at.......................on the..................day of................19 ....(Rank)

Commanding Officer

..................Wing

Note:-

To be modified in case of Army/Naval personnel by quoting the Corresponding law.

In this connection; it may also be noted that under Section 108 of the Air Force Act, 1950 (Section 107 of the Army Act, 1950), one of the duties of a Provost Marshal, which includes Deputy Provost Marshal and Assistant Provost Marshal is to take charge of persons confined for any offence. As a matter of fact, in the case of Commander KN Nanavati who was accused of a civil offence (Section 302 IPC) and was in the custody of civil police, on the application of the Naval authorities, that the accused be transferred to Naval custody in which custody he would continue to be detained, under the orders of Naval Provost Marshal, in exercise of his authority under Section 89 of the Navy Act, the Chief Presidency Magistrate Bombay did make an order, that the accused be transferred to Naval custody and he be detained in naval jail and detention quarters (Refer AIR 1961 SC 112).

Similarly, vide Section 106 of the Air Force Act, 1950 (Section 105 of the Army Act, 1950) in case of desertion, a Commanding Officer is authorized to give written information to such civil authorities, as in his opinion may be able to afford assistance for apprehending the deserter; and such civil authorities, on receipt of the written information by the Commanding Officer, are to take steps to apprehend the deserter in the same manner as if a warrant had been issued against him by a Magistrate. After apprehending, they are bound to deliver him to the nearest military authorities. A police officer has also been empowered to arrest without warrant any person whom he reasonably believes to be a deserter or travelling without authority. Immediately after the arrest, the said police officer has to bring such person before the nearest magistrate, to be dealt with according to law. (Section 10-6(2) Air Force Act, 1950; Section 105(2) Army Acts, 1950; Section 41 (i) Code of Criminal Procedure, (1973).

Safeguards against Arrest by Civil Police

Whilst on the subject of arrest by Civil Police, it would be in order to keep in mind the landmark judgement of the Hon'ble Supreme Court in the case of Joginder Kumar v. State of UP and others (1994 Supreme Court cases 260). In this judgement the Supreme Court held that no arrest can be made because it is lawful for police officers to do so. The existence of the power to arrest is one thing. The justification for the exercise of it is quite another. The Police Officer must be able to justify the arrest or exercise of his powers to do so. The Hon'ble Supreme Court also laid down important safeguards for a person before the Civil Police arrests him.

The right of the arrested person to have someone informed and to consult privately with a lawyer. This right is inherent in Articles 21 & 22 (1) of the Constitution and requires to be recognized and scrupulously protected. For effective enforcement of these fundamental rights the following requirements are must:

(a) An arrested person being held in custody, is entitled, if he requests to have one friend, relative or other person who is known to him or likely to take interest in his welfare to him or likely to take interest in his welfare to be told as far as practical that he has been arrested and where he is being detained;

(b) The Police Officer shall inform the arrested person when he is brought to the Police Station of this right;

(c) An entry shall be required to be made in the diary as to that he has been informed of the arrest;

(d) It shall be the duty of the Magistrate to see that when an arrested person is produced, he should satisfy himself that these requirement have been complied with;

(e) A person who is arrested has a right to be informed the offence for which he is being arrested.

The Supreme Court also said that these requirements are not exhaustive. The Director Generals of Police of all the States in India shall issue necessary instructions requiring due observance of these requirements. In addition, departmental instructions requiring due observance of these requirements. In addition, departmental instructions shall also be issued that the Police Officer making arrest should also enter in the case diary the reasons for making arrest.

These safeguards are very vital and knowledge of these is considered extremely important. For relevant orders of the State Police the individuals concerned should contact the

Civil Police and obtain a copy thereof. In case these instructions are not complied with, persons arrested should at the first available opportunity should inform the Magistrate of these ommissions for issue of necessary directions.

Whilst on the subject of arrest a few words about the legal provisions of bail would also be in order.

The provisions of bail are contained in Chapters XXIII of the Code of Criminal Procedures. As far as bailable offences are concerned, when a person appears or is brought before a court, the officer-in-charge of the Police Station or the Court must release him on bail if the arrested person furnishes the requisite bail bond.

The real difficulty may arise where a person accused is of a non-bailable offence and is arrested and applies for bail in the court of a Magistrate. Rules in this case are that such a person should not be released on bail, if there is a reasonable ground for believing that he is guilty of an offence punishable with death or imprisonment for life or such a person has previously been convicted of an offence punishable with death, imprisonment for seven years or more, or he is previously convicted on two or more occasions. On an information of a non-bailable cognizable offence, the rigidity of these rules would not however apply if the accused person is under the age of 16 years or is woman or sick or infirm. The rigidity of the rule may also be waived if the Court is of the view that it is desirable to release him on bail for any sufficient reason.

It is advisable for a servicemen or ex-serviceman, who is arrested by Civil Police, to bring to the notice of Magistrate that he belongs to the community of soldiers who are well-disciplines and have great regard for Law and the Rules. Since they are law-abiding, they would cooperate with the investigating authorities and the Court should grant him the bail. It is felt that these grounds would tend the magistrate to consider the application favourably.

Protection from Vexatious Prosecution

Section 130 and 131 of the Code of Criminal Procedure, 1973 (Sections 129, 130 and 131 of the Code of Criminal Procedure 1898) deal with the use of military force in dispersing unlawful assemblies, and the duties and powers of commissioned officers of the armed forces in this regard. Under these provisions, normally at the request of the magistrate of the highest rank present, the officer in Command of any portion of troops is authorized to use military force to disperse unlawful assemblies, to arrest and confine any person, as necessary. In certain circumstances when the public security is manifestly endangered by any unlawful assembly and no magistrate can be contacted, any commissioned officer of the armed force can disperse such assembly with the help of armed force under his command, and can arrest or confine any member of such assembly, so that he may be dealt with according to law. Under this clause, immediately when it becomes possible for the commissioned officer to communicate with the magistrate, he has to inform the magistrate and thereafter he has to obey the instructions of such magistrate.

Aid to Civil Power

It will be seen that under these sections, the members of the armed forces have been given certain magisterial and police powers under certain circumstances. In order to protect the members of the armed forces, from prosecution or criminal liability arising out of the exercise of these powers, the legislature has enacted Section 132 of the Criminal Procedure Code. According to this Section no inferior officer, soldier or an airman of armed forces, when he was doing any act in obedience to an order which, he was bound to obey, or the commissioned officer, who was acting in good faith under the powers given to him; under Section 131, would be deemed to have committed any offence. Further, no prosecution can be launched against such person for any offence alleged to have been committed by him whilst acting under these powers, unless the prior sanction from the Central Government is obtained. If this provision was not there, the members of the armed forces would possibly have been subject to unnecessary and numerous vexatious criminal prosecutions.

For requisitioning the use of the armed forces for dispersing unlawful assemblies and allied purposes, under Section 130 of Criminal Procedure Code there is no legal requirement that the requisition by the Magistrate should be in writing. However, in order to avoid any future complications, it is advisable that whenever any officer of the armed forces is called upon by the Magistrate to act under these sections, he should ask the magistrate to give the requisition in writing. The written requisition normally takes the following form:

I.............................Magistrate of the ....Class,

Acting under Section 130 of the Code of Criminal Procedure, require No......... Rank...........Name........................of the unit...............To disperse an unlawful assembly at.................O'clock (approximately) on the....................day of............. 19.........at.............

Countersigned........................ Signed...................

Military Officer Magistrate

However, when there is no time to give the request in writing, the officer should ask the Magistrate to repeat the request in presence of two service personnel and as soon as it becomes possible, to confirm the same in writing.

Once the requisition is given, it is the duty of the officer to obey the requisition, but the actual manner, the quantum of force, manpower, equipment to be utilized to achieve the objects is entirely within the officer's domain. It must however be remembered that the force used should be as little and the injury to persons and property should be as little as may be consistent with dispersing the assembly or arresting and detaining such persons. Further, it is also advisable that the officers should be fully conversant with their powers and duties in this regard. They have been elaborately laid down in Regulations for the Air Force, the Regulations for the Army and Manual of India Military Law. So long as the officers act in good faith which means with due care and attention and in accordance with these instructions, the officers will be protected.

It is also useful to note that according to Section 197 of the Criminal Procedure Code, no prosecution can be entertained against a public servant for an offence alleged to have been committed by him whilst acting or purporting to act in discharge of his official duties, without the sanction of the Government. The object of this provision again is to guard against vexatious proceedings against public servants and to secure well considered opinion of a superior authority before a prosecution is permitted to be launched against him. Prosecution, without the sanction of the government, in such cases is without jurisdiction and illegal.

Whilst on the subject of aid to civil power acting under Armed Forces (Special Powers Act 1958), a few DO's and DON'Ts for the service personnel are also relevant. These are:

DO's

1. Action before operation:
   - (a) Act only in the area declared "Disturbed area" under Section 3 of the Armed Forces Act of 1958.
   - (b) Power to open fire using force or arrest is to be exercised under the Act only by an Officer JCO/ WO or an NCO.
   - (c) Before launching any raid/search definite information about the activities to be obtained from the local civil authorities.

(d) As far as possible co-opt representatives of local civil administration during the raid.

2. Action during operation:

(a) In case of necessity of opening fire using the force against the suspect or any person acting in contravention to law and order, ascertain first that it is essential for maintenance of public order. Open fire only after due warning.

(b) Arrest only those who have committed cognizable offence or who are about to commit cognizable offence or against whom reasonable ground exists to prove that they have committed or about to commit cognizable offence.

(c) Ensure that the troops under command do not harass innocent people, destroy property of the public or unnecessarily enter into the houses/dwelling of people not engaged in any unlawful activity.

(d) Ensure that women are not searched/arrested without the presence of Female Police. In fact, women should be searched by female police only.

3. Action after operation:

(a) After arrest, prepare a list of persons so arrested.

(b) Hand over the arrested persons to the nearest Police Station with least possible delay.

(c) Whilst handing over to police, a report should accompany with detailed circumstances occasioning the arrest.

(d) Every delay in handling over the suspect to the police must be justified and should be reasonable, depending upon the place, time of arrest and the terrain in which such person has been arrested. Least possible delay may be two to three hours and extending to 24 hours or so depending upon a particular case.

(e) After raid make out a list of all arms, ammunition or any other incriminating material/document taken into possession

(f) All such arms ammunition, stores etc. should be handed over to Police Station along with seizure memo.

(g) Obtain receipt of persons and arms/ammunition stores etc. so handed over to the police.

(h) Make record of the area where operation is launched having the date and the time of the persons participating in such raids.

Privileges in the Matters of Choice of Courts

The most important privilege and safeguard granted by legislature to military personnel under the Criminal Procedure Code, is the privilege of the choice of the Court for the purposes of trial. Every person accused of an offence is liable to be tried by a criminal Court. The trials in criminal Court are normally prolonged, time consuming and expensive. If there was no provision like the one contained in Section 475 of the Code of Criminal Procedure, 1973 (Section 549 of the Code of Criminal Procedure, 1898) and the Rules made there under for trials of military personnel for civil offence, it would have caused serious complications and would also have subjected military personnel to great harassment, inconvenience and expense. Section 475 of the Criminal Procedure Code, 1973 empowered the Central Government to make Rules as to the choice of Court i.e., Criminal Court or the Court-martial, in which a person subject to military law, shall be tried. In pursuance of these powers, the Central Government has made Rules called "The Criminal Courts and Court-martial (Adjustment of Jurisdiction) Rules, 1978."

These Rules along with relevant provisions of the Army/Air Force Act regulate adjustment of jurisdiction, where an offender is liable to be tried both by the criminal Court as well as by a Court-martial. The Rules also outline the procedure to be followed in such cases. By Section 475 of Cr.P.C., the magistrates have also been directed to have regard to such Rules, and in proper cases when a person, subjects to military law accused of a civil offence is brought before them to deliver him to his Commanding Officer along with the statement of offence for the purpose of being tried by a Court-martial. The Criminal Courts and Court-martial (Adjustment of Jurisdiction) Rules, 1978 are reproduced below for ready reference:

The Criminal Courts and Court-martial (Adjustment of Jurisdiction) Rules - 1978 (Published vide SO 488 Dated 09 Feb 78)

1. These rules may be called the Criminal Courts and Court-martial (Adjustment of Jurisdiction) Rules, 1978.
2. In these rules, unless the context otherwise requires:-
   (a) "Commanding Officer"
      (i) in relation to a person subject to military law, means the officer Commanding the unit to which such person belongs or is attached;
      (ii) in relation to a person subject to naval law, means the Commanding officer of the ship or naval establishment or unit to which such person belongs or is attached; and
      (iii) in relation to a person subject to air force law, means the officer for the time being in command of the unit to which such person belongs or is attached;
      (v) in relation to a person subject to the coast guard law, means the Commanding Officer of the coast guard ship or establishment or unit to which such person belongs or is attached;

(b) "competent air force authority" means the Chief of the Air Staff or air or other commanding any Command, Group, Wing or Station in which the accused person is serving, or where such person is serving in a field area, the Officer Commanding the forces or the air force in the field;

(c) "competent military authority" means the Chief of army cops, division, area, sub-area or independent brigade in which the accused person is serving, and, except in cases falling under Section 69 of the Army Act 1950 (46 of 1950) in which death has resulted, the officer commanding the brigade or sub-area or station in which the accused person is serving.

(d) "competent naval authority" means the Chief of the Naval Staff or the Flag Officer Commanding-in-Chief, Western Naval Command, Bombay or the Flag Officer Commanding-in-Chief, Eastern Naval Command Vishskhapatnam or the Flag Officer Commanding, Southern Naval Area, Cochin or the Flag Officer Commanding,Western Fleet, Flag Officer Commanding, Eastern Fleet or Senior Naval Officer where the accused person is serving;

(e) "competent coast guard authority" means the Director General or Inspector General or Deputy Inspector General within whose command the Accused person is serving.

3. Where a person subject to military, naval, air force or coast guard law, or any other law relating to the Armed Forces of the Union for the time being in force is brought before a Magistrate and charged with an offence for which he is also liable to be tried by a Court-martial or coast guard Court, such Magistrate shall not proceed to try such person or to commit the case to the Court of Session, unless:-

(a) he is moved thereto by a competent military, naval air force or coast guard authority, or

(b) he is of opinion, for reasons to be recorded, that he should so proceed or to commit without being moved thereto by such authority.

4. Before proceeding under clause (b) of rule 3, the Magistrate shall give a written notice to the Commanding Officer or the competent military, naval, air force or coast guard authority, as the case may be, of the accused and until the expiry of a period of fifteen days from the date of service of the notice he shall not:-

   (a) convict or acquit the accused under Section 252, sub-section (1) (2) of Section 255 sub-section (1) of Section 256 of Section 257 of the Code of Criminal Procedure, 1973 (2 of 1974), or hear him in his defence under Section 254 of the said Code; or

   (b) frame in writing a charge against the accused under Section 240 or sub-section (1) of Section 246 of the said Code; or

   (c) make an order committing the accused for trial to the Court of Session under Section 209 of the said Code; or

   (d) make over the case for inquiry or trial under Section 192 of the said Code.

5. Where a magistrate has been moved by the competent military, naval, air force or coast guard authority, as the case may be, under clause (a) of rule 3 and such authority, subsequently, as the case may be, under clause (a) of rule 3 and such authority, subsequently gives notice to such Magistrate that, in the opinion of such authority, the accused should be tried by a Court-martial or coast guard Court, such Magistrate if he has not taken any action or made any order under rule 4 before receiving the notice shall stay the proceedings and, if the accused is in his power or under his control, shall deliver him together with the statement referred to in sub-section (1) of Section 475 of the said Code to the officer specified in the said sub-section.

6. Where within the period of fifteen days mentioned in rule 4, or any time thereafter but before the Magistrate takes any action or makes any order referred to in that rule, the Commanding Officer of the accused or the competent military, naval, air force or coast guard authority, as the case may be, gives notice to the Magistrate that in the opinion of such officer or authority, the accused should be tried by

a Court-martial or coast guard court the Magistrate shall stay the proceedings, and if the accused is in his power or under his control shall deliver him together with the statement referred to in sub-section (i) of Section 475 of the said Code to the Officer specified in the said sub-section.

7. (1) When an accused has been delivered by the Magistrate under rule 5 or 6. the commanding officer of the accused or the competent military, naval or air force or coast guard authority as the case may be, shall, as soon as may be, inform the Magistrate whether the accused has been *tried* by a Court-martial or coast guard Court or other effectual proceedings have been taken or ordered to be taken against him.

   When the Magistrate has been informed under sub-rule (1) that the accused was not been tried or other effectual proceedings have not been taken or ordered to be taken against him, the Magistrate shall report the circumstances to the State Government which may, in consultation with the Central Government, take appropriate steps to ensure that the accused person is dealt with in accordance with law.

8. Notwithstanding anything in the foregoing rules, where it comes to the notice of a Magistrate that a person subject to military, naval, air force or coast guard law or any other law relating to the Armed Forces of the Union for the time being in force has committed an offence, proceedings in respect of which ought to be instituted before him and that the presence of such person cannot be procured except through military naval, air force or coast guard authorities, the Magistrate may by a written notice require the commanding officer of such person either to deliver such persons to a Magistrate to be named in the said notice for being proceeded against according to law, or to stay the proceedings against such person before the Court-martial or coast guard Court if since instituted and to make a reference to the Central Government for determination as to the Court before which proceedings should be instituted.

9. Where a person, subject to military, naval, air force or coast guard law, or any other law relating to the Armed Forces of

the Union for the time being in force, has committed an offence which in the opinion of competent military, naval, air force or coast guard authority, as the case may be ought to be tried by a Magistrate in accordance with the civil law in force or where the Central Government has, on a reference mentioned in rule 8, decided the proceedings against such person should be instituted before a Magistrate, the commanding officer of such person under proper escort to that Magistrate.

Vide Section 71 of the Air Force Act, 1950/Section 69 of the Army Act, 1950 all civil offences are deemed to be offences under the Air Force Act/or the Army Act as the case may be, and as such, the offenders are also liable to be tried by Court-martial under the respective Acts for such offences. In such cases Section 124 of the Air Force Act, 1950, Section 125 of the Army Act, 1950 has given the right of choice of court (i.e. Criminal Court or Court-martial a person subject to military law shall be tried, to the Competent Air Force/Army authorities. If the civil Court holds a different opinion and considers that the accused should be tried by a Criminal Court and not by a Court-martial, it can ask the military authorities either to deliver the offender to the nearest magistrate to be proceeded against in accordance with law, or to stay the proceedings and make a reference to Central Government on this question is final as per Section 125 of the Air Force Act, 1950/Section 126 of the Army Act, 1950.

It would, therefore, be seen that initially the choice of the Court rests with; the military authorities. The trials by military Courts are normally speedy and less expensive. All facilities are provided by the State and the officers who constitute the Court are conversant with the ways of service life and can appreciate the position of the offender much better, having regard to the general service knowledge and exigencies of service. All these are important safeguards against possible miscarriage of justice. It also saves considerable harassment delay and expense. On the other hand, it was contended before the Honourable Supreme Court in Ram Swarup v.

Union of India (AIR 1965 SC 247) that the provisions of Section 125 of the Army Act were discriminatory and violated Article 14 of the Constitution and it acted against the interests of the accused. The Honourable Court after going through the various provisions of the Act and Rules with respect to the trials by Courts-martial, over ruled the plea. It was observed by them that the procedure followed by Court-martial was quite elaborate and it generally followed the pattern of the Criminal Procedure Code and that there were various provisions in the Act, to show the considerations by which the service authorities should be guided in making the choice, and the officers were expected to be guided by those considerations. Therefore, Section 125 of the Army Act, could not be said to infringe the provisions of Article 14 of the Constitution under the respective Service Acts and the Rules, the Commanding Officers have vast powers regarding the disposal of the charge Vide Rule 24 of the Air Force Rules, 1969 (and corresponding provisions of the Army and the Navy Regulations), a Commanding Officer may dismiss a charge brought before him even if the evidence shows that an offence under the Act has been committed, provided in his discretion he thinks/is satisfied, that the charge ought not to be proceeded with. Such a decision has to be governed among other considerations, by the service records, character and past conduct of the accused. Further, there is no obligation that once a case has been taken over from the Civil Court it must be tried by a Court-martial. The charge can be dismissed, summarily disposed off, or tried by a Court-martial as the case may, depending upon the facts of the case. Dismissal of the case, however, has to be after undergoing the formal judicial motion and not an administrative decision.

Vide Rule 5 of the Criminal Courts and Court-martial (Adjustment of Jurisdiction) Rules, 1978 normally a magistrate before whom a person subject to Army, Navy, or Air Force Act is brought and charged with an offence for which he is liable to be tried by a Court-martial shall not proceed with the case without giving a written notice to the Commanding

Officer or the accused person. By such notice he is to enquire whether the accused should be tried by a Court-martial or by a criminal Court. The Commanding Officer has to reply within 7 days of the receipt of such notice. A specimen form of reply to such notice is given below:(Performa Notice to be forwarded under Rule 5 of the Criminal Courts and Court-martial (Adjustment of Jurisdiction) Rules, 1978.

Name of Unit/Detachment

(Postal Address)

Telephone No.......... Date:

File Reference..........

......................Magistrate.

(Designation and address of Magistrate)

In the case of..............................

(personal particulars of accused)

(Case No...........)

Notice under Rule 5 of Criminal Courts and Court-martial (Adjustment of Jurisdiction Rules, 1978).

Reference is made to your notice No...........dated...............

Whereas the above named accused person, belonging/attached to this units/Detachments, who has been brought before you and charged with the offence(s) of..............is a person subject to the Air Force Act, 1950.

And Whereas I ....in respect of the above accused person, the competent authority as defined in Rule 2(b) of the above Rules;

Now therefore, I give you notice that in my opinion/in the opinion of aforesaid competent authority, the accused person, named above should be tried by Court-martial. You are accordingly requested to stay proceedings, and to deliver the above accused person, if he is in your power or under your control together with the statement prescribed in sub-section (1) of Section 475 Cr.P.C. to..............who is being instructed to report to you with this/a copy of this letter and whose two specimen signatures are given below:

Specimen signatures (1)..............................

(2)..............................

Signed at....................this the.............day of

Signatures

(Name)...................Rank

Officer Commanding

Unit/Detachment Stamp Name of Unit/Detachment

Note – To be modified in case of Army/Naval personnel by quoting the corresponding law.

If the Commanding Officer informs the Magistrate that in his opinion; the accused should be tried by Court-martial, the magistrate will stay the proceedings and if the accused is in his power or under his control, will deliver him, with the statement of the offence to the Commanding Officer.

Vide Rule 7 of the said Rules, when the accused has been delivered to the Commanding Officer, the Commanding Officer or the other competent military authority has to inform the magistrate whether the accused has been tried by Court-martial or other effectual proceedings have been taken or ordered to be taken against him. If however, the magistrate considers that the accused should be tried by him, and the military authorities do not agree he can require that the matter be referred to the Central Government for decision,, whose decision will be final.

There has been considerable controversy in judicial pronouncements with regard to the fact whether non-compliance of Section 549 of the Code of Criminal Procedure, 1898 (now Section 475 of the Code of Criminal Procedure, 1973) by the magistrate strikes at the basic root of his jurisdiction and thus vitiates the subsequent trial, or it is only a procedural irregularity not striking at the basic jurisdiction. It was held by Madras High Court in 1949. MAD Law Journal 44(61) that when a person subject to military law is brought before a magistrate, charged with an offence for which he is triable under the Army Act, the Magistrate is bound to follow the procedure and give notice to the Commanding Officer as required by the Rules. Failure to give the requisite notice renders the proceeding before the Magistrate illegal and without jurisdiction. Acquiescence on the part of the accused in such illegal proceedings will not regularize the proceedings. So also in Avadh Bihari Singh v. State, the Calcutta High Court (AIR 1967 CAL 323) held that the non-compliance of Rules framed under Section 549 was an illegality vitiating the trial. [Also see Major Gopinath v. State (AIR 1963 MP 2491970 P & H)] However, in Ajit Singh v. State of Punjab (AIR 1970 P & H 351), the Punjab High Court has held that whether the non-compliance of Section 549 and the Rules made thereunder was an illegality, vitiating the trial or would be a mere irregularity not vitiating the same, would depend upon the circumstances of each case. In that case a person; subject to Air Force Act, 1950 was brought before the magistrate for committal for an offence under Section 302 of the Indian Penal Code. The fact that he was in the Air Force was brought to the notice of the Magistrate only at the time of recording his plea after framing the charge against him, and in Sessions Court at the time of examination under Section 342 Cr.P.C. after closing of evidence at the trial. Apart from this, there was no material before those Courts to show that the accused had anything to do with the Air Force or that he was on active service. It was held that under the circumstances failure of the Courts in observing the provisions of Section 549 and the Rules made thereunder, was not an illegality, vitiating the trial, specially as no prejudice had been caused to the accused. It was mere irregularity curable under Section 537 of the Criminal Procedure Code. Similarly, in Joginder Singh v. State of M.P. (AIR 1971 SC 500) it was held that when the competent military authority knew well the charges against the accused and that investigations were being conducted by civil police, released him from military custody and handed him over to the civil authority, the surrender indicated the decision of the military authority not to try the accused person by Court-martial. On this subject a reference may also be usefully made to Lt. Col. Menon v. State (AIR 1967 RAJ 115) Lt. Col. SK Kashyap v. State AIR 1971 SC 1120m SPE DELHI v. Lt. Col. SK Loriya, AIR 1972 SC 2548). It has however, been held by the Supreme Court that merely because a police officer started the investigation, it does not debar the competent military authority to order that the accused would be tried by a Court-martial.

From the case law cited above, it would be seen that the question of non-compliance of Section 549 of the Code of Criminal Procedure, 1898 (Section 475 of Code of Criminal Procedure, 1973) is rather disputed. It is, therefore, advisable that when a person subject to military law and accused of a civil offence is brought before a Criminal Court, he should, at once, make it clear to the Court that he is a person subject to the military law and the attention of the Court should be drawn to the provisions of Section 549 of the Code of Criminal Procedure, 1898 (Now Section 475 of the Code of Criminal Procedure, 1973) and Criminal Court and Court-martial (Adjustment of Jurisdiction) Rules, 1978 and the Court should be requested to give notice to the Commanding Officer in terms of Rule 5 of the said Rules. Similarly, the military should be careful whilst handing over the accused person to the civil authorities for investigation where they intend that the accused should be tried by Court-martial, lest it may be construed as a decision of the competent military authority to surrender the accused person for trial by the Civil Court. In such a case it should be made clear that the handing over to the civil authority is only for the purposes of investigation and is not to be taken as decision to surrender the accused for trial by the Civil Court.

Regarding the concurrent jurisdiction for trial of offences under Section 162, 163, 165 or Section 165-A of the IPC or Section 5 of the Prevention of Corruption Act, 1947 alleged to have been committed by person subject to military law, upto 1966, the legal position was anomalous. By virtue of Section 7 of the Criminal Law Amendment Act, 1952, such offences were triable exclusively, by the special judges, appointed under the said Act. Section 475 of the Code of Criminal Procedure 1973 (Section 549 of Code of Criminal Procedure 1898) or the Rules made thereunder were therefore not applicable. It was held by the Hon'ble Supreme Court (AIR 1961 SC 1762) that Rule 3 of Criminal Court-martial (Adjustment of Jurisdiction) Rules, 1952 did not apply to a special judge constituted under the Criminal Law Amendment Act 1952 as by reading Section 6(i) and 8(2) of the Criminal Law Amendment Act, 1952, it was clear that the Court of special judge was at par with the Court of a sessions judge whereas, Section 549 of Criminal Procedure Code, 1898 and the Rules made thereunder, referred to, as to what was to be done by a magistrate. Similarly, it was held by the Calcutta High Court (AIR 1949 Cal 641, 644) that Section 549 did not apply to trial held by special tribunal constituted under West Bengal Criminal Law Amendment Act, (7 of 1947) because the special tribunal constituted under the Act was not a magistrate within the meaning of Section 549 of the Criminal Procedure Code, 1898.

Since the word civil offence is defined in the Army/Air Force Act, 1950 and Navy Act, 1957 as an offence which is triable by a Criminal Court and the Criminal Court, for that purpose, means a Court of ordinary criminal justice in any part of India, difficulties also arose as to whether these offences would be civil offences within the definition, since special judge, may not be within the meaning of "Court of ordinary criminal justice".

These lacunae caused considerable difficulties to the armed forces and created anomalous situations. In order to restore the jurisdiction exercisable by a Court-martial, for such offences alleged to be committed by person subject to military law, Section 11 of the Criminal Law Amendment Act, 1952 has been inserted by the Criminal Law Amendment (Amending)

Act, 1966. This Section clearly provides that nothing in the Criminal Law Amendment Act, 1952 shall affect the jurisdiction exercisable by or the procedure applicable to any Court or other authority under military, naval or air force law. It further declares that for the purpose of military, naval or air force law, the Courts of special judge shall be deemed to be a Court of ordinary criminal justice. Further the provisions of sections 350 and 549 of the Code of Criminal Procedure, 1973 shall, so far as may be, apply to the proceeding before a special judge and for the purpose of the said provisions, a special judge shall be deemed to be a magistrate.

With these amendments, the jurisdiction of the Court-martial to try persons subject to Military/Naval/Air Force law who are accused of these offences has been completely restored. It is submitted that the definition to civil offence as given in the Air Force Act, 1950 and the Army Act, 1950, is very wide and covers all offences triable by a Criminal Court irrespective of the Act under which it is punishable; and thus the priviledge of the choice of Court extends to all such offences.

Gist of case law

A gist of some of the important cases, decided by various Courts, on the subject of 'Aid to Civil Power' and the Criminal Courts and Court-martial (Adjustment and Jurisdiction) Rules, 1978 is appended below:

Section 130 Cr.P.C.

It is the duty of the officers of the armed forces to aid the civil authorities in quelling disorder.

AIR 1931 Bomb 57(59) - 32
Cri L Jour 403 (SB)

Sections 132, 197 Cr.P.C.

Cr.P.C. (1974) – Sections 132 and 197 – Prosecution of member of Armed Forces – Sanction to prosecute granted under Section 132. No sanction to take cognizance granted under Section 197 – Taking cognizance is illegal – Decision of Punjab and Haryana High Court reversed.

AIR 1987 SC 735

Section 549 Cr.P.C.

1. The provisions of this Section have to be constrained very strictly and jurisdiction should not be given up unless the plain meaning of the words of the statute so require.

   AIR 1949 Cal 641 (644)=51 Cri LJ 10=1LR (1950)2 Cal 45 (DB)

2. For the applicability of Section 549 it is necessary that both the ordinary Criminal Court as well as the Court-martial functioning under the Army Act should have jurisdiction.

   AIR 1958 Bomb 354(365)= 1958 Cri LJ 1144

3. The Section does not apply to a trial held by a Special Tribunal constituted under the West Bengal Criminal Law Amendment Act (7 of 1947).

   AIR 1949 Cal 641 (644)=51 Cri LJ 10=1LR (1950)1 Cal 45 (DB)

4. The Court of a special Judge under the Criminal Law Amendment Act, 1952, is on par with the Court of a Session Judge. It cannot, therefore, be said that the rules framed under Section 549 would have to be followed by the Court of a Special Judge.

   AIR 1958 Bomb 354 (365) = 1958 Cri LJ 928 = (1962) 1961 (2) Cri LJ 928 = (1962) 2 SCR 195

5. Where the attention of the Magistrate who tries the accused is not drawn to this Section or to the rules framed under and he does not act in accordance with the trial is illegal and the conviction and sentence must be set aside.

AIR 1945 Mad 289. Held no Longer good law in AIR 1970 Punj 351 in view of AIR 1961 SC 1762

6. When a person subject to the military law is brought before a magistrate is not absolved from; the statutory duty of acting according to the rules framed under Section 549, because the prescribed military authority under Section 69 of the Army Act had come to the conclusion that the proceedings should be instituted in an ordinary Criminal Court.

AIR 1967 Raj 221 (225)

7. Under Rules made by Government of India in 1935, accused in military service charge of theft before Magistrate – Magistrate not of opinion that he should try the accused – prosecution given opportunity to obtain permission of military authority for trial of the accused – Military authorities not moving magistrate to proceed with trial – Discharge of accused held valid.

AIR 1945 Bom 176 (198) (DB) Held no longer good law in AIR 1970 Punj 35s in view of AIR 1961 SC 1762

8. Accused delivered to Military authorities without statement under Section 549(1) or requisition under Section 549(2) – Rule issued under Section 491 was discharged as military authorities decided not to have trial by Court-martial and released accused on bail.

AIR 1945 Cal 340 (341)=47 CriL, 125 (DB)

9. Where the Central Government has already accorded sanction for the prosecution of military personnel by a Criminal Court, that sanction cannot be subsequently interfered with by the military authority.

AIR 1969 Raj 115 (118)=1969 Cri LJ 519 AIR 1970 Punj 351 (360)= 1970 Cri LJ 1119 72 Punj LR 396 (FS)

10. Accused, a serving sepoy subject to provisions of Army Act, tried and convicted under Section 4A of Madras Prohibition Act – Held in absence of any material for Magistrate to that accused was a sepoy, it could not be said that procedure followed by him was wrong.

AIR 1969 Mad 321 (32)=1969 Cri SJ 1143 = 1969 (2) Mad SJ 534
AIR 1970 Punj 351 AIR 1967 Cal 3323 & AIR 1945 Mad 289 AIR 1945 Bom 176, held no longer good law in view of AIR 1961 SC 1762

11. On receipt of notice from the military authority the Magistrate must stay proceeding and hand over the accused to military authorities.

AIR 1963 MP 249 Pra 249 251, 253=2; 253=1963 (2) Cri LJ 161 = 1963 MP LJ 382 AIR 12863 Mys 196, AIR 1960 J&K 145 (145) 147, 148

12. The provisions of Rule 3 (S.R.O. 709-D/-17.4.52) cannot be invoked in a case when the Police had merely started investigation. It applies to a case where the police has completed investigation and the accused is brought before the magistrate for submission of charge sheet.

AIR 1969 SC 414 (419)=1969 Cri LJ 663=(1969) 2 SCR 177

13. When the mandatory provisions of Section 549 and the rules made thereunder are not complied with the procedural defect is not merely an irregularity but is an illegality which affects the jurisdiction of the magistrate.

AIR 1967 Cal 323 (326)=1967 Cri LJ 471

Note: For additional cases, references can also be made to

AIR 1967 Raj 221, Cal Cr.Rev 41/70, AIR 1964, All 371, AIR 1965 SC 257, AIR 1960 J&K 139, 1946 Lah 103, AIR 1928 All 672

14. Sections 124, 125 and 72 – Criminal Courts and Court-martial (Adjustment of Jurisdiction) Rules, 1952 – Rr 3 to 6 – Criminal Procedure Code, 1973 – Section 475 – Jurisdiction punishable both under Air Force Act and other laws committed by a person while on active service of Air Force – inherent jurisdiction of Criminal Courts to try civil offences not barred – Provision of Air Force Act and Section 475 Cr.P.C. envisages an arrangement for proper exercise of such jurisdiction – Conflict of jurisdiction has to be resolved by the Central Government whose decision will be final – Accused has no option or right to claim trial by a particular forum – Criminal court must give notice to the Commanding Officer of the accused for exercising his option – But no particular form of such notice prescribed – Where full and complete information is provided to the authorities requirement of law would stand complied with irrespective of the fact whether such information was given by way of notice or otherwise. On facts, handing over of the custody of the accused to civil authorities in execution of warrant of arrest issued by the Criminal Court indicates that the authorities did not opt to try the accused by Court-martial – Army Act, 1950, Sections 125 and 126.

1995 (1) SCC 90

5

Legal and Financial Assistance to Personnel involved in Litigation

Having dealt with the subject of civil and criminal litigation, by or against the members of the armed forces in Civil Courts, it may also be useful to deal with the provisions regarding legal and financial assistance, admissible to them under the Departmental Rules. Although this is not a safeguard or a privilege granted by statute, yet considering its practical importance to the persons concerned, it is considered to be relevant to find place in this work.

Departmental Regulations

According to the Departmental regulations in the armed forces, if an airman or a soldier is charged with criminal offence and is being prosecuted by the Government in civil Courts, his defence is the responsibility of the Government provided the airman or the soldier was "At duty" at the time of commission of the alleged offence. "At duty" in this context means, in contrast to be "on leave" and therefore, if at the time of the alleged offence, the airman or the soldier was not on leave, he shall be deemed to be "At duty". In such cases the Station Commander/Brigade or Sub-Area Commander will consult the District Magistrate, and arrange with him for the selection and remuneration of a pleader, advocate, barrister etc. as the importance and necessity of the case may require. The procedures for employment of the counsel and the payment of his fees have also been laid down in the departmental regulations. Such assistance is available not only in the trial Courts, but also for appeals in the Appellate Court.

When any claim under the civil law is preferred by any party, against an officer or an airman or a soldier in respect of damages arising out of a M.T. accident, when; he was driving the M.T. vehicle on duty, the defence of the suit, is to be undertaken by the State. It will be undertaken irrespective of the fact whether the accident was or was not due to the negligence of the officer or the soldier concerned. In case an airmen or a soldier meets with an accident whilst driving service vehicle when not on duty, but with the permission of the competent authority, the state will undertake the defence only when, but for the sovereign immunity of the State, a claim would lie against the government as an employer. If the Station Commander/Brigade or Sub-Area Commander has any doubt on the subject, he should consult the specified civil law officer and seek his advice. In case of officers however, they will normally be left to undertake their own defence except in exceptional circumstances, in which case separate orders of the Central Government will be obtained.

A provision has also been made to sanction an advance from the Public Funds, to a M.T. driver, who has been involved in a traffic accident and had been subsequently fined by the Civil Court. This is to enable him to pay the fine, but is admissible when the Station Commander considers the retention of the driver's service in the interest of the State.

So far as a civil suit against an officer in his official capacity is concerned, departmental regulations provide that when he receives a notice under Section 80 of the Civil Procedure Code, 1908 he should report the circumstances to the superior authority along with detailed facts of the case. The specified authority after necessary examination would accord sanction for the defence of the suit at the Government expense. Before according sanction, however, the authority concerned will obtain legal advice on the case from the authorized civil law officer concerned. Similarly, if an officer is involved in a criminal case, for an act, purported to be done by him in exercise of his official duties, in such cases also the full facts of the case and the circumstances should be reported to superior authorities for sanction may be accorded depending upon the facts of each case. In other cases, to meet the expenses of litigation individuals concerned can in addition to other sources, apply and obtain advance from their provident funds under the relevant Provident Fund Rules. They may also apply for a grant or loan from the benevolent or other fund maintained for the welfare of troops. In appropriate and extreme cases, application can also be made for the financial assistance from the State, but this will be considered only in exceptional cases, where special circumstances so justify. In such cases also, the Central Government may sanction an advance or a special grant, depending upon the merits of the case.

Whilst on the subject of legal and financial assistance to those involved in litigation, let us have a look in brief on the matter of free legal aid, by the State, the constitutional mandate and various statutory provisions.

Free Legal Aid under the Law

India, being a welfare state and litigation being an expensive proposition, it has always been felt that a person should not be deprived of his right to seek justice merely because of his economic disability. Various commissions and committees have gone into this question, notable amongst them being the 14th Law Commission Report of 1969. As a result of the recommendations of these commissions Criminal Procedure Code was amended in 1974. Amended Section 304(1) lays downs that where in a trial before the Court of sessions, the accused is not represented by a pleader or advocate and where it appears to the Court that the accused does not have sufficient means to engage a pleader or advocate the Court shall assign a pleader for his defence at the expense of the State.

The Supreme Court in a number of cases has held that the right to free legal service is an essential ingredient of reasonably fair and just procedure implicit in Article 21 of the Constitution (Hussainara Khatoon v. State of Bihar AIR 1979 SC 1369). It has also been held in the case of Suk Das v. Union Territory of Arunachal Pradesh (AIR 1986 SC 991) that a conviction of an accused in a trial in which the accused was not provided free legal aid, where required, would be set aside as being violative of Article 21 of the Constitution.

To implement the concept of free legal aid, it was also included in the Constitution as Article 39 A. The Article states that the State shall secure that the operation of the legal system promotes justice on the basis of equal opportunity and shall in particular provide free legal aid by suitable legislation or scheme or in any other way to ensure the opportunities for securing justice are not denied to any citizen by reason of economic or other disability.

Other development in this field has been the enactment by Parliament on 11th October, 1987, of the Legal Services Authorities Act 1987 (Act No., 32 of 1987) which amongst others includes the recommendations of various commissions and committees set up for this purpose. This Act amongst others provides for the establishment of National Legal Service Authority, State Legal Services Authorities and the District Legal Services Authorities to be headed by the Chief Justice of India, Chief Justice of the High Court of the State as nominated by the Governor and the District Judge respectively.

A committee for implementation of Legal Aids has also been set up at the centre, which in turn has constituted Legal Air & Advice Boards at the Centre, States and Districts. Under this Supreme Court, High Courts and District Courts, Legal Aid Committees have been set up to provide free legal aid under this Act.

As per Section 12 of the Legal Services Authorities Act, amongst others, members of Scheduled Castes, Scheduled Tribes, women and children irrespective of their income are entitled for free legal aid under these schemes. For others, to be entitled, the upper income limit of the individual in cases upto High Courts is Rs. 6000/- p.a. and in cases in the Supreme Court is Rs. 12,000/- respectively. It will thus be seen that the servicemen and the ex-servicemen within the income limits as above and the families and children whether of serving personnel or ex-service personnel namely the widows, and those belonging to the S.C. or S.T. categories (irrespective of income) are eligible for free legal aid under these schemes. It is a real boon and the affected personnel should contact the State Legal Aid and Advice Boards and District Legal Aid and Advice Boards as available is annexed at the end of this chapter.

In addition to all these schemes, many of the Spirited Lawyers offer free legal aid particularly to the members and Ex-members of the Armed Forces and their families. For details of such lawyers the help of the respective Bar Associations may be useful.

Addresses of the state legal aid and advice boards:

1. Registrar (Management) &
   Secretary A.P. State Legal Aid &
   Advice Board, High Court Building,
   Hyderabad-500266, Andhra Pradesh

2. Secretary Law & Judl. Dept.,
Govt. of Arunachal Pradesh
Itanagar (Araunachal Pradesh)

3. Member Secretary
Assam State Legal Aid & Advice Board,
Legislative Deptt., Dispur,
Guwahati-78 006, Assam

4. Member Secretary,
Bihar State Legal Aid Board,
Near Police Station,
Ashram, 51(A)/C-Shree Drishnapuri
Patna-800 001

5. Member Secretary
Goa Free Legal Aid & Advice
Board, Law Deptt. (East)
Secretariat Annexe, Pundalik
Niwas Rua de Ourem
Panaji, Goa - 403001

6. Member Secretary,
Gujarat State Legal Aid & Advice
Board, High Court Compound,
Navrangpura, Ahmedabad-380009
Gujarat

7. Executive Director,
Haryana State Level Legal Service
& Advice Committee,
1609 Sector 34-D, Chandigarh-160022

8. Member Secretary,
H.P. State Legal Aid Board,
Craig Garden-3
Shimla - 171 002(H.P.)

9. Secretary (Jammu),
J&K State Legal Aid & Advice Board,
Civil Secretariat, Jammu Tawi (J&K)

10. Secretary, Karnataka Legal Aid Board
Director of Technical Education Building,
Palace Road, Bangalore - 560001

11. Executive Director
Kerala State Legal Aid & Advice Board,
Carrier Station Road,
Ernakulum South,
Kochi - 682016 (Kerala)

12. Member Secretary,
M.P. Legal Aid & Advice Board,
Second Floor 'B' Wing,
Vindhyachal Bhawan
Bhopal (M.P.)

13. Member Secretary,
Maharashtara State Legal Aid &
Advice Boarad,
(Law & Judiciary Department)
Mantralaya
Mumbai - 400032

14. Dy. Legal Rememberancer,
to Govt. of Manipur & Member,
Secretary, Manipur Legal,
Aid & Advice Board, Sectt.,
Law & Legislative Deptt.
Imphal - 795001

15. Secretary, Meghalaya State
Legal Aid Board,
Secretary(Law),
Room 222, Main Sectt.,
Shillong - 793001(Meghalaya)

16. Dy. Secretary to Govt. of
Mizoram & Member Secretary
Mizoram Legal Aid & Advice Board
Law, Judl & Parl. Affairs Deptt.
Aizawl (Mizoram)

17. Member Secretary, Legal
Advice Board, Deptt. of Justice
Law & Parl. Affairs,
Kohima (Nagaland)

18. Orissa Legal Aid & Advice Board,
SB 11-B, Cantonment Road,
Cuttack-753001 (Orissa)

19. Director/Member Secretary
Punjab State Legal Service Board,
SCO No. 3001-3002,
Sector 22D, Chandigarh-160022

20. Member Secretary,
Rajasthan State Legal Aid Board,
High Court Bench,
Jaipur (Rajasthan)

21. Joint Secretary (Law),
Sikkim State Legal Aid & Advice Board,
Tashiling Secretariat, Gangtok (Sikkim)

22. Secretary,
Tamilnadu State Legal Aid &
Advice Board, High Court Bldg.,
Chennai-600104 (Tamil Nadu)

23. Under Secretary to Govt of Tripura,
Tripura Legal Aid & Advice Board,
Law Deptt., Civil Secretariat,
Agartala West-799009
(Tripura)

24. Member Secretary,
UP Legal Aid & Advice Board,
3rd Floor, Jawahar Bhawan Annexe
Lucknow-226001(U.P)

25. Member Secretary,
WB State Legal Aid &
Advice Board,
Dy. Secretary Judl Deptt.,
Writers Building,
Kolkata-700401

26. Secretary(Law)
Andaman & Nicobar
Administration,
Secretariat, Port Blair

27. Legal Rememberancer-cum-
Director of Prosecution,
Chandigarh Administration,
Chandigarh

28. Social Welfare Officer
    Member Secretary,
    Daman & Diu,
    Free Legal Aid & Advice Board,
    Daman & Diu Administration,
    O/o the Chief Secretary,
    Secretariat, Daman
    Via Vapi, Pin 396220

29. Member Secretary,
    Delhi Legal Aid & Advice Board,
    Room No, 1, Patiala House,
    New Delhi-110001

30. Administrator,
    U.T. of Lakshadweep,
    Kavarati Islands-682555

31. Member Secretary,
    Pondicherry Legal Aid &
    Advice Board,
    Distt.Court Bldg.,
    Pondicherry-605001

32. Member Secretary,
    Supreme Court Legal Aid
    Committee, 109,
    Lawyers Chamber, Post Office Wing,
    Supreme Court Compound,
    New Delhi-110001

6

Exemption from Payment of Municipal Taxes

Besides the Central Government and the State Governments, the Municipal Corporations or Municipal Committees are also competent to levy certain taxes. They levy local taxes on persons residing within their respective jurisdiction and or on the properties situated therein. Such taxes are payable by all such persons and on all such properties unless they are specifically exempted by law.

Municipal Taxes

The Municipal Taxation Act, 1881, a Central Government enactment, is an enactment dealing exclusively with the exemption of levy of certain types of municipal taxes payable by persons in the Military, Naval or Air Force service, Vide Section 3 and 3(A) of the said Act, the Central Government and the State Governments, have been empowered, to prohibit levy of any specified tax or taxes by a Municipal Committee, payable by any person subject to the Army, Navy or Air Force Act, who is compelled by the exigencies of the military, naval or the air force duty to reside within the limits of the municipality.

Similarly, by notification No. 30-22/39-F&L dated 14th September, 1939 (Gazette of India 1939 Part I Page 1572) the Central Government has prohibited the levy of any tax of the following kinds, by any municipal committee, upon a person subject to the Army Act, the Navy Act or the Air Force Act, who by the exigencies of military duty is compelled to reside within the limits of the municipality:-

(a) municipal taxes on salaries;

(b) municipal taxes on profession, trades, calling, offices or appointments;

(c) municipal taxes on animals or vehicles in respect of:

  (i) any animal which such person is required to keep by the regulations of the service and

  (ii) vehicle which such person is permitted to keep in lieu of the animal, which in the absence of such permission, the said regulations would require him to keep.

Cantonment Board of Shillong has been prohibited to levy any tax on any person subject to the Army, Navy or Air Force Act, residing within the limits of that cantonment, vide notification No. 147 dated 6th Mar 43 published in Gazette of India, 1943 Part I Page 276. Similarly, Cantonment Boards of St. Thomas Mount, Pallavaram, Wellington, Cannanore, Barrackpore, Jalpahad, Lebong and Dimapur have been prohibited vide order No., 148 dated 6th March, 1943, with certain exceptions, to levy any municipal tax on military personnel within limits of their respective Cantonment Board (Gazette of India, 1943 Part I Page 276).

Exemption from House Tax

Some of the State Governments have also provided for exemption of house tax on the properties of ex-servicemen within their respective States with varying conditions and stipulations. The State where such exemptions have been granted include Haryana, Kerala, Mizoram, Punjab, Rajasthan, Sikkim, Tripura and Himachal Pradesh.

Whilst Haryana, Tamil Nadu and Mizoram provide for the exemption when the houses are occupied by the ex-servicemen themselves, Kerala and Rajasthan provide for exemption if the houses are occupied by the widows. Punjab provides for exemption if the income of the ex-servicemen is less than Rs. 15,000 p.a. Rules of Himachal Pradesh stipulate that rental value should not be more than Rs. 1,200 p.a. (which is under revision). Tripura rules stipulate exemption on those properties which are located within the municipality of Agartala only. For details, the Rajya Sainik Boards of the State concerned, whose list and addresses are given on pages 201-03 of this book, may be contacted.

Exemption from Payment of Tolls

By virtue of certain Act, Ordinances and regulations certain local authorities, municipalities, port-trusts companies, etc. are entitled to demand and receive tolls on persons and properties, passing through roads, and bridges within their jurisdiction or on being carried by means of ferry or embarking, disembarking or landing on any landing place within their jurisdiction. All persons and properties are liable for such tolls, unless specifically exempted by Law.

The Indian Tolls (Army and Air Force) Act, 1901 has been enacted to exempt persons and property belonging to Air Force and Army from payment of such Tolls.

Vide Section 3 (a) (i), all officers, soldiers and airmen of the Army and Air Force when on duty or on the march are exempted from payment of tolls.

Similarly, vide Section 3 (e) all members of the families of the officers, soldiers, airmen and authorized followers of the

Regular Forces are exempted from payment of tolls, when they are accompanying any body of troops or any officer, soldier or airmen on duty, or on the march.

Baggage, horse-carriages and persons employed in driving the carriages or in carrying the baggage of the officers, soldiers and airmen of the Regular Forces are also exempted vide Section 3(g) of the Indian Tolls (Army and Air Force) Act, 1901 when they accompany such officers, soldiers and airmen.

Section 3 also enumerates various other categories of personnel such as, the members of the Territorial Army, National Cadet Corps, personnel of the Indian Reserve Forces, prisoners under Military or Air Force escort, etc., and the circumstances in which such personnel and their luggage are exempted from payment of tolls.

Families, baggage, horses, carriages for the purposes of exemption are deemed to accompany forces, troops or persons, when their move is the direct result of or is connected with the move of such forces, troops or persons irrespective of the interval of space and time between the two moves.

The term "Toll" includes duties, dues, rents, rates, fees and charges but does not include custom duties or town duties on the import of goods.

The local authorities are in addition enjoined by Section 4, to provide such reasonable service and accommodation in respect of such vessels, troops, their families, luggages, carriages, etc., as may be required by the Central Government from time to time. This will be in addition to their duty of embarking or disembarking as such local authorities are otherwise required to perform.

Any person who demands and receives any toll in contravention of the provision of the Act, is liable to be punished with a fine, which may extend to Rs. 50/- only.

For claiming exemption from the payment of tolls under the Act, a pass is required to be presented on demand to the person authorized to demand the tolls. The pass has to be in the form shown on pages *97-98* and is to be signed by the Commanding Officer of the Unit or by the Station Staff Officer.

Vide rule 3(1) (a) (f) no pass is required in case of officers, soldiers and airmen of the Regular Forces when such officers, soldiers or airmen are accompanying any body of troops, on duty or on the march. The officers of the Regular Forces are further exempted from production of the required pass, if they are travelling of duty, though not in uniform. In such a case, the officer so travelling should furnish, if required, a statement in writing to the person authorized to demand the tolls, stating his name, rank and the fact that he is travelling on duty. In the context of roads being built in the private sector and the public sector where invariably the tolls will be charged, this exemption is of great significance.

Form of pass

Issued under the Indian Tolls (Army and Air Force) Act, 1901 (2 of 1901) this pass is issued subject to the rules on the reverse in respect of the persons and property specified in the annexed Schedule, and exempt from the payment of Tolls on the occasion of:-

Embarking or being shipped at..

Disembarking or being landed at...

Proceeding from.........................to.....................................

It will remain force from.............upto the.............9...............

SCHEDULE

Number Name of Corps Remarks

Part I

Persons

Officers..

Soldiers..

Airmen...

Members of the

Territorial Army or

The NCC

Authorized followers

Of Forces' or Corps.................................

Members of families of officers,

Soldiers, airmen or authorized

Followers..

Person in charge of carriages,

Horses, slaughter animals or

Baggage.....................................

Prisoners

PART II

Property

Horses as defined in the Act*..

Carriages...

Slaughter animals..

Baggage...

*'Horses" includes a mule and any beast of whatever description which is used for burden or draught or for carrying persons Section 2, clause (e).

Sd/..............

Place.................. Commanding Officer or

Station Staff Officer at............

(Endorsement)

(Here enter rules 1 to 3)

7

Exemption from Payment of Stamp Duty and Court Fees

The Indian Stamp Act, 1879, requires payment of stamp duty as specified, on various types of documents, receipts, deeds etc. Under the Act, these documents have to be affixed with stamps in the form of non-judicial stamps. Non-compliance of these provisions attract penal consequences. Similarly, the Court Fees Act, 1870, requires payment of specified amounts of Court fees on applications, plaints, appeals, etc., which are to be made or filed before Courts of law. These documents are affixed with judicial stamps. Without this the application, plaints' or appeal is not entertained.

However, there are certain provisions in these Acts, and other laws, which specifically exempt the payment of stamp duty or the Court fee payable by military personnel. In addition, Central Government has also been authorized to exempt certain documents from the payment of such duty or the fees.

According to Section 19(1) of the Court fees Act, 1870, a Power of Attorney executed by member of the Armed Forces for instituting or defending a suit, is exempted from the payment of Court fees. Similarly, under the Air Force Act,

Section 32 (Section 32 of the Army Act and Section 24 of the Navy Act) an application for speedy disposal of the suit, an application for the supply of a copy of the reasons for not disposing of the case within the specified period, or a copy of such order, by persons subject to the Army/Air Force/Navy Act, are all exempted from the payment of any Court fees.

Under the Indian Stamp Act Schedule-1, Article 4(a) an affidavit or declaration as to condition of enrolment under the Army, Navy or Air Force Act is exempted from the payment of Stamp Duty.

Similarly, under Article 53(d) of the same Schedule the receipts for pay and allowances drawn by N.C.Os, Petty Officers, Soldiers, Sailors or Airmen of the Indian Armed Forces when serving in such capacity are exempted from stamp duty. Under Article 53(e) & (f) receipts given by holders of family certificates in cases where the persons from whose pay and allowances the sum comprised in receipt, has been assigned, is a non-commissioned officer or petty officer, or soldier, sailor or airman and serving in such capacity, and the receipts for pension or allowances by person receiving such pensions or allowances in respect of their services as such N.C.O., Petty Officer, soldier, sailor or airman and not serving the Government in any other capacity are also exempted from the payment of stamp duty,. Vide notification No. 6 dated 12th September, 1931, issued under Section 9(a) of the Indian Stamp Act, 1899, stamp duty chargeable on the following documents which are executed by the persons in military employ has been remitted:

(a) Mortgage-deed executed by an officer of Government in civil or military employ for securing the payment of an advance received by him from the government for the purpose of constructing, purchasing or repairing a dwelling house for his own use.

(b) Instrument of re-conveyance of mortgaged property executed by Government in favour of any person; who is or has been in the civil or military employment of the Government on the repayment of an advance received by him from the Government for the purpose of constructing, purchasing or repairing a dwelling house for his own use.

(c) Instrument of re-conveyance executed by Government in respect of property mortgaged by an officer of Government or his surety as security for the due execution of an officer, or the due accounting for money or other property received by virtue thereof.

(d) Mortgage deed or agreement executed by an officer of the Government for securing the payment of an advance received by him from the Government for the purpose of purchasing a motor car, a motor boat, a motor cycle, a horse, a cycle, or a type writer.

(e) Agreement executed by an officer of the Government relating to the repayment of an advance received by him from the Government for defraying the cost of passes for himself or his Family or both.

(f) Receipt given for pension or allowances paid by the Government to an heir of a deceased by the Government to an heir of a deceased non-commissioned officer or soldier in respect of service in His Majesty's Army or in His Majesty's Indian Army.

(g) Authority in writing, executed under Rule 1, Order XXVIII of the Code of Civil Procedure, 1908, (Act V of 1908) by any officer or soldier actually serving the Government in a military capacity authorizing any person to sue or defend in his stead in a civil Court.

Miscellaneous Exemptions

Vide Government of India Finance Department notification No. 6 dated 22nd November, 1941, stamp duty chargeable on receipt for pay executed by prisoners of war confined in the Indian Union has been remitted.

Similarly, vide notification No. 5 dated the 25th September, 1941, issued by the Finance Department (Central Revenues), Government of India, under section 9 of the Indian Stamp Act, the stamp duty chargeable under the Act on receipts for advance of pay drawn and allowances received locally by Commissioned Officer, J.C.Os and Warrant Officers of the Military forces, who are on the war system of pay accounting have been remitted provided that in case of Commissioned Officers the concession shall be admissible only when they are authorized to draw advances on personal cheque books. In so far as the Navy is concerned vide, Notification No. 20 dated 9th September, 1944, stamp duty payable on receipts for advance of pay drawn and allowances received locally by commissioned and warrant officers, midshipmen of the Indian Navy and its reserves and civilians personnel paid from the defence service estimates, who are authorized to draw advances on personal cheque books, or who are serving in field service areas or in ships operating on seas which are declared to be open to the same degree of risk as field service areas, has been remitted.

The State Governments have also granted various exemptions by their own Stamp Duties Acts. These have been dealt with separately, whilst dealing with privileges granted by the respective State Governments.

8

Privileges in Matters of Succession

Execution of Wills

The Indian Succession Act, 1925 is an Act enacted to lay down the law regarding the intestate and testamentary succession. The Act *inter alia* also deals with the execution, attestation, construction, proof etc., of a Will.

A Will means a legal declaration of the intention of a person with respect to his property which he desires to be carried into effect after his death.

Section 63 of the Act contains the manner in which normally the Wills are to be executed by Hindus, Sikhs, Buddhists and Jains. According to this Section, the Will has to be in writing and has to be signed by the testator and has to be attested by two or more witnesses; and each witness has to sign the attestation in the presence of testator. Therefore, for persons belonging to these religions, there can be no oral Will to be legally valid, although a Mohammedan under his personal laws can always make a nuncupative Will.

Though no particular form of Will is required by law but in practice, to avoid future disputes and possible complications it is drawn up elaborately in a highly technical language.

Further, if it is not properly executed or the requirements of law are not strictly complied with, the Will cannot be regarded as having been properly executed. Practically, therefore, if a person has to make a Will he has to seek necessary legal assistance and preferably register it under the Indian Registration Act. Such a procedure is quite cumbersome and expensive.

Soldiers Wills

The members of the Armed Forces whilst on active service may at times, be placed in such situations when they cannot comply with the above requirements, in which case they would suffer from a disability and they would be deprived of the opportunity of making a valid Will. Further, the Will is in its nature, being ambulatory and revokable until death, every person with a disposing mind has a right to make a Will revoking the previous one, if any, till the last breath of his life. The exercise of this inherit right would also be rendered difficult if not impossible, if the formalities required under Section 63 of the Indian Succession Act were to be complied with, when a person is engaged in active service, with a bullet in his throat and a bomber over his head.

To cater for such a situation, the Indian Succession Act had made special provisions regarding the execution of Wills by the soldiers engaged in actual warfare. Such Wills are called the privileged Wills.

According to Section 65 of the Indian Succession Act, 1925, any soldier being employed in an expedition or engaged in actual warfare, or an airman so employed or engaged or any mariner being at sea, may if has completed the age of 18 years, dispose of his property by a Will made in the manner, provided for making privileged Wills. A privileged Will, according to Section 66 need not be in writing. It can be oral as well. The soldier, the airman or the mariner placed in the situations mentioned in Section 65 can make his Will by a word of mouth, by declaring his intentions before two witnesses, present at the same time. Such an oral Will, however, becomes null, if after the expiration of one month, the testator, being still have, has ceased to be entitled to make a privileged Will. The privileged Will can also be in writing. If it is in the handwriting of the person making the Will, it need not be signed by him or attested by any witness. If it is written wholly or in part by any other person and signed by the testator in such cases it need not be attested. Similarly, if the solider, airman or mariner has given written instructions for the preparation of his Will, but has died before it could be prepared and executed, such instructions shall be considered to constitute his Will. For other details, a reference should be made to Section 66 of the Indian Succession Act, 1925.

It would be noticed that the persons entitled for making the privileged Wills are only soldiers and airmen employed in an expedition, or engaged in actual warfare, or any mariner being at sea. The word "soldier" of the airman is not restricted in the sense as it is understood in the service to mean the other ranks only but it also includes officer.

The expression 'being employed in expedition' or 'engaged in actual warfare' does not mean that the person concerned must be actually fighting, it would include the other soldiers also who may not be actually fighting. For example, a medical officer attached to a regiment which is actually employed in expedition, is a solider employed in an expedition, within the meaning of this Section, but an Admiral, who commands a Naval Force, lives on shore and only occasionally goes on board his ship, is not considered at sea, and, therefore, cannot make a privileged Will. However, if a mariner is on board a ship which is temporarily on shore, while she is lying in harbor, he is for the purposes of this Section mariner at sea, and can make a privileged Will.

There has been considerable controversy, as to whether these provisions regarding 'Privileged Wills' and its mode of execution are applicable to soldiers who are Hindus, Buddhists,

Sikhs, Jains and Mohammedans by religion. According to Section 57 (which is the opening Section of Part VI of the Indian Succession Act, 1925 which part contains Sections 65 and 66 i.e. the provisions regarding privileged Wills) only those provisions of this part, which are set out in Schedule III, shall (subjects to the restrictions and modifications specified therein) apply to the Wills and codicils made by any Hindu, Buddhist, Sikh and Jain. A perusal of Schedule III reveals that Section 65 & 66 i.e. the privileged Wills are excluded. The result of this exclusion would appear to be, that these provisions are not applicable to soldiers who are Hindus, Buddhists, Sikhs or Jains. Similarly, vide Section 58 of Indian Succession Act the provisions of this part (which include provisions regarding Privileged Wills) do not apply to the testamentary succession to the property of any Mohammedan. It would thus appear, that if a soldier is a Hindu, Buddhist, Sikh, Jain or a Mohammedan, he would have to make the Will according to the normal Law, applicable to him and he cannot make Will in accordance with Sections 65 & 66 of the Indian Succession Act. If this be the correct position, it would lead to a paradoxical situation, operate harshly and would reduce the provisions of Sections 65 and 66 to a near nullity because most of the Indian soldiers belong to these religions. The purpose of the legislature would also be defeated. On further examination it would be seen that Section 63 which lays down the manner of executing unprivileged Wills for Hindus, has been amended to specifically exclude, the testators who are soldiers employed on an expedition or engaged in actual warfare or an airman so employed or engaged or mariner at sea. It therefore, clearly indicates that this manner of executing the normal Wills or the unprivileged Wills is not applicable to such soldiers, etc., showing the intention of the legislatures that such soldiers should have the privilege of making privileged Wills. If the earlier view is accepted it would as stated earlier, create paradoxical situation. It may not operate harshly on Mohammedan soldiers, as under their personal law, they are entitled at all times to make nuncupative Will, but Hindus after 1st January 1927 cannot legally make an oral Will. It appears that when provisions of Section 63 were extended to all Hindus in India, after the initial passing of the Indian Succession Act the legislature by oversight omitted to extend Section 65 and 66 also to them. In view of the aforesaid and to create harmony in the various provisions, it is submitted that these provisions regarding privileged Wills should be held to be applicable to soldiers who are Hindus, etc., and if necessary, these Sections should be amended at an early date.

Will Bequeathing of Property to one Person

Whilst on the subject of Wills, it would be in order if we briefly touch upon as to how to execute an ordinary Will. Will is the last testamentary disposition of the property of an individual. It contains his directions as to how his property both movable and immovable will be dealt with after his death. It is not necessary that the Will should be in highly technical legal language. It should be simple, at the same time clear so that no ambiguity is left. A specimen of an ordinary Will bequeathing of property to one individual after his death is given below.

Will Bequeathing of Property to one Person

This is the last Will and testament of me

(a)................................of...etc

I hereby revoke all Wills and Testamentary dispositions by me heretofore made.

I hereby bequeath to my wife...

Her heirs executors or administrators for her use and benefit absolutely and for ever all my property, both movable and immovable whatsoever and of what nature and quality so ever....

And I hereby appoint her the said..

sole executor of this my Will in Witness Whereby I the said..have hereto, signed at...................this..........day of.......................at..........

Signature of the Testator

Signed by said Shri...

In the presence of us present at the same time, who in his presence and in the presence of each other have signed as witnesses hereto

(1) WITNESS NO. 1

(2) WITNESS NO. 2

It is not necessary that the Will should be on stamp paper or it should be registered. But practically for all purpose both are desirable. It should be executed on a non-judicial stamp paper of Rs. 10/- and should be registered with the Registrar of Documents, so that after the death its authenticity is proved and in case of loss, an authentic copy of the Will can be obtained. The registration is also helpful as on its being probated succession certificate is not required. Various government departments dealing with moneys and properties like DDA, Banks etc also require a registered Will for any further action in respect of the said property.

Disposal of Private Property

While dealing with the matter of succession, it is also useful to deal with the privileges regarding the disposal of private property of the deceased officers and men of the Army and Air Force, given under the Army and Air Force (Disposal of Private Property) Act, 1950. (In case of Navy please see Chapter XIX of the Navy Act, 1957, Sections 171 to 183).

In case of death normally the next of kin can take the estate of the deceased, including the money from the banks, etc. only after obtaining a succession certificate from a court of competent jurisdiction. This obtaining of succession certificate etc., is cumbersome, time consuming and expensive. However, for the estate of the deceased members of the armed forces, a simplified procedure has been given under the Army Air Force (Disposal of Private Property) Act, 1950. This is partly because of peculiar nature of service in the armed forces and partly to help the next of kin to obtain an estate without much difficulty.

Under Sections 3 and 4 of this Act, the Commanding Officer of the deceased person (Committee of Adjustment in case of officers) has been authorized to secure all movable properties belonging to the deceased to draw all pay and allowances due to such person, and to collect all money left by the deceased in any banking company, Post Office Saving Bank, Society or any other institution receiving deposits howsoever named. Vide sub-section 2 of Section 3 it has been enjoined upon the managers, agents of such banking companies, etc., to deliver such money to the Commanding Officers/Committee of Adjustment on receipt of the requisition to that effect, notwithstanding anything contained to the contrary in the rules of such banking company, society or other institution.

After the money and properties belonging to the deceased have been collected, and if the representative of the deceased gives security to the satisfaction of the Commanding Officer, for payment of regimental and other debts in camp or quarters, the Commanding Officer will deliver money and property to that representative. Representative means any person who has taken out representation, but does not include Administrator General. If no such security is given, the Commanding Officer after securing all the properties, will make arrangements for payments of regimental and other debts in camp or quarters and the expenses incurred by him out of the money received, collected or realize, and thereafter arrive at the surplus.

In case of airmen or soldiers, if the surplus, that is, the amount collected after payment of debts, etc., is not more than Rs.1,000 the Commanding Officer can pay the surplus to any person appearing to be entitled to receive it or administer the estate of the deceased, without requiring such person to produce any probate, letter of administration or succession certificate, etc. (Disposal of Private Property) Act, and Rule 25 of Army and Air Force (Disposal of Private Property) Rules refers.

In case the surplus exceeds Rs. 1000 but does not exceed Rs. 10,000 in cases of airmen, the AOC-in-C of the Command or Group Headquarter, concerned or, Director of Personnel Services, Air Headquarters in respect of airmen serving in units directly administered by Air Headquarters, is the prescribed authority, who if he thinks fit, can authorize the delivery of property or payment of money, to any person appearing to him to be entitled to receive it, without requiring such person to produce any probate, letter of administration, succession certificate, etc. The prescribed authority for persons subject to the Army Act other than officers is the Brigade or equivalent Commander.

In case of officers, the securing of the movable property, drawing of pay and allowances, collecting the money from the banks, etc. and all other functions of the Commanding Officer are to be performed by a Committee of Adjustment, and the surplus is to be paid to the prescribed person, who is the Joint Secretary in Ministry of Defence Vide Rule 24 of the Army and Air Force (Disposal of Private Property) Rules, 1953, the Joint Secretary, Ministry of Defence can authorize the payment of the surplus to any person, appearing to him to be entitled to receive it, without requiring such person to produce any probate, letter of administration or succession certificate, if the amount does not exceed Rs. 10,000.

It has been further laid down vide Rule 30 that in determining the person to whom the property or surplus may be delivered or paid under Section 110, without production of any succession certificate, etc., the authorities shall take into consideration the law or customs of succession applicable to the deceased, and his wishes, if any, in this respect.

It would thus be seen that the families and next-of-kin of the deceased officers are spared of the cumbersome, technical, and expensive procedures for obtaining the properties of the deceased members of the armed forces by virtue of the Army and Air Force (Disposal of Private Property) Act, 1950.

Gist of case law

For the benefit of the keen reader a gist of some of the decided cases on privileged Wills is given below:

1. A soldier under training cannot be said to be, in the absence of any other evidence, employed in an expedition, or engaged in a actual warfare. The Will made by him cannot be said to be a privileged Will within the meaning of Section 65.

2. Where an apprentice under the age of 22, and in the employment of a Steamship Co. while ashore in England on leave executed a Will and again within the next week returned to the ship, which sailed away, the executant was at the material time a seaman at sea within the meaning of Section 11 of the Wills Act, 1837 (C 26). As explained by Section, 1 of the Wills (Soldiers and Sailors) Act, 1918 the Will having been executed while in contemplation of sailing a fresh voyage.

   (1951) All E.R. 841 (851).

3. Will altered by striking out bequest at date unknown and alteration was before or after execution of Will presumption held was that alteration was made while deceased was at sea. The deceased was a chief officer employed by the Anglo Saxon Petroleum Co. Ltd. in their marine department. On January, 11th, 1946 he went on furlough in England until April 15th, 1946. He was then awaiting re-appointment to an other ship. On April 25th,

1946 the deceased received instruction from the employer to proceed to Sunderland to join a ship on April 30th. On April 27th, while at his sister's house, he made a nuncupative Will, by saying in the presence of his mother and other witnesses: if anything happens to me, I want everything to go to my mother". Held, that the deceased made this nuncupative Will in contemplation of sailing that particular voyage and therefore he was a seaman at sea, within the meaning of Section 11 of the English Wills Act, 1837, when he made the Will; that the Will was valid and that the letter of Administration could be granted with the contents of nuncupative Will annexed.

(1952) All E.R. 852 (853)

4. The deceased entered the Royal Air Force in February, 1942, he was sent overseas to Canada for training in operational duties on service as an airman. In March, 1943, while on this service, the deceased wrote out what he described as Will and signed it but did not get it attested. On August 11th, 1943 the deceased, who had become a pilot instructor, died from injuries received as the result of an aircraft accident. The question was whether the document could be admitted to probate as a valid Will. Held, that the words "actual military service" in Section 11 of the Wills Act (English) 1937 meant "active military service" and the adjective 'Active' in this connection confined the military service to such service as was directly concerned with operations in a war, which was or had been in progress or was imminent. The deceased was therefore at the time, when he made the Will, in "Actual military service" and therefore, the document should be admitted to probate as a valid Will.

(1948) 2 All E.R. 908 (911)

5. A testator who was 19 years of age and on leave in England from the British Army of Rhine, executed a Will in May, 1954, which was prepared on the advice of a solicitor and property executed according to Section 9 of

the Wills Act (Eng), 1837. In May 1954, the British forces were in military occupation of certain areas in Germany. By virtue of the unconditional surrender of 1945, the status and position of the forces in occupation were that of an Army in occupation of a foreign country by force of arms. The executor of the Will applied for a grant of probate. Held, that despite the lapse of almost nine years since the unconditional surrender, the service of the testator was directly concerned with a war which has been in progress and that the testator was in "actual military service" in May, 1954 within the meaning of the Wills Act (Eng), 1837, and that the Will by virtue of Section 1 of the Wills (Soldiers and Sailors) Act (Eng), 1918, the fact that the testator was in fact in England and was not in Ops Council because he had the advantage of a solicitor to guide him, was immaterial, since the testator was only on a fortnight's leave and knew that he was returning to his duties as a member of the occupying forces. The grant of the probate as sought should be made.

(1958) 1 WLR 457 (461)

6. There is no legal obligation on the part of the military authorities to prepare a kindered roll. It is a document prepared by the military authorities for enabling them to communicate to the next-of-kin, if the soldier happens to die. An entry in a kindered roll prepared by the military authorities on the basis of the information furnished by the soldier cannot be considered as a Will.

1958 Andhra Pra 336 (337)

7. Where the language of the oral statement of the deceased soldier on the eve of embarkation clearly stated what he wanted to be done with his property after his death, it is immaterial for it to operate as a Will, whether he knew it could have any testamentary effect and it is equally immaterial whether other people thought or whether he thought that he could only do that by referring to a document which was then in existence.

1949-2, All E.R. 659 (661)

9

Privileges under the Arms Act, 1959

Sections 3 and 4 of the Arms Act, 1959 require all persons in India to have a license, issued in accordance with provisions of the Act, for acquiring, possessing, or carrying any arm or firearm. The Act and Rules have laid down the procedure for the issue of license, the categories of persons to whom a license can be issued, payment of license fees, and other allied matters. Penal provisions for contravention of the Act have also been made.

The word 'Arms' for the purpose of this Act in simple words means as any article of any description, designed or adopted as a weapon for offence or defence, and includes fire arms, sharp edged and other deadly weapons but excludes weapons incapable of being used otherwise than as toys, or of being converted into serviceable weapons.

The term 'Fire-arms' means, arms of any description designed or adopted to discharge a projectile or projectiles of any kind, by the action of any explosive or other forms of energy.

If a person, therefore, wishes to possess any of the above

mentioned articles, he has to obtain the requisite license, from the proper licensing authority on payment of the necessary license fees. He has also to comply with the provisions of the Arms Act, Arms Rules and the condition of the license. Failure to do so entails serious consequences.

Vide Section 41 of the Arms Act, however, it has been enacted that when the Central Government is of the opinion that it is necessary and expedient; in the public interest to do so, it may, by notification in the official gazette, exempt any person, or class of persons or exclude any description of arms or ammunition from the operation of all or any of the provisions of this Act.

For the benefit of the members of the Armed Forces, under this provision, the Central Government has issued notification No. GSR 991 dated 13th July 1962, exempting certain categories of persons and certain categories of arms and ammunition from the operation of the Arms Act, subject to the conditions mentioned therein.

According to entry No. 5 in Schedule 1 of the notification, every serving member of the Armed Forces and every Commanding Officer of a unit of the Armed Forces or of Territorial Army, are exempted from the operation of Sections 3 and 4 of the Arms Act, for such arms and ammunition, as are provided for sporting purposes by the Government, or are provided from a regimental fund under the authority of the Officer Commanding Unit, provided such persons are in possession of a pass granted and signed by their Commanding Officer to that effect. The exemption applies in case of the members of the Armed Forces, only in respect of such arms and ammunition and to the areas and for such dates, which are specified in the pass.

Under the same notification, vide entry No. 1 (7 and 8) of Schedule II, all arms which are in possession of a regiment or military mess as trophies, or curios, or otherwise solely for the purpose of ornament or display, and sights for rifles imported for the use of or for sale to Officers, WOs, JCOs and Petty Officers or NCOs of the Army, Navy or the Air Force or the Indian Territorial Army, are exempted from all provisions of the Arms Act.

The uniform swords, and dirks of recognized military or official pattern, when possessed by, or intended to be supplied to persons entitled to wear them as a part of their uniform, swords of honour possessed or carried by persons, or by the heirs of persons to whom they were awarded by the Central or State Government, are exempted from the operation of Section 4 of the Arms Act. Similarly, swords imported for presentation as prizes, for members of the Regular Forces or Auxiliary Forces, are exempted from the operation of Section 4 and Section 10 of the Arms Act, (Entry Nos., 3, 4 and 5 of Schedule II). Kirpans possessed and carried by Sikhs; and Khukris possessed by Gurkhas of all classes, are also exempt from the provisions of section 4 of the Act, Vide entry Nos. 1 and 2 of Schedule II.

For obtaining the license for any arms including fire arms, as it is well known, a certain amount of license fees has to be paid by the applicant. Vide Rule 57(#) of the Arms Rules, however, the Central Government has been authorised to grant exemption/reduction of the fees payable in respect of any licence by making a general or special order. In pursuance of this provision, the Central Government has, by general order G.S.R. 993 dated 13th July 62 exempted certain categories of persons, from the payment of licence fees for the specified arms and ammunition, in public interest.

According to Items I in the table annexed to the above mentioned order, all JCOs, WOs, Petty Officers, NCOs, soldiers of Armed Forces, whether in service or retired, (in case of soldiers only through Commanding Officer), are exempted from payment of fees for the grant or renewal of any licence in form III, for one sporting gun or rifle together with a reasonable quantity of ammunition for the same. Similar concessions have been granted to the personnel of the Territorial Army, members of the corps of volunteers, officers and warrant officers of Assam Rifles and certain other Forces subject to certain conditions. Ex-Indian Commissioned Officers of the Army, Navy or the Air Force are also exempted from the payment of fees for the grant or renewal of the licence for revolvers, automatic pistols which form part of their equipment when in employment as such officer, together with a reasonable quantity of ammunition for the same, so long as he is entitled to wear the uniform of such force. (Item 2 of the table annexed of G.S.R. 993 dated 13th July 61).

Vide Item VIII of the same table-Indian citizens who have been awarded gallantry awards like Param Vir Chakra, Maha Vir Chakra, Vir Chakra, Ashok Chakra, Kirti Chakra, Shaurya Chakra, the Distinguished Service Cross etc. are also exempted for payment of licence fee for such arms or ammunition as may be considered reasonable by the authority or the officer issuing the licence.

Section 45 of the Arms Act, 1959 has laid down that nothing in the Act shall apply to the acquisition, possession, or carrying the arms and ammunition:-

(a) by or under the order of the Central Government;

(b) by a public servant, in the course of his duty as such public servant;

(c) by members of the N.C.C. Territorial Army or members of any other Force raised and maintained; under any Central Act, officer, or enrolled person.

According to the departmental regulations for the Army and the Air Force, which have been issued under the authority of the Central Government, the officers of the Armed Forces are permitted to possess fire arms for the purpose of sports upto any number and of any type, except the prohibited bores, in the discretion of the license issuing authority, provided before purchase they obtain the licence on payment of fees for possession of such arms. The officers of the Armed Forces are also entitled to hold a pistol/revolver of any description excluding prohibited bores, as a part of their personal equipment without licence. Government of India, vide Ministry of Home Affairs letter No. 9/88/49-Police (i) dated 4th July, 1950 has specified the type and quantity of arms, which will form such part of personal equipment. By this order dated 4th July 1950, the Central Government has notified, that all Indian Commissioned Officers are authorized for one pistol each, as personal issue so long as they are on the active list. They can also keep in addition, one privately owned revolver/pistol. The Junior Commissioned Officers are authorized one pistol/revolver/machine StenGun each as indicated by the establishment of the Unit. The weapons so authorised, are unit equipment but are normally retained by the individuals whilst serving with their units. Khukris/Dahs are also authorized for Gurkha, Garhwal and Assam Battalions. In an emergency, officers and JCOs may be issued with one rifle/Sten Machine carbine each. When so issued, these weapons will constitute personal equipment of these officers. For the officers of the Indian Navy including Warrant Officers the personal equipment will comprise one sword, one pistol/revolver 38 (Service Calibre). One pistol automatic of any calibre and one Dirk for carrying, acquiring or possessing of which, no licence under the Arms Act, is required.

It would thus be seen, that considerable relaxation have been made under the Arms Act, for persons in the Armed Forces. These relaxations are mostly due to the nature of their duties, but a number of them also confer personal privileges in recognition of their meritorious services and special standing in society.

10

Houses, Rent and Evictions

Historical Background

The modern legislation relating to the control of rents and evictions is in fact the posthumous child of war. In the First World War, the germs of such legislation were formed in England. The conditions after the war necessitated the intervention of legislature in the so-called field of "Contract of Letting". The necessity of such legislation became more acute during and after the Second World War. The so-called personal freedom of contract and action was restricted and curtailed on the ground that the individual freedom was to give way to social liberty. The restrictions had to be brought forth because due to great shortage of space accommodation and upward movement in the economic conditions of the country. The undue profiteering motive of the landlords, which became prominently evident, also had to be checked.

In addition, the industrial revolution had also brought in its wake a radical change in the life of the people. Besides bringing about a sea change in the economy, it also sowed the seeds of rapid urbanization. People left their traditional vocations like agriculture and migrated to industrial centres in search of more lucrative occupations. The population of the cities thus began to swell in arithmetical progression. Whilst a large number of migrants managed to get better paid jobs, they however, had to sacrifice on the quality of their lives. Open space and large houses became a thing of the past. A house thus became a prized possession and the landlords began to cash on it. The helpless tenants had to pay exorbitant rents and would constantly nurse the fears of being dislodged from the house, the moment he was unable to meet their ever increasing demand for rent. This also had to be remedied to maintain social balance. The Industrial Revolution thus marked the beginning of social legislation which was primarily meant to make or mitigate the ill-effects of the Industrial Revolution. Rent control was one such social legislation. This legislation made its debut in India in 1918. The first Act passed by the Indian Legislature was the Act of 1918 i.e. the Bombay Rent (War Restrictions) Act, 1918. It was enacted on 10th April, 1918. This Act was followed by Bombay Rent (War Restrictions) Amendment Acts of 1920 and 1923. Similarly, in the presidency town of Calcutta, the Calcutta Rent Control Act, 1920 was passed. These legislations were only temporary measures.

They were found insufficient to meet the conditions arising out of Second World War, which worsened the plight of poor tenants living in big cities. In order to prevent the flow of persons back to villages, lest it entails the closure of factories/ big establishments the Bombay Rent Restrictions Act, 1939 was passed in order to restrict the increase of rent of premises. In the year 1942, in exercise of the powers conferred by the defence of India Rules, the Bombay Rent Restrictions Order, 1942 was promulgated which also underwent several amendments till it was followed by the Bombay Rents, Hotels and Lodging House Rates Control Act, 1947. Similar was the story in other places too. This clearly shows that the rent control legislation was born and brought up in the lap of war.

The Changing Scenario

The social economic changes brought in over the years has greatly altered the scenario. The tenant who was generally from the weaker sections of society may not be necessarily so these days. With the rise of middle class, most of them have become better off over the years and form an influential class by itself. By continuing to occupy the rented premises, some of the tenants have not only started harassing the landlords by not vacating the premises even when genuinely required by the landlords but in some cases have even stopped paying the rents.

Similarly, not all the landlords are necessarily from the upper classes. A fair number of them may be even those who have acquired or built a house after investing their whole life savings or by procuring loans through various sources. The situation being what it is today, the famous quote of Bernard Shaw "Fools build houses for wise men to live in them" has not remained merely poetical. Thus, it is time now for the scales to tilt somewhat in favour of the landlords also and a fair and equitable balance is maintained amongst conflicting interests, based solely on equity and fair play.

Model Rent Control Law

Eviction is only one part of the problem arising out of existing rent control legislation in various States. The legislation has not only soured the relationship of the landlord and the tenant, but has also given rise to various social problems like bribery, corruption, pugrees and so on. On the top of it, it has adversely affected the housing activity and thus the shortage. Considering all these problems, the Government of India taking cognizance of all these malaise have recently (1992) approved a national housing policy and have come with Model Rent Control Act. Since the subject of Rent Control is exclusively within the domains of the State Governments, the Central Government can only advise and guide and leave it to the State

Governments to adopt it subject to such modification(s) as may be required, keeping in view the local conditions of each State. Such a model legislation has been presented to parliament and in view of the legal position; it can at best take note of it. Further, to assist in expeditious disposal of cases it has been proposed to exclude the jurisdiction of the Civil Courts and place it exclusively with the rent controllers. It has also been proposed to exclude the writ jurisdiction of the High Court and in its place constitute State level tribunals on the lines of tribunals contemplated under Article 323 B of the constitution. For this purpose, a constitutional amendment has been approved by the Parliament and is awaiting the assent of the President.

The detailed examination of the model Rent Control Act is not relevant to the present subject but suffice it to say that it also specifically contains a provision for the right to recover immediate possession to certain specified categories of population like retiring/retired government servant, widows, persons in the armed forces aged and the handicapped.

How it takes a final shape in the legislation of various States and how it works, time along will reveal.

Special Need for Protection in case of Armed Forces Personnel and Efforts in that Direction.

The members of the armed forces constitute a class by themselves. By the terms of their employment, nature of their duties and exigencies of their profession, they have to move from one place to another too frequently and that too in national interest. The result is that they cannot live in their own houses and perforce have to rent out their premises. If they can not get their houses vacated when they need them either on retirement or any other eventuality, it is bound to adversely affect their morale. It is, therefore, in the national interest that some special provisions are made in this regard and their legitimate interests are safeguarded.

This has also been long-standing problem engaging the attention of the personnel and the service headquarters. It must be said to the credit of the government that it also realizes the magnitude of the problem and has been seriously addressing itself for its genuine redressal. Since the subject falls within the jurisdiction of the States, its role has been advisory, persuasive and recommendatory. But over the years, it has been able to bring round most of the States to address the problem and give the legitimate redressal. Most of the States have also shown their earnestness and amended their rent control legislation to give relief to this category of personnel, of course in the larger national interest, but subject to their own constraints.

As a part of its efforts the government of India way back in 1968, at the level of the Cabinet Secretary, sent a detailed letter to the Chief Secretaries of all the State Government and Union Territories urging them to bring out the amendments to their respective Rent Control Acts to enable the retired and released members of the Armed Forces and the families of personnel who have served in forces to get back the possession of their houses speedily. Government of India, Ministry of Defence letter No. 17(27/56/B(Acl) dated 2nd March, 1968. Again on 26th July 1976, the Director General Rehabilitation and Resettlement, Ministry of Defence submitted a paper on the legal protection to Serving/Ex-Service personnel, their widows and dependants for restoration of their residential premises. This paper was considered by the Chiefs of Staff Committee and as a result a central legislation was drafted for this purpose. However, this could not be enacted as rent control was a State subject being listed in list II of the Constitution.

On 29th October, 1980, the then Prime Minister, whilst chairing the 14th meeting of the Kendriya Sainik Board directed that all such State enactments should lay down a maximum time limit for settlement of cases already filed or pending in the various Courts, with particular reference to the Union Territory of Delhi. She also referred the issue to the Economic Reforms Committee presided over by late Shri L K Jha.

Again on 3rd December, 1980 a D.O. letter was sent from the RRM to all the Chief Ministers of the States and all the Lt. Governors of the Union Territories for this purpose. In June, 1983, the then Home Minister Shri P C Sethi also wrote a letter to all the Chief Ministers of the States and Lt. Governors of the Union Territories, urging them to consider the problems of servicemen sympathetically.

Next, the high level committee of the government of India, for the problems of ex-servicemen, constituted in 1984 and chaired by Shri K P Singh Deo also deliberated on this issue. One of the recommendations of the committee was that when service personnel came back to their place on retirement the rent control Act should provide for their getting back their houses for self occupation on a time-bound basis and under a summary procedure. If necessary, legislation may be undertaken by all the State governments. Pursuant to this recommendation, a letter addressed to the Chief Ministers of all States and Lt. Governors of Union Territories was sent requesting the State Governments/Union Territories for making suitable amendments to rent control legislation and tenancy laws to assist ex-servicemen to re-occupy/regain the possession of their houses. A letter was also sent by the Additional Secretary to the Chief Secretaries of all the States to make necessary amendments to the rent control legislation in the interest of the Ex-servicemen.

Present Position

As a result of all these efforts and the follow up with the States, the position that emerged on this score in various States as on 15th July 1986 was as under:-

(a) Provisions had/have already been made in the relevant Acts in the States of Gujarat, Haryana,

J&K, Kerala, Karnataka, Madhya Pradesh, Maharashtra, Punjab, Tripura, Uttar Pradesh and West Bengal.

(b) Only partial provisions exist in States of Himachal Pradesh, Orissa and Tamil Nadu.

(c) There was no problem on this score in the State of Manipur, Nagaland, Meghalaya and Sikkim.

(d) Provisions had yet to be made in the States of Andhra Pradesh, Assam, Bihar and Rajasthan.

Thereafter also, efforts have been continuing and some more States have fallen in line.

As of now the information regarding the following States is available:-

1. Maharashtra 2. Punjab 3. Haryana 4. Himachal Pradesh 5. Kerala 6. Karnataka 7. Tamil Nadu 8. West Bengal 9. Uttar Pradesh 10. Jammu & Kashmir 11. Rajasthan 12. Union Territory of Delhi 13. Union Territory of Chandigarh 14. Madhya Pradesh.

Basic Fundamentals

Before we discuss the situation as existing in various States, it would be necessary to highlight some basic premises.

Firstly, what is the basic structure, objective and scope to properly understand and interpret the same.

Secondly, who are all the persons who are entitled to these safeguards and privileges i.e. what the scope and meaning of the word 'Armed Forces' is for this purpose.

And thirdly, what is the nature of relief?

Objectives

As regards the first, a scrutiny of the various preambles of the existing Rent Acts enacted by the States reveal the following objectives:

(a) To control and regulate rents and letting.

(b) To prevent un-reasonable eviction of tenants from leased property.

These statutes are beneficial and remedial so far as their objects are concerned. Although in effect they are prohibitive and restrictive legislation affecting the contractual rights of the landlords and tenants. The Rent Control Acts of various States may be classified in three following groups:

(a) Acts purely supplementary to the Transfer of Property Act such as Rajasthan Act.

(b) Acts partly supplementary such as Bombay and Madhya Pradesh, in which no doubt additional protection is given to the tenants, but the ordinary machinery of the civil suit, is not disturbed. To this category belong the Acts of a large number of states.

(c) And the Acts which are self contained codes with special machinery of rent Control Tribunals, for application for eviction and orders for eviction, such as Madras Act of 1960.

Although all the Rent Acts in India may seemingly appear to be identical, but they have vital differences, both in statutory structure and legislative intendment. Therefore, whilst interpreting the different Rent Laws great care has to be taken as to in which of these groups, they fall and what is the legislative intent.

Nexus between Landlordship and being a member of the Armed Forces

It is significant to note that right to get eviction of a tenant is given to the landlord who is either a member or a retired member or a released member of the Armed Forces. There must be co-existence between the landlordship and the membership of the Armed Forces at some point of time. If at no point of time the landlordship and the membership of the

Armed Forces is combined together in a person, the benefit of the provision would not be obtainable by such a person. Therefore, if a retired Army Officer or the widow or the heirs of the retired Army Officer purchases a property in occupation of a tenant, he/she will not be entitled to take the benefit of the provision on the ground that although he/she or his/her predecessor entitle was a member of the Armed Forces. Looking to the object and the policy of the Act, the benefits of the provisions is only available to those persons, who fill up the character of landlordship and membership of the Armed Forces. This legislative intent is also very well manifested by the fact that some of the Acts even prescribe the period with in which the application or proceedings for eviction on this ground has to be initiated. It is further significant to observe that looking to the phraseology of the sections, it also appears that the letting of the premises of which the benefit can be obtained by landlord must be prior to retirement. If the landlord after retirement, lets all the property to a tenant and thereafter files an application for his ejectment on the ground that he is a retired member of the Armed Forces, the benefit of the provision would not be available, because his landlordship and membership of the armed forces at no point of time combined together. If the ground is permitted in such a case, then the object of the Act is to protect the tenant, would be to a large extent frustrated. Thereafter, it seems to be the proper construction that only those premises can be got vacated, for purpose of residence by a member of an ex-member of the Armed Forces or his dependents, which was let out to the tenant whilst in service, so that the retired member of the armed force may have a roof of his own over his head.

It is appropriate to note that as a rule, the accommodation which a person belonging to the Armed Forces desires to be vacated must be needed for residence. If the accommodation is needed for non-residential purposes the benefit of the provision would not be available, unless it is provided otherwise explicitly or by implication. For example Section 13 (3) (a) (V) and Section 13 (3-4) of the Haryana Act are unique and deal with the requirement of residential as well as non residential accommodation (emphasis added) Section 13(3)(A)(V) deals with residential accommodation and enacts that if a landlord makes an application to the authority that he is a member of the Armed Forces of the Union and requires it for the occupation of his family and produces a certificate to the prescribed authority under the Indian Soldiers Litigation Act, 1925 that he is serving under special conditions within the meaning of Section 3 of the Act, the ejectment of the tenant would be ordered. The occupation as brought out above, connotes occupation for residence as well as business. Therefore under clause (V) he may seek eviction of the tenant from residential accommodation, if he needs it for occupation of this family irrespective of the purpose of occupation. Whereas under Section 13(3)(A) a non residential building may be got vacated for personal use within a period of three years from the date of retirement or discharge if the landlord is a retired or discharged Non Commissioned Officer from the Armed Forces. Thus the Haryana Act makes provision for both types of necessity, whereas the other enactments are limited exclusively to residential accommodation only.

Section 11 A of the Kerala Act and Section 10 (3A) of the Tamil Nadu Act are applicable to residential buildings for residential necessity. But Section 20A of the Madhya Pradesh Act use the general words and are not confined to a particular category of accommodation or to a particular kind of requirement. Section 29B of the West Bengal Act deals with the necessity covered by Section 13(i) (f) namely for his own 'occupation'. As brought out earlier the term occupation covers occupation for residence or for business. Thus different Acts have different spheres to operate and cover different areas.

Nature of Relief

Members of the Armed Forces have been given treatment in the Rent Control Acts, with reference to making their needs as a specific ground for eviction and presenting a special mode of brief and summary procedure for meeting their requirements. Some Acts have even made special provision as to the manner of evidence and proof of the fact of the requirements. It has been specifically enacted in some that if the member of the Armed Forces produces a certificate from the competent prescribed authority about certain facts specified in that the mere production of the certificate would be enough to satisfy the Court under the rent law, to decree the claim without any further regular proof. Thus, it would imply that other and normal modes of proof are excluded and are dispensed with.

Whilst at the nature of the relief is also pertinent to note that the service Acts i.e. Army Act, 1957 and the Air Force Act, 1950 have made specific provisions in the respective Acts for priority in respect of litigation in which the members subject to these Acts are a party. (See Section 32 of the Army Act, Section 24 of the Navy Act and Section 32 of the Air Force Act 1950. For details refer to Chapter One at p. 9). Under these provisions the Commanding Officer of the person is authorized to give a certificate, containing the particulars referred there in for priority in matters of litigation. On presentation of the certificate Courts are required to hear and as far as possible to decide the case within the period of leave granted for that purpose. A specimen of the form of such a certificate is given at page 10. It may also be noted that the High Court of Punjab and Haryana in the case of one Parkash Saini v. Daljit Singh (AIR 1980 p. 185), has held that the Court of the rent controller is a Court for this purpose.

Further, the Indian Soldiers (Litigation) Act, 1925 has been enacted amongst other for speedy disposal of civil and revenue litigation of the Indian Soldiers serving under special conditions viz. when serving under War conditions or overseas or under orders to proceed on field service or whilst being a prisoner of war. It is noteworthy in this context that Punjab High Court case of Yadav Ram Singh, Lt. Col. V. Gurwati Devi & Others (AIR 1968 P & H 26) that held existence of special conditions or War conditions is not a justifiable matter. It has been further held that the Court cannot require the soldiers counsel to disclose his place of posting. For other and detailed privileges under that Act reference may be made to Chapter one.

Armed Forces – Members of the Armed Forces – Meaning

The Constitution-makers gave and for good reasons used the term "Defence Forces" and "Armed Forces" in different context to denote different connotations. Whereas the term "Armed Forces" has a wider meaning to include other forces like the BSF, Coast Guard, CRPF etc., the term "Defence Forces" connote the Army, Navy and the Air Force. Therefore, Defence Forces in this context means the regular Army, Navy and Air Force or any part of any one or more of them. Members of the Defence Forces are the persons governed by the Army, Navy or Air Force Acts. Members of the para military forces would also fall in this category, if the term used is "Armed Forces".

Army

The Army Act, 1950 is applicable to the following persons:-

(a) Officers, Junior Commissioned Officers and Warrant Officers of the Regular Army.

(b) Persons enrolled under the Army Act.

(c) Persons belonging to the Indian Reserve Forces.

(d) Persons belonging to the Indian Supplementary Force, when called out for Service or when carrying out the annual test.

(e) Officers of the Territorial Army, when doing duty as such officers and enrolled person of the said Army, when called out or embodied or attached to any regular forces, subjects to such adaptations and modifications as may be made under Section 9 of the Territorial Army Act, 1948.

(f) Persons holding commissions in the Army in Indian Reserve Forces when ordered on any duty or service, for which they are liable as members of such reserve force.

(g) Officers appointed to the Indian regular Reserve Forces, when ordered for any duty or service for which they are liable as member of such reserve force.

(h) Persons not otherwise subjects to Military law, who on active service in camp, on the march or at any frontier post specified by the Central Government by notification in his behalf are employed by or are in the service of, or the followers of, or accompany any portion of the Regular Army. (Section 2 of the Army Act, 1950).

Air Force

The Air Force Act, 1950 is applicable to the following:

(a) Officers and Warrant Officers of the Air Force.

(b) Persons enrolled under the Air Force Act.

(c) Persons belonging to the Regular Air Force Reserve or Air Definite Reserve or the Auxiliary Air Force, in circumstances specified in Section 26 of the reserve and Auxiliary Air Force Act, 1952 (62 of 1952).

(d) Persons not otherwise subject to Air Force Law, who on active service in camp, on the march, or at any frontier part specified by the Central Government by notification in this behalf, are employed by, or are in the service of, or are followers or, accompany any portion of the Air Force.

Navy

The Navy Act, 1957 is applicable to the following persons:

(a) Every persons belonging to the Indian Navy during the time that he is liable for service under the Navy Act.

(b) Every person belonging to Indian navy reserve force when he is:

   (i) On active service or

   (ii) In or any property of the Naval Service, including Naval establishment ships and other vessel, aircraft, vehicles and armouries, or

   (iii) Called upon for training or under going training in pursuance of Regulations made under Navy Act unit he is duly released from his training or

   (iv) Called up into actual service in the Indian Navy in pursuance or regulations made under Navy Act until he is duly released there from.

(c) Members of the regular Army and the Air Force when embarked on board any ship or aircraft of the Indian Navy to such extent and subject to such conditions as may be prescribed.

(d) Every person not otherwise subject to Naval law who enters into an engagement with the Central government under Section 6.

(e) Every person belonging to any Auxiliary Forces raised under the Navy Act to such extent and subject to such conditions as may be prescribed and

(f) Every person, who, although he would not otherwise be subject to Naval law, is by any other Act or during active service by regulations made under this Act is subject to such conditions as may be prescribed.

It would thus be seen that it is not only the uniformed officers and men of the Army, Navy or the Air Force, who only as understood in common parlance, are subject to these Acts, but also certain civilians, when serving under the special conditions as laid down in these Acts and members of the Regular Army, Navy and the Air Force. For example certain civilians of the defence establishments i.e. Cooks, Chowkidars, Barbers, Tailors etc. under certain conditions answer the description of the members of the Armed Forces.

For this purpose, reference may be made to the Judgements of the Supreme Court in the following cases:

O K Nayyar v. Union of India AIR 1976 SC 1179

Gopal Upadhaya v. Union of India AIR 1987 SC 413.

R Viswan & others v. Union of India AIR 1983 SC 658

Further, if a person attached for the time being to unit forming part of a force which is engaged in operation against an enemy, he will be deemed as member of the Armed Force, such as Civilian Officers Works Engineers in Defence service do. In this connection see:

Sachdev v. Union of India 1964 J & K 21.

Kartar Sing v. King Emperor

Cr. Miss Case 68/44 Lahore.

Having seen the broad parameters of the Rent Control laws as relating to the Armed Forces in general, we will now examine the situation prevailing in each of the respective States. For Rent Control in each State, kindly see under the provisions of the safeguards provided by each State given in Chapter XI.

Maharashtara

Bombay Rents, Hotels and Lodging House Rates Control Act, 1947 came into force on 19th January 1948, Section 13 of the Act lists the grounds on which a landlord may recover possession of the premises from the tenant. As per Section 13 (i) (g) of the above Act, a landloard may recover possession on the ground that the premises are reasonably and bonafidely required by the landlord for occupation by himself or by any person for, whose benefit the premises are held.

A landlord seeking to evict his tenant u/s 13(i) (g) has to satisfy the Court that his (landlord) requirement is not only reasonable but is also bonafide. While considering the proof of bonafide and reasonableness of the requirement, a number of factors come into play. The Bombay High Court has held that the words "reasonably and bonfide" are not intended to be used disjunctively (AIR 1972 Bom 46). Further, Section 13(2A) of the Act puts an important limitation on the ground stated in Section 13(1)(g). If the premises are let to the Government, in a cantonment area and such premises are being used for residence by members of the Armed Forces or their families, then a landlord shall not be entitled to recover possession of the premises under Section 13(10).

Section 13 A-1 has been introduced in the Bombay Rents, Hotels and Lodging House Rates Control Act, 1947, to provide valuable relief to serving and retired members of the Armed Forces who want to settle down in their houses after evicting the tenants, Section 13A-1 stipulates:

(a) Landlord, who is a member of the Armed Forces of the Union, or who was such member and is duly retired (which term shall include premature retirement), shall be entitled to recover possession of any premises, on the ground that the premises, are bonafidely required by him for occupation by himself or any member of his family (which term shall include a parent or other relation ordinarily residing with him and dependent on him), the Court shall pass a decree for eviction on such ground if the landlord, at the hearing of the suit, produces a certificate signed by the head of his service or his commanding officer to the effect that:

(i) he is presently a member of the armed forces of the Union or he was such member and is now a retired ex-serviceman,

(ii) he does not possess any other suitable residence in the local area where he or members of his family can reside.

Where a member of the Armed Forces of the Union dies while in service or such member is duly retired as stated above and is within five years of his retirement his widow who is or becomes a landlord of any premises, shall be entitled to recover possession of such premises on the ground that the premises are bonafidely required by her for occupation by herself or any member of her family (which term shall include he and her husband's parent or other relation ordinarily residing with her), and the Court shall pass a decree for eviction on such ground, if such widow, at the having of the suit, produces a certificate signed by the Area or Sub-Area Commander within whose jurisdiction the premises are situated to the effect that:

(i) She is a widow of a deceased member of the armed forces as aforesaid,

(ii) She does not possess any other suitable residence in the local area where she or the members of her family can reside.

Explanation 1: For the purposes of clause (a) of this section, the expression "the Head of his service" in the case of officers retired from the Indian Army includes the Area Commander, in the case of officers retired from the Indian Navy, includes the Flag Officer Commander-in-Chief, Western Naval Command and in the case of officers retired from the Indian Air Force include the Station Commander.

Explanation 2: For the purpose of this section any certificate granted thereunder shall be conclusive evidence of the facts stated therein.

Yet another advantage of the new provision (incorporated vide Maharashtra Amending Act 52/75) is that the prohibition under Section 13 (2A) does not apply to Section 13A-1. Thus even if the premises area let to the Central Government in a cantonment area and the premises are being used for residence of members of Armed Forces for their families), still the landlord may petition u/s 13A-1 and will be entitled to vacant possession.

Procedure for Eviction

After above amendment came into force, on 25th October, 1972 HQ Western Naval Command finalized the modalities of the procedure in consultation with the Maharashtara Government. A copy of the format of the application to be submitted by the personnel as also a copy of the certificate to be issued by the Defence authorities, are at pages 161-63 respectively. The following is the existing procedure for recovery of possession:

(a) A valid notice should be served on; the defendant giving 30 days time to hand over vacant and peaceful possession of premises in question.

(b) The court of Small Causes is the Court of competent jurisdiction and a suit is to be filed and contested in Court No. 10 of the SCC at Bombay.

(c) Any decree or order passed by the above Court is appealable and an appeal lies with the Bench of the Court of Small Causes.

(d) Although the decision of the above bench is not appealable the same can be challenged in the High Court at Bombay by filling a special civil application.

(e) Lastly, the decision of the High Court can also be challenged in the Supreme Court.

The question whether the benefit of Section 13A-1 would be available to ex-member of the Armed Forces in respect of premises, the ownership of which he acquired after his retirement, came up before the Supreme Court in the case of Mrs. W. Ress v. Mrs Ivy Fanseca (AIR 1984 SC 458). The Supreme Court held that Section 13A-1 has to be read as conferring benefit only on those members of the Armed Forces who were landlords of the suit-premises while they were in service even though they may avail of it after their retirement. The Supreme Court further held that Section 13A-1 cannot be liberally interpreted to cover all retired members of the

Armed Forces irrespective of the fact whether they were landlords while they were in service or not, as such a liberal interpretation is likely to expose it to a successful challenge on the basis of Article 14 of the Constitution. Thus a retired Army Officer, who had become landlord of the 'suit premises', already in possession of the tenant, by way of gift after his retirement could not avail of the benefit of Section 13A-1. In this case, the Supreme Court also expressed the view that Section 13A-1 did not govern the case of a person who had retired long back from the Armed Forces and was gainfully employed elsewhere and while so employed had let out his premises with open eyes.

Punjab

East Punjab Urban Rent Restriction Act, 1949 lays down grounds and procedure for eviction of tenants. Section 13(3)(1-a) of the said Act provides that, 'In the case of residential building, if the landlord is a member of the Armed Forces of the Union of India and requires it for the occupation of his family and if he produces a certificate of the prescribed authority, referred to in Section 7 of the Indian Soldiers (Litigation) Act, 1925, that he is serving under special conditions within the meaning of Section 3 of that Act.

Explanation – The certificate of the prescribed authority shall be conclusive evidence that the landlord is serving under special conditions. Family means such relations of the landlord as ordinarily live with him and are dependent upon him.

Where an application is made by member of Armed Forces, it shall be disposed of as far as may be, within a period of one month and if the claim of the landlord is accepted the controller, shall make an order directing the tenant to put the landlord in possession of the building on a date to be specified in the order and such date shall not be later than fifteen days from the date of the order.

It would be seen from the above provision that it only extends to those members of the Armed Forces who are serving under special conditions within the meaning of Section 3 of Indian Soldiers (Litigation) Act, 1925. Hence the extent of effect of this provision is quite minimal.

Haryana

Haryana Urban (Control of Rent and Eviction) Act 1973 Section 13(3)(a)(v) stipulates that 'a landlord may apply to the Controller for an order directing the tenant to put the landlord in possession in the case of residential building if he is a member of the armed forces and requires it for the occupation of his family and produces a certificate from the prescribed authority (authority competent to sanction leave of absence) that he is serving under special conditions within the meaning of Section 3 of Indian Soldiers Litigation Act, 1925 (as per Section 3 of OSL Act) and Indian Soldier shall be deemed to be serving under special conditions when he is or has been serving under war conditions, or overseas or at any place beyond India or at any such place within India as may be specified by the Central Government by notification in the official Gazette".

For Non-residential Building

As per Section 13 (3a) of Haryana Urban (Control of Rent and Eviction) Act, 1973, "Landlord who stands retired or discharged as a NCO from the Armed Forces or who was a minor son at the time of death of the deceased landlord, and requires it for his personal use, may within a period of 3 years from the date of retirement or discharge or attaining the age of eighteen years apply to the Controller for an order directing the tenant to put the landlord in possession.

Time Limit for Eviction

A landlord who seeks to evict his tenant shall apply to the Controller for direction to that effect. If the Controller, after giving the tenant a reasonable opportunity of showing cause is satisfied, the Controller may make an order directing the tenant to put the landlord in possession of the building within such period as stipulated or extended.

If the application is made by a member of the Armed Forces, it shall be disposed of, as far as may be within a period of one month and if the claim of the landlord is accepted, the controller shall make an order directing the tenant to put the landlord in possession of the building or land on a date to be specified in the order and such date shall not be later than 15 days from the day of the order.

Himachal Pradesh

Himachal Pradesh Urban Rent Control Act, 1971 stipulates the grounds and procedure by which tenant can be evicted by a landlord Section 14(3)(e) states:- A landlord may apply to the Controller for order directing the tenant to put the landlord in possession.

(1) In the case of residential building, if the landlord is a member of the Armed Forces of the Union of India and requires it for the occupation of his family and if he produces a certificate of the prescribed authority referred to in Section 7 of the Indian Soldier's (Litigation) Act, 1925, that he is serving under special conditions within the meaning of Section 3 of that Act or is posted in a non-family Station.

Explanations – The purpose of this sub-clause:

(1) The certificate of the prescribed authority shall be conclusive evidence that the landlord is serving under special conditions or is posted in a non-family station.

(2) "Family" means parents and such relations of the landlord as ordinarily live with him and are dependent upon him.

A landlord who is a member of the Armed Forces may apply to the controller for an order directing the tenant to put the landlord in possession of the premises for the occupation of his family. The landlord is to produce a certificate from his CO that he is serving under special conditions within the meaning of the Section 3 of that Act or is posted in a non-family station.

Delhi

For the benefit of members of the Armed Forces, Delhi Rent Control Act was amended in 1988 by insertion of Section 14 B, vide Delhi Rent Control (Amendment) Act, 1988 (57 of 1988) Section 14 B provides:

Right to recover immediate possession of premises to accrue to members of the Armed Forces, etc.:

(1) Where the landlord:-

(a) is a released or retired person from any armed forces and the premises let out by him are required for his own residence; or

(b) is a dependent of a member of any armed forces who had been killed in action and the premises let out by such members are required for the residence of the family of such member, such person or, as the case may be, the dependent may, within one year from the date of his release or retirement from such armed forces or, as the case may be, the date of death of such member, or within a period of one year from the date of commencement of the Delhi Rent Control (Amendment) Act, 1988, whichever is later, apply to the Controller for recovering the immediate possession of such premises.

(2) Where the landlord is a member of any of the armed forces and has a period of less than one year preceding to the date of his retirement and the premises let out by him are required for his own residence after his retirement, he may at any time, within a period of one year before the date of his retirement, apply to the Controller for recovering the immediate possession of such premises.

(3) Where the landlord referred to in sub-section (1) or (2) has let out more than one premises, it shall be open to him to make an application under that sub-section in respect of only one of the premises chosen by him.

Explanation - For the purpose of this section, 'armed forces' means an armed force of the Union constituted under an Act of Parliament and includes a member of the police force constituted under Section 3 of the Delhi Police Act, 1978 (34 of 1978).

For the term " armed forces" in this context reference may be made to Saraswati Devi v. District Magistrate of Deoria decided where it was held:

Armed Forces: The expression "armed forces" has also not being defined anywhere in the Act. However, the explanation to Section 14B states that for the purpose of Section 14B, "armed forces" mean an armed force of the Union constituted under an Act of Parliament and includes a member of the police force constituted under Section 3 of the Delhi Police Act, 1978. The explanation enlarges the scope of the expression "armed forces" by including a member of the police force constituted under Section 3 of the Delhi Police Act, 1978.

Armed Forces of the Union means the regular Army, Navy and Air Force or any part of any one or more of them as defined in the Army Act, and it could never have meant the members of the National Cadet Corps who are not part of the regular Armed Forces of the Union.

Saraswati Devi v. District Magistrate of Deoria

AIR 1936 All 236

Jammu & Kashmir
J&K Houses and Shops Rent Control Act, 1966
II-A Restoration of Possession to Defence personnel

Notwithstanding anything to the contrary contained in this Act, possession of a residential building shall be restored within one month from the date of application, if:

(a) the landlord is member of the Defence Force and requires it for occupation of his family and produces a certificate from his Commanding Officer showing that he is serving under special condition within the meaning of Section 3 of the Indian Soldiers (Litigation) Act, 1925.

(b) the landlord is a member of the Defence Forces and requires it for his own occupation on retirement, release or discharge from the Defence services and produces a certificate from the Commanding Officer evidence of his release, retirement or discharge; and

(c) if the landlord is the wife of a deceased member of Defence Forces, who requires it for her own occupation and produces certificate from the Commanding Officer of his deceased husband to the effect that her husband died while serving under special conditions within the meaning of Section 3 of the Indian Soldiers (Litigation) Act, 1925.

Amendment to Section 13 Act XXXIV of 1966 In Section 13 of the Principal Act

(i) For the brackets and letter "(b) wherever occurring the brackets and letter"(h)" Shall be and shall always be deemed to have been substituted:

(ii) in sub section (i), for the words and figures section or because of section 11A" substituted.

Amendment under SRO 396 Dt. 8th September, 1981

Rule 6 provides that the Rent Controller will get the premises physically vacated within 7 days of passing the orders, after he has made the brief enquiries to satisfy himself.

Union Territory of Chandigarh

The East Punjab Urban Rent Restriction Act (Extension to Chandigarh) Act, 1974. (Act No. 54 of 1974)

An Act to extend the East Punjab Urban Rent Restriction Act, 1949, to the Union Territory of Chandigarh. (See AIR March, 1975).

Uttar Pradesh

The State of Uttar Pradesh has provided three fold safeguards in its rent control laws in favour of the Armed Forces.

One in relation to a landlord who is a member of the Armed Forces, two, in relation to such a tenant and third in relation to heirs of the member of the Armed Forces who have died whilst serving under special conditions.

In relation to such a landlord Section 14(3) (iii) of the UP Urban Buildings (Regulation of Letting & Eviction) Act, 1972 provides that a landlord may apply to the controller for order directing the tenant to put the landlord in possession of the residential building if the landlord is a member of the Armed Forces of the Union of India and requires it for the occupation of his family and if he produces a certificate of his prescribed authority referred to in Section 7 of the Indian Soldiers Litigation Act, 1925 that he is serving under special conditions within the meaning of Section 3 of that Act or is posted in a non-family station.

The explanation to the sub-section provides that the certificate of the prescribed authority shall be conclusive evidence that the landlord is serving under special conditions or is posted in a non-family station. The word 'Family' means parents and such relation of the landlord as ordinarily live with him and are dependent upon him.

For a member who is a tenant, Section 21 of the same Act provides that no application for eviction shall be entertained in case of a residential building against any tenant, who is a member of the Armed Forces of the Union and in whose favour the prescribed authority under the Soldiers Litigation Act, 1925 has issued a certificate that he is serving under special conditions within the meaning of Section 3 of that Act or where he has died by enemy action whilst so serving there against his heirs.

So also Section 20 which deals with bar of suits for eviction of tenant except on specified ground for the arrears of rent the period of four months has been increased to six months in relation to person serving under special conditions or where he has died whilst so serving there in relation to his heirs.

Section 21 of the said Act after its amendment in the explanation provides yet another valuable provision.

It states that where the landlord of any building is a serving or retired Indian soldier as defined in the Indian Soldiers Litigation Act, 1925 and such building was let out at any time before retirement or a widow of such soldier and such building was let out at any time before the retirement or death of her husband, whichever occurs earlier. And such landlord needs such building for occupation by himself or member of his family for residential purposes, his representation that he needs the building for residential purposes for himself or the member of his family shall be deemed sufficient for the purpose of clause (a) and where such landlord own more than one building this provision shall apply in respect of one building only.

For the Ex-servicemen and their families in the state of UP there is a very valuable judgement in the case of Mohinder Pal Singh v. Additional District Judge, Dehradun Civil Miscellaneous Writ Petition No. 2791 of 1989 dated 03-11-92 (AIR 1993 Allahabad 176). In the said landmark judgement the Hon'ble High Court has held that vide section 21(1) proviso 4 explanation clause (3) (As amended by UP Act, 31 of 1985) that the said provisions for soldiers contained in the amendment applies to all types of buildings and to retired soldiers or their widows. They noted the fact that the explanation as originally enacted was confined to a "Residential Building" and to the members of the family of a Indian soldier serving under special conditions, whereas after its amendment by UP Act 31 of 1985 Clause (III) of the explanation has made it applicable to "all building" and to any soldier that is serving or retired and his widow, it does not effect any of the vested rights of the tenant of such building.

It also held that under section 21 (IA) application by the specified landlord – landlord in occupation of public building which he is to vacate on cessation of employement – prescribed authority has no option but to order eviction provision of sub-section (IA) are mandatory – non-obsentents clause in section 21(IA) giving it over-riding effect of section (2) further established its mandatory nature.

In the facts of these cases the respondent was serving as a colonel in the Indian Army and was occupying a public building at 27, The Mall, Delhi Cantonment. He stood superannuated with effects form 21st July, 1982 and vacated his official residence on 30th September, 1982. Whilst examining the relevant provision, the learned High Court said that the authority has not been given any option with regards an order of eviction in case covered by sub-section (IA).

Madhya Pradesh

Section 20-A has been inserted in the Madhya Pradesh Accommodation Control Act, 1961, to provide for special provision for recovery of possession of the premises by the members of family of landlord, who is killed whilst in active service in Army, Navy or the Air Force.

It provides that where the landlord in respect of any accommodation being a member of the Naval, Military, Air or other Armed Forces of the Union dies on active duty and the said accommodation or a part thereof is required for the bonafide residence of a member of his family, the Court may on an application by such member of the family, place him in vacant possession of such accommodation or part thereof, as the case may be, by evicting the tenant or every other person who may be in occupation thereof if the Court is satisfied:

(a) That the landlord was the owner of such accommodation and,

(b) That the member of the family is in need of the accommodation or a part thereof for his residence and no other suitable alternative accommodation is possessed by him.

It is pertinent to note that in this provision not only members of the Army, Navy or the Air Force are covered but also members of other armed forces of the Union such as BSF, Coast Guards or the CRPF.

Rajasthan

On 22nd May, 1987 the Governor of Rajasthan promulgated the Rajasthan Premises (Control of Rent and Eviction) (Amendment) Ordinance amending Section 13 of the Rajasthan premises (Control of Rent and Eviction) Act, 1950.

It now enables the retired members of the armed forces of the Union as also a war widow or other legal representative of a deceased member, to seek eviction of their tenants in a summary manner by moving an application to the District Magistrate on the ground that the premises are required for the use and occupation of such member. A bill to this effect will be tabled before the Rajasthan State Assembly shortly.

Tamil Nadu

Tamil Nadu Building (Lease and Rent Control) Act, 1960 stipulates the grounds and procedure for evicting a tenant from the premises.

Section 10 sub-section 3-A (a) Tamil Nadu Building (Lease & Rent Control) Act, 1960 stipulates that:

(a) A landlord who has been or is a member of the Armed Forces can obtain the possession of the premises if he,

   (i) is released or has retired from service and the building is bonafidely required for his residence;

   or

   (ii) is stationed at a place where on account of Military exigencies, he cannot live with his family or dies or is on active duty and the building is bonafidely required for the residence of his family.

The Controller shall, on application made by the landlord who is a member of the Armed Forces or the member of his family, as the case may be, if he is satisfied that the claim of the landlord or the member of his family is bonafide, pass an order directing the tenant to put the landlord or the members of his family in possession of the building and if the controller is not so satisfied he shall make an order rejecting the application.

Notwithstanding anything contained in clause (a) of Section 10(3A) where the landlord who is a member of the armed forces or the member of his family produces a certificate from the prescribed authority under the Indian Soldiers (Litigation) Act, 1925 (Central Act IV of 1925) that the landlord is serving under special conditions within the meaning of Section 3 of that Act, the application referred to in clause (a) shall be disposed of, as far as may be within a period of one month and if the claim of the landlord of the members of his family is accepted, the controller shall pass an order directing the tenant to put the landlord or the member of his family in possession of the building on such date as may be specified in the order which shall not be later than one month from the date or such order.

Explanation – For the purpose of this sub-section "Member of the Armed Forces" means a person in the service of the Air Force, Army or Navy of the Union of India and includes a seaman and "seaman" includes a master, pilot or apprentice employed or engaged as a member of the crew of a ship or a sailing vessel to which the Merchant Shipping Act, 1958 (Central Act 44 of 1958) applies.

Provided that if a question arises whether any person is a member of the Armed Forces, such question shall be decided by the controller and his decision shall be final.

Mysore (Karnataka)

Mysore (Karnataka) Rent Control Act, 1961 stipulates the grounds and procedure for evicting a tenant from the premises.

Section 21(b) contains special provisions for recovery of premises by members of Armed Forces or a member of a deceased member of such Forces. It provides that notwithstanding anything contained in the Act:

(a) A landlord, who is a member of the Armed Forces of the Union, or who was such a member and is duly retired which term shall include premature retirement shall be entitled to recover possession of any premises on the ground that the premises is bonafidely required by him for occupation by himself or any member of his family and the court shall pass a decree for eviction on such ground, if the landlord, at the hearing of the suit, produces a certificate given by the head of his service or his Commanding Officer, to the effect that:

(i) he is presently a member of the Armed Forces of the Union or he was such a member and is now retired, and

(iii) he does not possesses any other suitable accommodation in the local area where he or the members of his family can reside.

(b) Where a member of the Armed Force of the Union dies while in service or such member is duly retired as stated above and dies within five years of his retirement, his widow who is or becomes a landlady or any premises shall be entitled to recover possession of such premises on the ground that the accommodation is bonafidely required by her for occupation by herself, or for any member of her family and the Court shall pass a decree for eviction on such ground, if such widow at the hearing of the suit, produces a certificate signed by the area or sub-area Commander within whose jurisdiction the accommodation is situated to the effect that:-

(i) She is the widow of a deceased member of the Armed Forces as aforesaid, and

(ii) She does not possess any other suitable accommodation in the local area where she or the members of her family can reside.

Explanation – For the purposes of clause (a) of this section, the expression 'the head of his service' in the case members retired from the Indian Army includes the Area Commander, in the case of members retired from the Indian Navy includes the Flag Officer Commanding-in-Chief and in the case of the members retired from the Indian Air Force includes the Station Commander.

For the purpose of this section, any certificate referred to in sub-section (i) shall be conclusive evidence of facts stated therein.

Kerala

Kerala Building (Lease and Rent Control) Act, 1965 specified the grounds and procedure for evicting a tenant from the premises. Extract of Section 11A of the Kerala Building (Lease & Rent) Act, 1965.

Notwithstanding any thing contained in Section 11, in the case of a residential building where the landlord is a member of the Armed Forces of the Union of India, and the building is required for the occupation of himself on his release from services, and he makes an application for eviction of the tenant to the Rent Control Court, or where on the occurrence of death in action of a member of the Armed Forces, a member of his family requires recovery of possession of the building for his own residence or where on the posting of a member of the Armed Forces to serve under special conditions, a member of his family requires recovery of possession of the Building for his own residence and an application is made to the Rent Control Court for eviction of the tenant, the Rent Control Court shall dispose of the same, as far as may be within one month, and if the claim of the landlord or member of his family is accepted, the Court shall make an order directing the tenant to put the landlord or the member of his family as the case may be in possession of the building on a date to be specified in the order, and such date shall not be later than fifteen days from the date of the order.

Provided that an application under this section for recovery of the possession of a building on the ground that the landlord is serving under special conditions of service shall not be entertained by the Rent Control Court unless the same is accompanied by a certificate of the prescribed authority referred to in Section 7 of the Indian Soldiers (Litigation) Act, 1925 that the landlord is serving under special conditions within the meaning of Section 3 of the said Act.

Explanation – For the purpose of this section "Family" shall mean such relations of the landlord as ordinarily live with him and are dependent on him.

West Bengal

Extract of Section 298 (ii) of West Bengal Tenancy Act, 1956 (1979 Amendment) Provision to Section 29 (b) (ii):

(a) Where the landlord has retired, or will retire within a period of less than one year, as Member of the Naval, Military or Air Force of the Union of India, a certificate by the Area or Sub-Area Commander within whose jurisdiction the premises are situated or by the Head of his service or his Commanding Officer that he has retired, or will retire, as such member and that he requires the premises for his own occupation and for the occupation of his family after retirement, or

(b) Where the landlord is the parent or the wife of such member of the naval, military or air force of the Union of India, as aforesaid, a certificate by the Area or Sub-Area Commander within whose jurisdiction the premises are situated that he or she is the parent or the wife, as the case may be, of such member of the naval, military or air force of the Union of India and that he or she requires the premises for his or her own occupation and for the occupation of his or her family after the retirement of such member, or

(c) Where the landlord is a relation (other than a minor child or the widow) and a dependent of a member of the naval, military or air force of the Union of India, and ordinarily resides with him or a minor child or the widow or such member who dies while in service or within five years of retirement, a certificate by the Area or Sub-Area Commander within whose jurisdiction the premises are situated. That he or the relation and dependent as aforesaid or the minor child of the widow, as the case may be of the deceased member of the naval, military or air force, and requires the premises for his or her own occupation of his or her family, shall be produced before the Controller while filing the application, and such certificates shall be conclusive evidence of the fact stated therein.

No Civil Court shall entertain any application by a landlord being a government employee, and who being in occupation of any residential premises allotted to him by his employer to vacate such residential accommodation, or in default to incur certain obligations on the ground that he owns a residential accommodation either in his own name or in the name of his wife or dependent child at or near the place where he is posted for the time being or by a landlord who has retired or will retire within a period of less than one year as a member of the Naval, Military or Air Force of the Union of India, or by a landlord who is a relation (other than a minor child or widow) and a dependent of a member of the naval, military or air force of the Union of India and ordinarily resides within or a minor child or the widow of such member who dies while in service or within five years of retirement for the recovery of possession of any premises. Section 13(h) of the same Act also provides that where a landlord is a member of the Armed Forces of the Union of India and requires it for occupation of his family and produces a certificate of the prescribed authority of Indian soldiers

(Litigation) Act, 1925 that he is serving under special conditions, that certificate shall be conclusive evidence that the landlord is serving under special conditions or is posted in a non-family area.

The family for this purpose means parents and such relations of the landlord as ordinarily reside with him and are dependent on him.

Agricultural Land

As mentioned earlier, Rent Control legislation does not deal with Agricultural land, that is dealt with by the respective Land Reforms Act of the State concerned. It has been confirmed from reliable sources that following states/Union Territories have already made special provisions for resumption of agricultural lands by the servicemen and their dependents on retirement or demise.

(a) Andra Pradesh (b) Assam (c) Goa (d) Gujarat (e) Haryana (f) Himachal Pradesh (g) Jammu and Kashmir (h) Kerala (i) Karnataka (j) Madhya Pradesh (k) Maharashtra (l) Manipur (m) Mizoram (n) Punjab (o) Rajasthan (p) Tamilnadu (q) Tripura and (r) U.P.

Since that matter is not subject matter of this chapter, it has not been dealt with. Personnel requiring the same may refer to the relevant Land Reforms Act of the State and in case of any practical difficulty may approach the Rajya/Zila Sainik Board through District Soldiers, Sailors and Air men Boards, who are under instructions to render all help.

11

Pension and Gratuities

Introduction

It was in mid fifties, when I was serving in a flying-cum-training institution of the IAF that I became very friendly with one Sqn. Ldr. David, the Chief Flying Instructor, an officer par excellence and equally outstanding flying instructor. An evening with him and his charming lady and two small kids was a treat worth remembering and an envy for many.

One unlucky Saturday afternoon, the entire station was plunged into grief and darkness, the bad news was that Sqn. Ldr. David had died in an air crash whilst on an operational duty. My thoughts naturally went immediately to the service and exemplary deeds of the officer and his shattered family. I became too philosophical and said that cruel fate does not spare even noble souls. Last rituals and mourning period over, our concern obviously shifted to the settlement of ill-fated charming lady and the innocent children and lot, to our horror, we found that with, no significant special family pension, no worthwhile death-cum-retirement gratuity, no family assistance scheme, no Group Insurance cover, no Wives Welfare Association and no significant contribution from IAF Benevolent Fund, she was destined to live on a paltry monthly pension of

Rs. 230 only. The fate had snatched not only Sqn. Ldr. David, but also right of his family to live a decent existence. We, all the officers at the Station, then decided to contribute our half a month's salary so that she could have a decent start in life.

Today, things are vastly different. There are a number of funds and schemes and of course grants and enhanced pensions and gratuities. So long as a service man retires or even dies whilst in service, he himself or his colleagues in service and authorities take care of various aspects. But after his retirement, where he has severed his connections with service authorities and colleagues and often lives far away in cities, towns or villages, on his demise the families face a different situation. This is compounded by the facts that, most often such personnel often do not educate their families on various reliefs available to them, either due to delicate nature of the subject or some sheer superstitious beliefs.

It is, therefore, imperative that as the sun sets, the families and the next of kin know, what exactly are their legal entitlements from the government, the service and various institutions. For immediate relief and reference, the various authorities which should be contacted should be known. It is precisely for this reason that a need for a separate chapter in a work of this nature was felt. For sake of convenience, the matter has been divided under four groups, one from – the government, which is applicable to the personnel of all the three Services and one each for Army, Navy and Air Force personnel. In the first group, where rank of one service is indicated, for the other services; the corresponding rank would apply. At one stage it was also considered to attach samples of Forms that are required to be filled by various authorities/ agencies with this Chapter. However, with computerization and even changing forms, it was realized that listing the addresses of various authorities/agencies who should be contacted would be more practical.

Pensions – Historical Overview

The law on the subjects has travelled a long way to reach the present stage. Earlier, the rules or at least the impression about these rules was quite to the contrary. Thanks is not due to the officialdom but to the judiciary whose progressive look has brought this sea change. To have a proper appreciation of this revolution, a peep into the past is necessary.

Presidency Regulations on Pensions 19th Century

At the earlier stages, the law relating to the pensions was distributed over 9 Regulations of the Bengal, 3 Regulations of the Madras and 2 Regulations of the Bombay Courts as well as the 3 Acts of the Governor-General in Council. The main provisions of the law as expressed in Bengal Regulation` XXIV, 1793, Section 17, XXXIV, 1795, Section 14, XXIV, 1803, Section 16, VI, 1817 and the Madras Regulations IV 1831, Section 2 is the reservation to the Government of the right to determine on all claims to the continuance of pensions, and the exclusion of the jurisdiction of the ordinary Courts of judicature in regard to such claims. The Bengal Regulations, that were expressly applicable only to Bengal and the NW Provinces was practically in force throughout the British Provinces except a portion of the Bombay Presidency.

As the Civil Courts in the country had nevertheless assumed the jurisdiction in such cases, a need was felt to curtail the same. This was essentially based on the principle that the jurisdiction elsewhere was disallowed. As the principle was founded on perfectly equitable considerations, it was therefore considered fit for a uniform application. It was in effect the assertion of the right of the State to reserve to itself the power of granting or withholding at pleasure concessions which are made gratuitously and without consideration.

Pension Act 1871

Accordingly, Pension Act, 1871 was brought in which came into effect on 8th August 1871. The object behind the Act was to reserve to the Government determination of all questions affecting grant of money bestowal of which was an act of grace or State policy or part of the Government. The Pension Act which came into being tends to restrict the ordinary legal rights of the subjects to have recourse to the Courts for remedy of grievances Section 4 of the Pension Act refers "which *inter alia* stipulates "Bar of suits relating to pension" -

"Except as hereinafter provided, no Civil Court shall entertain any suit relating to any pension or grant money or land revenue conferred or made by the Government or by any other former Government whatever may have been the consideration for any such pension or grant or whatever may have been the nature of the payment, claim or the right to which such pension or grant may have been substituted."

In 1956, All. 564(567)(DB), it was held that where the Government refuses to pay pension to a claimant it cannot be said that such a claimant has alternative remedy by means of a suit.

The words "any suit relating to any pension" in Section 4 are quite indicative of the position that suits relating to such pensions are barred under that Section and it is immaterial whether the Government is or is not a party to such suit (Beldeo Jha v. Ganga Prasad AIR 59 Pat. 17).

It is pertinent however to note that the above Section (Section 4) cannot over-ride or affect the jurisdiction of the High Court under Article 226 of the Constitution as the Constitution is supreme. The remedy under Article 226 cannot be barred by a substitute (K R Erry v. State of Punjab (AIR 1967 Punj). In S H Baig Mirza v. The State (AIR 1959 All 969); it was held that an order refusing to grant pension on extraneous or irrelevant ground should normally be interfered with by the High Court and set aside.

Immunity from Attachment

Having seen in brief the historical background of the law on pensions, let us see the legal safeguards so far as the pension and gratuity of the persons belonging to the armed forces are concerned. In that context, it must be remembered that Section 11 of the Pension Act provides a very valuable safeguard which is applicable also to the members of the armed forces.

It states:

11. Exemption of pension from Attachment – No pension granted or continued by government on political considerations or on account of past services or present infirmities or as a compassionate allowance.

And no money due or to become due on account of any such pension or allowance, shall be liable to seizure, attachment or sequestration by process of any Court at the instance of a creditor, for any demand against the pensioner, or in satisfaction of a decree order of any such Court.

This Section applies also to pensions granted or continued after the separation of Burma from India, by the Government of Burma.

Pension – C.P.C. immunity from attachment

In this context Provisions of Section 60 Civil Procedures Court 1908 are equally important, which should also be kept in mind. It reads:-

60. Property Liable to Attachment and Sale in execution of Decree. (1) The following property is liable to attachment and sale in execution of – a decree, namely, lands, houses or other buildings, goods, money, bank-notes, cheques, bills of exchange, hundis, promissory , Government securities, bonds or other securities for money, debts, shares in a corporation and, save as hereinafter mentioned, all other saleable property, moveable or immoveable, belonging to the judgment-debtor,

or over which, or the profits of which, he had disposing power which he may exercise for his own benefit, whether the same be held in the name of the judgment-debtor or by another person in trust for him or on his behalf.

(g) stipends and gratuities allowed to pensioners of the Government, or payable out of any service family pension fund notified in the Official Gazette by the Central Government or the State Government in this behalf, and political pensions;

(h) the wages of laborers and domestic servants, whether payable in money or in kind;

(i) salary to the extent of the first two hundred rupees and one-half the remainder in execution of any decree other than a decree for maintenance:

Provided that, where such salary is the salary of a servant of the Government or a servant of a railway company or local authority, and the whole or any part of the portion of such salary liable to attachment has been under attachment, whether continuously or intermittently for a total period of twenty-four months, such portion shall be exempted from attachment until the expiry of a further period of twelve months and, where such attachment has been made in execution of one and the same decree, shall be finally exempt from attachment in execution of that decree;

(i)(a) one-third of the salary in execution of any decree for maintenance;

(j) the pay and allowances of persons to whom the Air Force Act, 1950, or the Army Act, 1950 applies, or the persons other than Commissioned Officers to whom the Indian Navy Act, 1957 applies;

(k) all compulsory deposits and other sums in or derived from any fund to which the Provident Funds Act, 1925 for the time being applies in so far as they are declared by the said Act not to be liable to attachment; (o) any allowance declared by any Indian law to be exempt from liability to attachment or sale in execution of a decree; and

Explanation 1. The particulars mentioned in clauses (g), (h), (i), (j), (k) and (o) are exempted from attachment or sale whether before or after they are actually payable and in the case of salary of a servant of the Government or a servant of a railway company or local authority the attachable portion thereof is exempt from attachment until it is actually payable.

Explanation 2. In clause (h) and (i), 'salary' means the total monthly emoluments, excluding any allowance declared exempt from attachment under the provisions of clause (1), derived by a person from his employment whether on duty or on leave.

Pensions – Armed Forces

As regards pensions for the members of the armed forces, i.e. Army, Navy & Air Force, they are governed by the provisions contained in Pension Regulations for the Army, Part 1 (1961); Pension Regulations for the Air Force, part 1 (1961); and the Navy (Pension) Regulations (1964);

As per these regulations, full rate of pension or gratuity shall not be granted unless the service rendered has been satisfactory. If the service has not been satisfactory, the competent authority may make such reduction in the amount of pension or gratuity as it thinks proper. Further as per these regulations future good conduct shall be an implied condition of grant of pension or allowance. Regulations also stipulate that in special cases to be determined by the President as may be specified in the Regulations the pensions service, disability or family children allowance or gratuity to be granted or given to an individual or any portion of it, may be withheld, suspended or discontinued. In exceptional cases, payment of part or whole of the pension, allowance or gratuity suspended or withheld by the order of the President can be made to the wife or other dependents of the pensioner.

These pension regulations are administrative regulations and thus are amended or clarified by various instructions issued by the Government. Though the legal status and enforceability of these regulations and instructions have yet to be judicially pronounced, but in practice the courts have been very zealous in safeguarding the rights flowing there from to the various beneficiaries.

Before we proceed to examine the various cases decided by the Courts to bring out the change in the law of pensions and how they have interpreted various provisions, it must be mentioned that the government has also constituted various appellate authorities within the government to decide on appeals concerning matters relating to pensions. In matters of disability pensions, and special family pension, the first appeal can be preferred within 6 months of the date of communication of orders to a committee known as Pensions First Appellate Committee on Pensions within the Ministry of Defence. This appeal lies aggrieved, he can prefer a second appeal. This appeal lies to committee called the Defence Minister's Appellate Committee on pensions. This Committee is headed by the Defence Minister himself, and consists of three Chiefs of Staff, the DGMS, representatives of the Ministry of Defence and Ministry of Finance. It also has on it the Judge Advocate-Generals or their representatives. In appropriate cases, the aggrieved personnel should in the first place explore these avenues. The existence of these committees, however, lit not a bar to invoke the jurisdiction of the Courts, as these committees are not the creation of any statute. Bur still, it is advisable that an affected individual should explore these avenues in the first instance.

Exemptions from Income Tax – Pension Gallantry Award Winners

Pensions payable to the grantee of award winners including Vayu Sena Medal (Gallantry) and their dependents are exempt from income tax by the Govt. of India, Ministry of Finance Notification No. S.O. 1048(E) dated 24th November, 2000 published vide Gazette of India Extraordinary Part 11 dated 29th January, 2001.

Gratuities Commuted Pension – Exemption from Income Tax

Gratuity – Under Section 10(10), Income Tax Act, gratuity received by employees is exempt from tax subject to the conditions and to the extent permitted under the Act.

Sub-section (10) provides for tax exemption of gratuities in the following manner. In the case of Government employees, the following payments by way of gratuities are exempt from tax.

Death-cum-retirement gratuities received under: The Revised Pension Rules of the Central Government, or the Central Civil Services (Pension) Rules, 1972, or any similar scheme applicable to the members of civil services of the Union, or gratuity received under the pension Code or Regulations by holders of posts connected with defence or of civil posts under the Pension Code or Regulations by holders of posts connected with defence or of civil posts under the Union, or the members of All India Services or the members of Civil Services of a state or holders of Civil posts under state, or the employees of a local authority.

Pension – Commuted pension received by a Government employee is wholly exempt from tax under Section I O(I OA). Even in the case of a Government servant absorbed in a public undertaking, lump sum received on commutation of pension is wholly exempt from tax – C K Karunkaran v. Union of India (1980) 4 Taxman 178 (Delhi) and S Ranganatha Rao v. Accountant General (1981) 6 Taxman 224 (Kar).

Pensions, a bare 'gratuity' after trial by a Court Martial

List of Same decided on Armed Forces in India

The two petitioners herein had put in a number of years of service. Major G.S. Sodhi has put in about 171/2 years of service and was also awarded some medals for his meritorious service. Likewise, Lt Col. S K Duggal, the other petitioner had rendered about 21 years of service without any blemish. Therefore, their services upto the date of punishment have been satisfactory. On two earlier occasions, this court had granted similar reliefs to the officers who were Court-martialed and removed from service. In Lt Col. T S Harbans Singh Sandhu v. Union of India of (writ petition no. 553/72 decided on 22.11.1978) a bench of three judges of this Court passed an order in favour of the army officer who was cashiered holding that he was entitled to be paid the entire pension and gratuity under the rules. In passing such an order the Court took into consideration the fact that no other penalty forfeiting the pensionary benefits was passed. Therefore, he cannot be deprived of his pensionary benefits by applying any of the regulations. Similarly, order was also pâssed on Religious Teacher Ex N Sub R K Sharma v. Chief of Army Staff & Others (Cr MP 349/80 in WO(CR) No. 244/80 dated April 29th, 1980).

In instant case also the Court Martial had also not inflicted any other punishment of forfeiture of pension. Therefore, they are also entitled to these benefits.

Maj. G S Sodhi v. Union of India
AISL Jv. 1992(2)

Pension Regulations for the Army. Pt. I (1961) – Regulation 22 – Gratuity Entitlement to – whether cut is permissible.

Services of the appellant terminated by the President under the pleasure doctrine. President granting the appellant gratuity. 50% cut imposed on gratuity. No provision to impose cut. Provision envisaging either payment of retiring gratuity or its refusal. Imposition of cost not permissible.

HELD – Appellant entitled to full retiring gratuity.

Ex Capt N D Sharma V. Union of India

1987(I) SLR 443(Del)

Navy (Pension) Regulations, 1964 – Regulation 79 – Qualifying Service for Pension

The respondent R C Jain joined the Indian Naval Organization as a "Boy" on August 2nd, 1959 as Artificer Apprentice and continued as such till August 23rd, 1963, where after on August 24th, 1963, he was promoted as Electrical Artificer (Power) V Class which rank is equivalent to "Leading Seaman". This was the first promotion of the respondent in the Navy.

The issue for determination before the single Judge (B N Kirpal J) was as to whether the training of R C Jain for the period from August 22nd, 1959 to August 23rd, 1963, as Artificer Apprentice was to be counted or not for determining the qualifying service for the pension/gratuity or the same was to be reckoned with effect from August 24th, 1963, on which date he was promoted as Electrical Artificer (Power) V Class on completion of his training.

HELD – The date of August 22nd, 1959 is to be counted for the purpose of calculating the pensionary benefits.

On appeal by the Union of india a DB (Rajinder Sachar and Jagdish Chandra J J) ruled that the subject judge had erroneously held R C Jain to be entitled to pensionary benefits with effect from the initial enrolment even though the relevant rule i.e. Rule 79 of the Navy (Pension) Regulations (1964) entitled him to pensionary and gratuity benefits only on his advancement to the rank of ordinary Seaman".

Union of India v. R C Jain
1984(I) SLR 591 (Del)

Pension Regulation for the Army 1961 (Pt I)

Regulation 173 – Disability Pension, Negligence in providing proper medical service, Boarded out of service. Held attributable to or aggravated by military service.

The petitioner was recruited in the Indian Army in 1954. Whilst on posting to J&K he developed pain in his eyes. He was given treatment in military service, but the pain subsisted and his eye-sight deteriorated as the army authorities neglected to provide glasses, for a period of eight months, as recommended by the eye specialist.

He was subsequently examined by the Board and his medical category was down-graded. The disability was assessed at 40% for the purpose of pension. The petitioner was discharged from service on May 5th, 1960.

Averment in the petition to the effect that the disability was attributable to the army service has remained uncontested, Regulation 173 of the Pension Regulation for the Army, 1961 (Pt. 1) provides that unless otherwise specifically provided, a disability pension may be granted to an individual who is invalidated from the service on account of disability which is attributable or aggravated by military service.

HELD – Petitioner is entitled for disability pension.

Darshan Singh v. Union of India
1986(3) SLR 451 (P&H)

Pensionary Benefits – Right to pension is property – under Article 19 and 31 (I) of the Constitution.

Pensionary benefits – Right to pension flows from the ranks and not the order granting the pension.

Pension Act 1871 S 4 Bar of suits does not bar the High Court in writ jurisdiction.

... Pension is not a bounty payable on the sweet will and pleasure of the Government and that on the other hand the right to pension is a valuable right vesting in the government servant. Right to receive pension is property under Article (1) and by a mere executive order the State has no power to withhold the same. Similarly, the said claim is also property under Article 19(I)(f) same. Similarly, the said claim is also property under Article 19(I)(1) and is not saved by sub-article (5) of Article 19.

... The grant of pension does not depend upon an order being passed by the authorities to that effect. It may be that for the purpose of unifying the amount having regard to the period of service and other allied matters. It may be necessary for the authorities to pass an order to that effect, but the right to receive pension flows to the officer employee, not because of the said order but by virtue of the ranks.

... Though a Civil Court is barred from entertaining suit relating to pension but bar does not stand in the way of a writ of Mandamus being issued to State to property consider the claims of a servant for payment of pension according to law.

Deokinandan Parsad v. State of Bihar & Others
AIR 1971 SC 1409

Civil Services (Commutation of Pension) Rules 1981
Period of 15 years – This benefit must be given also to Armed Forces Personnel.

The age of superannuation used to be 55 until it was raised to 58. It is not necessary to refer to the age of the computing pensioner when the benefits would be restored. It is sufficient to indicate that on expiry of fifteen years from the period of retirement such restoration would take place. The 15 years formula need not be disturbed.

In dealing with a matter of this nature it is not appropriate to be guided by the example of Life Insurance. Equally unjust it would be to adopt the interest basis. No separate period need be fixed for the Armed Forces personnel and they should also be entitled to restoration of the commuted portion of the pension on the expiry of 15 years as is conceded in the case of civil pensioners. And for them also the effective date should be from April 01, 1985.

"Common Cause" & others v. Union of India
AIR 1987 SC 210

Commuted Pension, Pension Act 1871 S. I to words money due or to become due - Recovery from

Words "money due or to become due on account of pension" include commuted portion of the pension payable to a retired employee. Rent due from such employee for occupying government quarters cannot be deducted from the amount of commuted pension.

Union of India v. Sqn. Ldr. R R Hingorani
1987 LAR IC 627 SC
AIR 1987 SC 808

Pension Regulation for the Air Force. Regulation 16(a) – Applicability.

It would apply only if an officer is cashiered or dismissed or removed from service by way of punishment and not for dismissal or removal in exercise of Presidential pleasure – show cause of opportunity is mandatory.

Regulation 16(a) empowers the President to forfeit the pension of an officer who has been dismissed or removed or cashiered. It covers cases where an officer has been dismissed or cashiered as a measure of punishment. After all, an order forfeiting pension is a serious matter and has far-reaching consequences. It is well-settled that pension is not a bounty payable at the sweet will and pleasure of the government and the right to pension is valuable a right vested in a government servant. Not only the right of the petitioner to receive pension is a right to property under Article 31(l) and by a mere executive order the State has no power to withhold the same.

If as a consequence of a contractual or enquiry under the Act and Rules a person is dismissed or cashiered where he has had full opportunity to meet and prove his innocence, but he has failed and therefore an order forfeiting pension is made, in such a case the officer would know the reasons for proceeding against him and could answer to proceedings under the Regulations 16(a) showing that no order of forfeit or total forfeiture of pension should be made. But whereas in the present case the dismissal is in essence of Presidential pleasure under Article 310 of the Constitution read with Section 18 of the Act, it is apparent that no reason will be told or known to the officer. In such a case if Regulation 16(a) could be invoked it will virtually amount to condemning and depriving a person of his pension without giving him an opportunity. Action taken under Regulation 16(a) is not justified.

Hazara Singh v. Chief of Air Staff
Writ Petion no. 1 129 of 1979
1981 (2) SLR-517

Pension Regulations – Qualifying Service – Should be 30 years

In view of the decision of this Court in Common Cause v. Union of India (AIR 1987 SC 2) the 15 years period or the age of 70 years as fixed therein has to apply and the learned counsel for the petitioners does not dispute. The only other question which require determination is whether the appropriate period of service should be 30 years or 33 years. At the relevant period when each of the petitioners superannuated, the retiring age was 55 years. We are of the view that the period of qualifying service as indicated therein should therefore be 30 years.

The petitioners should be entitled to the benefit on the aforesaid basis. A direction is accordingly issued to the Union of India to extend the benefits on such basis.

Raghunandan Lal Choudhury & Others v. Union of India
AIR 1988 SC 1225

Family Pension – Definition of the term "Family" for the Purpose of grant of family pension – marriage after retirement

As per Central Civil Service (Pension) Rules 1972, where the marriage took place after retirement of the government servant, the spouse was not entitled to family pension. Similarly children born after retirement or legally adopted after retirement were also not covered under the definition of family and position was the same for the armed forces persons as well.

Two cases relating to the grant of family pension, one from the widow of a subedar from the army and the other concerning a railway employee were before the Supreme Court. The Court quashed the existing definition of the term "family" as being violative of the Article 14 of the Constitution. The Court observed that retirement pension as well as family pension was linked to the past service rendered by the employee. Hence distinction between marriage during service and marriage after retirement was arbitrary. The children born after retirement were held by the Court to be without the ambit of the definition of "family".

Smt. Sharada Swamy v. Union of India
Smt. Shagwanti v. Union of India
Writ Petition nos. 1298 and 1204 of 1988

Regulation 48 of the Pension Regulation 1961 (Army) Read with Rule 2, 4 and 6.

A person travelling even partly at public expense to his leave station is a person on duty and he will be entitled for disability pension if he is disabled in the course of journey due to accident.

Whilst answering the question if the petitioner was entitled to disability pension in terms of Regulation 48, the Court held:

The provision in Rule 6(c) is intended to lay down when the officer can be deemed or considered to be "on duty". It provides that he will be considered to be 64 on duty" when proceeding to his leave station or returning to duty from his leave station at public expense. As pointed out above in a situation like the one in which petitioner was, the journey to or from the leave station would be partly at public expenses and partly "not on duty". This odd anomalous result can be avoided by interpreting the words "at public expense" in Rule 6(c) in one two ways viz.:

(1) that they mean that entire journey from starting station to the destination and back should be "wholly" public expense, or

(2) may mean that the said journey may even be partly at public expense. In order to avoid an odd result in the application of Rule 6(c) in a situation like this, the question then is as to which of the two interpretation is to be preferred. The answer we consider is to be found in Rule 4 in Appendix 11 to the pension regulations. The said rule provides that in deciding on the issue of entitlement of an officer to disability pension, all the evidence, both direct and circumstantial, will be taken into account and the benefit of reasonable doubt will be given to the claimant.

...In that view we hold that the petitioner was traveling "at public expense" within the meaning of Rule 6(c) and was therefore "on duty" at the time of the accident. He was therefore entitled to disability pension under Regulation 48 of the Pension Regulations.

Harbans Singh v. Union of India
AIR 1971 Del 213

Regulation 74 of the Pension Regulations 1961 – Special Family Pension – who is entitled – widow of the officer/alone can claim cannot be subject matter of testamentary disposition by the husband.

It is unquestionably established that special family pension sanctioned by the President of India to the widow of an officer of the IAF under Rule 74 could not be subject matter of testamentary disposition by the husband of the widow.' It is irrelevant whether the deceased had shown his wife as his dependent or not.

HELD – Special family pension is payable to the widow on the death of the officer. It is not payable in his lifetime. What is not payable during the lifetime of the deceased over which he has no power of disposition cannot form part of his estate. In the event of his death that provides the eligibility qualification for claiming special family pension. Such qualifying even which can only occur on the death of the deceased and which even confers some monetary benefit on someone other than the deceased albeit related to the deceased, cannot form part of the estate of the deceased which he can dispose of by testamentary disposition. The special family pension is admissible on account of the status of the widow and not on account of the fact that there was some estate of the deceased which devolved on his death to the widow. Decision of Punjab High Court affirmed.

Jodh Singh v. Union of India & others
AIR 1980 SC 2081

Pension Regulations for the Air Force 1961. Regulation 93 & 79. Widow alone is entitled to special family pension and family gratuity, not the parents.

Smt. Deepa Shikha Agha v. Smt. Rani Agha & Others.

When admissible.

The petitioner was examined by the release Medical Board which certified that the petitioner suffered from 30% disability aggravated by the military services. The Re-survey Medical Board, opined that the petitioner's disability was to the tune of 20%. Once again, the pension authorities thought that the disability of the petitioner was less than 20% and rejected the claim of the petitioner. It was argued on behalf of the respondents that the power to sanction disability pension rests with the President of India and Controller of Defence Accounts (Pensions) and, therefore the authorities of CDA (Pension), Allahabad had every right to alter the percentage of the disability of the petitioner. The Court while rejecting the stand observed that the interpretation of the authorities was misconceived. The respondents were directed to grant disability pension to the petitioner by treating his disability to bed 20%.

Wg Cdr R L Sharma v. Union of India & Other
in the High Court of P&H
Civil Writ Petition No. 12913/93

Pension Regulations, 1961 – Regulation 37 – Disability Pension – when admissible.

Grant of disability pension to retired Air Force officers reduction in pension without giving the petitioner an opportunity of hearing – Action held as invalid.

Sqn. Ldr. G S Cheema v. Union of India – 1991 (1) SLR 213 (P&H)

Labour and Services – Pension – Government servants have Right to receive pension under statutory rules

Constitution of India – Article 14 – Making of classification and further

Classification must be for a valid purpose – Over-classification may be hit by Article 14.

The Central Government servants on retirement from service are entitled to receive pension under the Central Civil Services (Pension) Rules, 1972. Under the earlier pension scheme the pension was related to the average emoluments during 36 months just preceding retirement. On May 25th, 1979, the Government of India, Ministry of Finance issued Office Memorandum No. F-I9(3)-EV-79 whereby the formula for computation of pension was liberalized but made it applicable to the Government servants who were in service on March 31st, 1979 and retired from service on or after that specified date. By the Memorandum of the Ministry of Defence No.B/40725/AG/PS4-C/1816/AD (Pension)/Services dated September 28th, 1979, the liberalized pension formula introduced for the Government servants governed by the 1972 Rules was extended to the Armed Forces personnel subject to limitations set out in the memorandum with a condition that the new rules of pension would be effective from April 1st, 1979 and may be applicable to the service officers who become/became non-effective on or after that date. The liberalized scheme introduced a slab system for computation of pension, raised pension ceiling, and provided for average emoluments with reference to last I 0 months' service. Consequently, the pensioner who retired prior to the specified date had to earn pension on the average emoluments of 36 months' salary just preceding the date of retirement. Thus they suffered triple jeopardy viz. lower average emoluments, absence of slab system and lower ceiling. Being so aggrieved they filed the present writ petitions in Supreme Court contending that the memoranda were in violation of Article 14. Petitioners I and 2 are retired pensioners of the Central Government who retired prior to the specified date and petitioner 3 is a society registered under the Societies Registration Act, 1860 formed to ventilate the legitimate public problems and consistent with its objective it is espousing the cause of the pensioners all over the country. Allowing the petitioner the Supreme Court.

HELD – (1) Pension is neither a bounty nor a matter of grace depending upon the sweet will of the employer, nor an ex-gratia payment. It is a payment for the past services rendered. It is a social welfare measure rendering socio-economic justice to those who in the hey-day of their life ceaselessly toiled for the employer on an assurance that in their old age they would not be left in lurch. Pension as a retirement benefit is in consonance with the furtherance of the goals of the Constitution. The most practical raisond'etre for pension is the inability to provide for oneself due to old age. It creates a vested right and is governed by the statutory rules such as the Central Civil Services (Pension) Rules which are enacted in exercise of power conferred by Article 309 and 148(5) of the Constitution.

D S Nakara and others v. Union of India
Writ Petition Nos. 5939-5941 of 1980
1981 Supp SCC 87.218

Pension. Dearness relief to re-employed ex-servicemen.

Held – The denial of Dearness Relief on pension, family pension in case of those ex-servicemen, who got re-employed or whose dependents got employed is legal and valid.

"For the disposal of the present case it is not necessary to express any opinion on this aspect of the matter inasmuch as, according to us, even if Dearness relief be an integral part of pension, we do not find any legal inhibition I disallowing the same in cases of those pensioners who get themselves re-employed after retirement. In our view this category of pensioners can rightfully be treated differently from those who do not re-employed; and in the case of re-employed pensioners it would be permissible in law to deny D.R. on pension in as much as the salary to be paid to them on re-employment takes care of erosion in the value of the money because of rise in prices, which lay at the back of grant of D.R., as they get Dearness Allowance on their pay which allowance is not available to those who do not get re-employed. We, therefore, hold that the ex-servicemen were rightly debarred from Dearness Relief on their pension after they got themselves re-employed to any civil post under the Government of India".

Union of India and Others v. G Vasudevan and Others
JT 1995 (1) SC 417

Pension. Army Brigadier's claim for pension. Regulation 16 (a) and Court-martial. Section 71.

HELD – There is no inconsistency between Section 71 (h) and Regulation 16(a). Pensionary benefits are payable only under Regulations and can be withheld or forfeited as provided under Regulations.

"Regulation 16(a) contemplates a situation where an officer is cashiered, dismissed or removed from service and provides how his pension is to be dealt with. Where as Section 71(h) provides the punishment which can be awarded by the Court-martial. Section 71(h) contemplated a punishment awarded at the conclusion of the Court martial. While Regulation 16(a) contemplates a stage subsequent to the awarding of punishment of Court martial and its confirmation. The nature and content of both the impositions is altogether different and distinct. So is the field occupied by clause (k) of Section 71. Wholly distinct from Regulation 16(a). We are, therefore, unable to see any inconsistency between Section 71 (h) and Regulation 16 (a)."

Held – It is true that Pension Regulations are not statutory in character. But as held earlier by this court that pension benefits are provided for and are payable under those regulations".

Union of India v. Brigadier P K Dutta
JT 1995 (1) SC 413

Note: The court has not overruled Maj. G S Sodhi's case. In my view this need a review after some time.

Pension: Dearness Relief over pensions to ex-servicemen re-employed. Dearness Relief becomes integral part of pension.

Since D.R. in such cases becomes an integral part of pension and because of this it cannot be discontinued after re-employment.

Narayanan v. Union of India
Kerala 1994 (1) KLT 897

Pension – Dearness Relief on Pension to re-employed ex-servicemen.

Held – The decision to reduce the enhanced pension pay of those ex-servicemen only who were holding civil posts on 1.1.1986 following their re-employment is unconstitutional.

"We find no logic and basis for classifying the re-employed persons on the basis of their being on employment on 1.1.1986. Indeed, no justification had been canvassed before us. The decision which held the field before the impugned Memorandum is not taking note of pension while fixing pay of the ex-servicemen on re-employment, which was based on good reason for its reversal, as enhanced pension was not confined to those who were in employment on 1,186. The impugned decision is, therefore, arbitrary and is hit by Article 14 and 16 of the Constitution. We, therefore, declare the same as void."

Union of India and Others v
G Vasudevan Pillay and Others
JT 1995(I) SC 417

Pension. Commutation of Pension, DCRG, cash in lieu of accumulated leave. Army JCO Court martialed and dismissed from service. Court-martial not awarding punishment of forfeiture of pension.

Held – Petitioner is entitled to all such benefits.

"The petitioner was Court-martialed and was dismissed from service on 2nd April, 1989. Subsequently, on Ist August, 1989, he was relieved from his unit. The appeal filed by the petitioner was rejected. Petitioner is aggrieved by the refusal to pay him pension, commutation of pension, DCRG, cash in lieu of accumulated leave etc. consequent on the termination of the service by dismissal".

"In CW 2720 of 1992 Hari Dev Gian Chand v. Union of India & Others it was held that even though the Court Martial had imposed the punishment of dismissal it had not deprived the petitioner of his pensionary benefits and of gratuity, therefore, the petitioner will be entitled to the benefits of pension and gratuity and other retirement benefits. The decision was rendered on 20th May, 1993. The decision refers to the decision of the Supreme Court in the case of Major G S Sodhi v Union of India reported in 1992(2)".

"In view of the above, the present petitioner is also entitled to a similar relief. The write petition is, accordingly allowed. Respondents are directed to pay the petitioner all the pensionary benefits due to the petitioner, if already not paid.

Respondents to comply with the order within three months from today. Petitioner be paid a sum of Rs. 3500/- as costs".

CW 917/91 & CM 1483/91
Delhi High Court
Decided on 9th August, 1994.

Pension and Gratuity. An Army JCO convicted by Court-martial, sentenced to dismissal and RI. No sentence of forfeiture of pension passed. Can the pensionary benefits be denied under Pension Regulations - No.

"Learned Counsel appearing for the petitioner submitted that the petitioner is entitled to relief on the ground that no punishment forfeiting his pension and other pensionary benefits was imposed to him. In this regard he has invited my attention to Section 71 (h) of the Army Act, 1950. He has also relief upon the decision of the Supreme Court in Major G S Sodhi v. Union of India 1992 (2) SLJ 91 in support of his submission. Besides, he has placed on record a certified copy of the judgment of a Single Judge of this Court in CW 917/91 dated August 1 1994 whereby the petitioner in that case, who was Subedar and was dismissed by the General Court-martial, was granted relief on the basis of the judgment in Sodhi's case (supra).

"In the counter-affidavit the respondents have relief Regulation No. 113 of the Pension Regulation, according to which a junior commissioned officer who is dismissed from service will not be entitled to pension or gratuity except where the President in its discretion grants pension and gratuity at the rate not exceeding that for which he would have been qualified had he been discharged. The Regulation does not come in the way of the petitioner as the rights are governed by a statute and Section 71(h) provides for forfeiture of pension or other benefits only if such a punishment is imposed on the person and not otherwise. The Regulation must be read in the light of the statutory provision and if so read pensionary benefits can be withheld under it only when punishment of forfeiture of pension etc. is imposed on a dismissed junior commissioned officer".

"In view of the foregoing, the petitioner would be entitled to the grant of pension and commuted pension and other allied benefits. I order accordingly. The writ petition succeeds and is disposed of in terms of the aforesaid observations and directions".

Subedar Ram Rakh v. Union of India
Delhi High Court CW 2651 of 1991
Decided on 1st February, 1995

Constitution of .India, Articles 311 and 300 (A) – Retirement dues delay in payment liability of the government to pay interest at market rates commences from the expiry of two months from the date of retirements. Non-Production of Last Pay Certificate.

Held – It was due to lapse of issuing authorities i.e. Government liable to pay, interest.

Pension and Gratuity are no longer a bounty to be distributed by the Government to the employees on their retirement, but are Fundamental Rights in their hands. Any culpable delay in settlement and disbursement thereof must be dealt with the penalty of payment of interest at the current market rate till actual payment. The liability to pay interest on these dues at the current market rate commences on the expiry of two months from the date of retirement.

State of Kerala and Others v. V M Padhmanabhan Nair
AIR 1985 (SC 356)

Army Act. Section 123 Pension Regulation 1961 – Regulation 16(a) whether a retired officer of the Army could be tried under the Army Act even after retirement.

Held – Yes.

"We do not agree even with the second contention advanced by the learned counsel. The provisions of Regulation 16(a) are clear. Even if it is assumed that the Pension Regulations have no statutory forces, we fail to understand and how the provisions of the State Regulations are contrary to the Statutory Provisions under the Act or the Rules. The pension has been provided under these Regulations. It is not disputed by the learned counsel that the pension was granted to the said appellant under the said Regulations. The Regulations which provide for the grant of pension can also provide for taking it away on justifiable grounds. A show cause notice was issued to the appellant. The reply was considered and thereafter the President passed an order forfeiting the pension and death cum retirement gratuity. We see no infirmity in the order. The appeal is therefore, dismissed. No costs."

Note: The Hon'ble Court has not overruled G S Sodhi's case. It is submitted that in view of the fact that a forfeiture of pension is a specific punishment awardable by a Court-martial, as a Statutory Punishment, an order under the Administrative Regulations may not be justifiable. It is submitted that the case may require reconsideration at some later stage.

Pension Regulation for the Air Force 1961 (Para 11) Para (III). Qualifying service rendered prior to attaining the age of 17 years is treated as not qualifying service.

Held – Regular service of 15 years is to be read as 15 years service which is qualifying service for pension as per Para (III) of the Regulations. Airman legally entitled for pension.

In this case the Airman's qualifying service for pension has fallen short by 180 days and the Competent Authority was eligible to condone only for 180 days. If he wanted to avail of the pension he had to work for six years in reserve. Refusal of work for four days to enjoy his pension not right. The Airman was eligible for pension.

High Court of Judicature Andhra Pradesh at Hyderabad
Writ Petition No. 12517 of 1988

Pension Regulation 1961 para 423(d) disability pension no note of it made at the time of individuals acceptance for service. Clause 'D' of Regulation 423.

Held – Disability will as made at the time of the individual's acceptance for service. Clause 'D' described only the mode by which the aforesaid assumption can be scaled over i.e. if the Medical Board or the Medical Officer had certified with reasons that the disability is not attributable or aggravated by service, then the opinion of the Medical board can be regarded as final.

There is no case that any medical board had considered the matter and expressed the opinion that the disability which led to the discharge was not attributable to the service. We find no reason to interfere with the direction issued by the learned single judge. Appeal is accordingly dismissed.

High Court of Kerala
Writ Appeal No. 594 of 1995 'c'

Memorandum of Ministry of Finance, Department of Expenditure dated 01-08-75 stating pensioner is not eligible to draw any relief during the period of reemployment.

Held – Dearness Relief on pension to servicemen re-employed in any department/office of the Central Government not entitled to.

Further Held – Dearness Relief of pension of re-employed in any government department/office can be legitimately denied. Office Memorandum dated 22-4-87 (sub-para 5 of Annexure 1) states that Dearness Relief will be suspended when the Central Government pensioner is re-employed in the department/office of Central Government.

There are materials of records to show that any person including ex-servicemen would not be entitled to Dearness Relief on hire-employment to any department/office of the Central Government.

Supreme Court of India
Civil Appeal No. 3543-46 of 1990
Decided on 08-12-94

Pension Regulation. Denial of dearness relief on family pension on employment.

Held – It can justly be denied. In some of the cases, we are concerned with the denial of Dearness Relief on family pension on employment of dependents like widows of ex-servicemen.

This decision has to be sustained as the official document referred on that point also mentioned about the denial of Dearness Relief of family pension on employment. The refusal of this decision in granting of dearness allowance by the dependents on their pay which is drawn following employment, because of which Dearness Relief on family pension can justly be denied as has been done.

Supreme Court of India
Civil Appeal No. 3543-46 of 1990
Decided on 08-12-94

Pension Regulations. Reduction of enhanced pension from pay of those ex-servicemen who were holding civil posts on 01-01-86 following their reemployment.

Held – is unconstitutional.

According to office memorandum dated 11-9-87 the pay of ex-servicemen who were in employment in civil posts as on 01-01-86 following their re-employment is required to be reduced by an amount equivalent to the enhanced pension made available pursuance to the report of the Fourth Pay Commission. We find no logic and basis for classifying the re-employed persons on the basis of their being on employment on 01-01-86. The impugned decision is, therefore, arbitrary and hit by Article 14 and 16 of the Constitution. We, therefore, declare the same as void.

Supreme Court of India
Civil Appeal No. 3543-46 of 1990
Decided on 08-12-94

A. Service Law – **Pension Regulations for the Army, 1961** – Regn. 16(a) – Provision in, for forfeiture of pension – Validity and scope Held, neither inconsistent with, nor contrary to, S. 71 of Army Act Regn. 16(a) and S. 71 cover different fields and have different objects – Army Act, 1950, Ss. 71(h) & (k) – pension Forfeiture of

B. Service Law – **Navy (Pension) Regulations, 1964** – Regn. 15(2) Provision in, for forfeiture of pension – Validity and Scope – Held, neither inconsistent with, nor contrary to, S. 81 of the Navy Act, Regn. 15(2) and S. 81 cover different fields and different objects – Navy Act, 1957, S. 81 (m) – Pension Forfeiture of

C. Service Law – **Pension Right to Conditions Precedent** – pension, although not a bounty, held, is earned on satisfactory completion of qualifying service subject to the further condition that the person concerned is not otherwise disentitled thereto

D. Service Law – **Pension Regulations for the Army, 1961** – Regn. 16(a) – Forfeiture of pension under, of a person dismissed or cashiered consequent to trial by General Court-martial – Permissibility Notwithstanding that the General Court-martial while imposing other punishments, had not ordered under S. 71(h) or (k) of the Army Act forfeiture of service of such a person for the purposes of pension, forfeiture of his pension under Regn.16(a), held, is nonetheless permissible and does not amount to double jeopardy Army Act, 1950, Ss. 71(h) & (k) and 73, Pension Forfeiture of – Double jeopardy - Doctrine of - When not applicable - Maxim - "Nemo debet bis vexari, si constat curiae quod sit prouna et eadem causa" Constitution of India, Act 20(2) (Para 25)

E. Service Law – **Navy (Pension) Regulations, 1964** – Regn. 15(2) Forfeiture of pension under, of a person dismissed consequent to trial by General Court-martial Permissibility – Notwithstanding that the General Court-martial, while imposing other punishments, ordered under S. 81 (m) of the Navy Act, had not ordered forfeiture of service of such a person for the purposes of pension, forfeiture of his pension under Regn. 15(2), held, is nonetheless permissible and does not amount to double jeopardy – Navy Act, 1957, S. 81 (m) – Pension Forfeiture of

F. Service Law – **Pension Regulations for the Army, 1961** – Regn. 16(a), 3, 4 and 2 A(4) – Power of forfeiture of pension under Regn. 16(a) - factor relevant for the exercise of such power, held, is whether the very terms of that Regulation are satisfied or not – Hence, in the case of a person cashiered or dismissed or removed from service, such power can be exercised for that very reason. There is not further requirement of considering whether his prior service was satisfactory. Further held, this principle applies also to gratuity – Distinction between the situations governed by Regn. 16(a) and 3 pointed out Army Act, 1950, S. 71.

G. Service Law – **Navy (Pension) Regulations, 1964** – Regn.15(2) Power of forfeiture of pension under – Conditions for exercise of – In the case of persons cashiered otherwise than with disgrace, held, Central

Union of India and another
v. P D Yadav & others
1 Supreme Court Cases 405 (2002)

Some of the other important cases on Pension for armed forces personnel as decided by the Supreme Court which may greatly help the persons to solve their case of pension are given below:

1. Union of India v. Harjeet Singh Sandhu (2001) 5 SCC 593 ARMED FORCES – Army Act, 1950 S.19 and 122. Army Rules, 1954 – R.14 – Power under S. 19 r/wR. 14(2) when can be exer....
2. Commander Head Quarter v. Capt Biplabendra Vhanda (1997) 1 SSC 208 SL – Pension-Entitlement – New/Revised rules reducing the requisite qualifying service coming into effect prospective
3. Common Cause v. Union of India (1987) 1 SCC 142 SL – Pension-Commutation of Releif....
4. D K Jain v. State of Haryana, 1995 Supp (1) SCC 349 SL – Seniority – Determination of Seniority – Length of Service – Military service during proclamation of emergency on....
5. D S Nakara v. Union of India (1983) 1 SCC 305

   SL – Pension - "Pension" – Meaning – Reasons for grant of....

6. Ex-Capt. Ashwani Kumar Katoch v. Union of India, 1995 Supp (4) SCC 715 SL – Departamental Enquiry – Penalty/Punishment – Punishment Removal from service with terminal benefits determined as the qua...

7. Ex-Subedar Joginder Singh v. Union of India, (2001) 9 SSC 602

   SL – Pension Eligibility – Army person dismissed under S. 52(a) of the Army Act for committing theft of government property....

8. Indian Ex-Services League v. Union of India, (1991) 2 SCC 104 SL – Pension – Armed Forces – Liberalized pension scheme – 'One rank. One pension' for all retirees of Armed Forces irrespective

9. Jodh Singh v. Union of India (1980) 4 SCC 306 WILL – Special Family Pension granted under Reg. 74 of Pension Regulations for Indian Air Force to widow of deceased officer...

10. K C Arora v. State of Haryana, (1984) 3 SCC 281.

11. Lt. Col. (T S) Harbans Singh Sandhu v. Union of India (2002) 1 SCC 427 SL – Pension Regulations for the Army, 1961 – Regn. 16(a) – In the absence of any order under, held, the pension or gratuity...

12. Madan Singh Shekhawat v. Union of India, (1999) 6 SCC 459 IOC – Basic R – Beneficent construction, Held – it is the duty of the court to interpret a provision, especially a beneficiary...

13. Major G S Sodhi v. Union of India, 1994 Supp (2) SCC 173 SL – Pension-Entitlement to – Army Service Contempt...

14. Major-Gen (Old Capt) Virender Kumar v. Chief of Army Staff, 1994 Supp (2) SCC 303 SL – Relief-

Interest – Group Insurance Scheme – Provident Fund – Children's Education Fund – Gratuity – Pension...

15. Raghu Nandan Lal Chaudhary v. Union of India, (1988) 2 SSC 406 SL – Pension – Pension of defence personnel – Pension equivalent of gratuity recoverable from January 1st, 1986...
16. Sansar Chand Atri v. State of Punjab (2002) 4 SCC 154 SL – Appointment – Reservation/Concession/Exemption/Relaxation – Reservation – Ex-servicemen-Exemption "ex-servicemen"
17. State of Bihar v. Bal Mukund Sah (2000) 4 SCC 640 COI – Art. 233, 234, 235, 236(b) and 309 and 245 and Sch. VII List II Entry 11-A – Judicial service – Recruitment of District.....
18. Union of India v. Baljit Singh (1966) 11 SCC 315 SL – Pension – Disability pension – Entitlement to Army
19. Union of India v. Brig. P K Dutta (Retd), 1995 Supp (2) SCC 29 SL – Pension – Withholding or forfeiture of, under non-statutory regulations – Legality
20. Union of India v. Lt. Col. P S Bhargava (1997) 2 SCC 28 SL – Terminal benefits – Entitlement to, on resigning....
21. Union of India v. P D Yadav (2002) 1 SCC 405 SL – Navy Pension Regulations, 1964 – Regn. 15(2) – Forfeiture of pension under, of a person dismissed consequent of trial by....
22. Union of India v. R K L D Azad, 1995 Supp (3) SCC 426 SL – Pension – Person dismissed from service under the provisions of Army Act, 1950....

12

Privileges in Matters of Civil Employment and Re-Employment

The members of the armed forces, due to nature of their duties, exigencies of service and the national imperative retire, at much early age than their civil counterparts. At the same time, they are highly qualified and a vast reserve of trained manpower, both technical and non-technical and all not only well trained but also highly disciplined.

To allow such a vast trained manpower to remain idle would be a great national catastrophe. So, also many service men become disabled due to war or other exigencies of service. Also to give recognition to their services in the nation building, it is equally necessary to provide for some reservations for their employment after the retiremet from the service. Keeping the national interest and requirements the central government has vide "The Ex-servicemen (re-employment in Central Civil Services and posts) rules, 1979 provided for reservations vacancies and posts in their favour. Extract from these rules and their subsequent amendments are reproduced as Appendix to this chapter.

The state government also have similarly introduced such reservations of vacancies in various departments under their control to suit not only the national requirement but also the requirement of the concerned states. Since, there are nearly 28 states, in the Union to reproduce them, would only add to the bulk of the book. A reference has however been made to them whilst dealing with the concessions by the various state governments. The persons concerned may contact their respective Rajya, soldiers, sailors and Airman boards of their respective states.

Some of the provisions regarding concessions to Ex-serviceman with respect to their employment in these states services as current update are given below:-

Andhra Pradesh

1. 2 per cent reservation in Group II-B and IV posts. Govt. of Andhra Pradesh has equated Defence Service Trades with Civil Trades vide G.O. Ms. No. 16, dt. 12th Apr 99 of Labour Employment and Training and Factories (Emp) Department.

Arunachal Pradesh

1. 5 per cent, 10 per cent and 20 per cent reservation in Group "B", "C" and "D" posts respectively.

Assam

1. 2 per cent reservation of vacancies for ex-servicemen in Group "C and D" posts in the State Govt Deptts.

Bihar

1. Priority in Govt Jobs in Group III & IV posts.
2. Compassionate employment in Group C and D posts.

Delhi

1. Priority (1) Employment for disabled ex-servicemen vide Govt of NCT of Delhi letter no.: F.16/146/98/S-III/457 dt. 24/2/99.

2. Reservation of 10 per cent and 20 per cent in Group C and Group D posts respective in Delhi Police vide letter no.: 3431/D.II(PHQ) dtd. 13/3/97.
3. Reservation of 10 per cent and 20 per cent in Group C and Group D Posts in Govt. jobs and 14.5 per cent and 24.5 per cent in PSUs.
4. Priority-II An Employment for widows/dependents of service personnel killed in war/peace (death attributable to military service) vide Govt. of NCT of Delhi letter no. F.16/146/98/S-III/457 DT. 24/2/99.

Goa

1. Reservation of 2 per cent posts in Group C & Group D.

Gujarat

1. 10 and 20 per cent reservation in Group C and Group D posts respectively in SPSUs, Panchayat and Gujarat Civil Services.
2. 25 per cent reservation vacancies in Veterinary service. (Animal Husbandry services) Class I & II which are filled by direct selection.

Haryana

1. Reservation of 5 per cent posts in Group I & II and 15 per cent in Group III and IV posts for ex-servicemen. Reserved vacancies are being carried forward for two years. Age relaxation for ex-servicemen to the extent of his Military service + 3 years. Ex-Servicemen/their dependents candidates sponsored against reserved vacancies by RSBs/ZSBs are allowed free travel in Haryana Roadways buses for attending the interview.

Himachal Pradesh

1. 15 per cent reservation in each of the Groups A, B, C and D posts.

2. Preference to ex-servicemen for the post of Jail Warden/Guard posts.

Jammu & Kashmir

1. Relaxation of educational qualification to the ex-servicemen for appointment in Group C and D posts Matric Pass for Post C and Middle pass for Post D.

Karnataka

1. 10 per cent reservation in each of the Groups A, B, C and D Posts.
2. Relaxation of age limit for ex-servicemen for civil employment to the extent of number of years of military service plus three years.

Kerala

1. Vacancies in Sainik Welfare Deptt and NCC are exclusively for ex-servicemen.
2. Reservation of Seats
3. Details may be obtained from Kendriya Sainik Board.

Maharastra

1. 15 per cent Horizontal Reservation in Group C and D posts.

Manipur

1. Reservation in Group B Posts – 2 per cent, Group C – 3 per cent and Group D – 5 per cent.

Mizoram

1. Priority I for employment of disabled ex-servicemen and priority III for ex-serviceman.
2. Reservation in Group C posts – 10 Per cent and Group D posts – 20 per cent.
3. Induction of ex-serviceman at suitable levels in State Police Force.

Nagaland

1. 5 per cent reservation in Group C and Group D Posts.

Punjab

1. Reservation of 13 per cent SEATS IN EACH OF THE GROUP A, B, C and D posts. Vacancies are carried forward for two years. State has also amended recruitment rules in respect of age and educational qualification of ex-serviceman.

Rajasthan

1. Reservation of seats in Group C posts – 12.5 per cent and Group D posts – 15 per cent reserved vacancies are carried forward for one year. Recruitment rules have been amended in respect of age and educational qualification of ex-servicemen. 100 point roster followed.

Sikkim

1. 3 Per cent reservation in both Group C and D posts. Recruitment rules amended in respect of age and educational qualification of ex-servicemen. (State Govt. notification No. 87/Gen/DOP dated 23 Mar 98).

Tamilnadu

1. Reservation in Group D posts – 10 per cent, Forest Guards – 10 per cent, Forest watcher – 5 per cent and 25 per cent in NCC Department (for the Post of Lascars, Drivers, Watchman) Basic Service 10 per cent, Live Stock Inspector course – 5 per cent.
2. Age relaxation for appointment to State Government Service upto 53 years for OBC/SC & 48 years for others.

Tripura

1. 2 Per cent reservation in each of the Group A, B, C and D posts. Recruitment rules amended in respect of

age and educational qualification of ex-servicemen. Provision to carry forward unfilled vacancies for one year exits.

West Bengal

1. 5 and 10 per cent reservation in Group C and D posts.

Andaman & Nicobar Islands

1. Reservation in Group C posts – 10 per cent and Group D posts – 20 per cent.

Chandigarh

1. 10 per cent reservation in Group C Posts and 20 percent in Group D posts.

Pondicherry

1. Reservation in Group C and D posts at the rate of 10 per cent and 20 per cent respectively.

Gist of case law

Gist of some of the decided cases by the Supreme Court and the High Courts on the above subject is given below:-

Service Law – Appointment Reservation

Vacancies reserved for ex-serviceman, application of merit criteria, Ex-servicemen disabled to an extent within eligibility limits (between 20 per cent and 50 per cent) although sponsored by Rajya Sainik Board and appointed on ad hoc basis, held, not entitled to automatic regular absorption in preference to dependants of those killed non-selection of such an ex-serviceman for his failure to secure minimum marks prescribed for viva voce by the selection Board, held, justified – Government of Haryana Instructions dated 06.03.1972 (criterian e) and 21.05.1979 Satyapal Sing v. Haryana State Subordinate Service Selection Board, 1994 Supp (2) SCC 578: 1994 SCC (L&S) 1155: (1994) 28 ATC 74:

(1994) 2 SLR 670. Bench Strength 2. Coram: K Ramaswamy and N Venkatachala, JJ. (Date of decision: 07.04.1994) Service Law, Promotion Eligibility Seniority.

Benefit of seniority under R. 5 of Demobilized Armed Forces Personnel (Reservation of Vacancies in the Punjab State) (Non-Technical Services) Rules – Acquisition of necessary qualification to apply for the post when the first opportunity to occupy the same became available to the demobilized army personnel during military service, held, not a condition precedent for the availability of such benefit, requirements of the said provision clarified, Demobilized Armed Forces personnel (Reservation of Vacancies in the Punjab State) (Non-Technical Services) Rules, 1968, s. 4 (a) & (b), 5 and 3 Reservation/concession-Ex-servicemen-promotion-Eligibility-Qualification requirement if bar to avail seniority benefit.

Rule 4(a) and (b) and Rule 5, read together, suggest that it is not necessary that the individual concerned should have been qualified to apply for the post when the first opportunity to occupy the said post became available to him while he was in military service. Charan Singh v. State of Punjab (1998), 9 SCC 283: 1998 SCC (L&S) 1181.

Bench Strength 3. Coram: P B Sawant, S C Sen and K Venkataswami, JJ. (Date of decision: 10.05.1995)

Service Law-Seniority particular instances/rules

Released Emergency Commissioned officers and short service commissioned officers (Reservation of Vacancies) Rules, 1971 – Benefit of seniority available under, on entering reserved vacancies in Central Civil Services, non-availability of such benefit on joining non-reserved posts, held, not hit by Art.14. More so where the recruitment to reserved posts was through a different method-further held, quantum and shape of such benefit are matters to be decided exclusively by the executive, such policy matters can be interfered with by the courts only on the ground of illegality, irrationality or procedural impropriety, policy in question did not suffer from any such infirmity.

It is not correct to say that the impugned rules classify the officers into two categories: holders of reserved posts and non-reserved posts. Infact a policy decision was taken to give some benefits to those servicemen who had stood with the people when the country was invaded and had rendered useful service during the emergency in question. How much benefit and in what shape it ought to have been given are not matters on which courts can have any say, these are exclusively for the executive to decide. The courts come into picture in such policy matters if the same be either illegal or irrational or were to suffer from procedural impropriety (Para 3).

There is no such infirmity in the policy at hand this is not all. As the recruitment for the reserved post is through separate method, there is no possibility of some of the released officers obtaining reserved posts with the benefit available under the Rules, and others obtaining non-reserved posts with no benefit visualized by the rules. So the two types of incumbents have to be taken as belonging to two different categories; the one having no clash of interest with the other, the other being denied no benefit available (Para 4). All India E-Emergency commissioned Officers and Short commissioned officers welfare Assn. v. Union of India, 1995 Supp (1) SCC 78: 1995 WCC (L&S) 258.

Bench Strength 2. Coram: Kuldip Singh and B L Hansaria, JJ. (Date of decision: 20.09.1994) Tata Cellular v. Union of India (1994) 6 SCC 651, followed.

Service Law - Judiciary Ex-servicemen (Reservation of vacancies in the Himachal Pradesh – Judicial service)

Preamble and Rr. 5 (1) and 3 – Constitutionality of the 1981 Rules – Held, ultra vires the constitution and void. Hence high courts orders granting the benefit of the period of approved service to the appellant in H.P. Judicial Service, held, had-the appellant having been promoted as Senior Sub-Judge-cum-Chief Judicial Magistrate consequent to the said orders about eight long years ago, the appellant restrained from being reverted on that ground alone. Constituion of India, Art. 234 and 309-Rules for appointment to State Judicial Service framed without consulting the High Court-validity..... judiciary, demobilized Indian armed forces (Reservation of Vacancies in H.P. Judicial service) Rules, 1975, Rr. 4 (1) and 2. Brief history of the 1975 rules, considered seniority miscellaneous, rules enabling assignment found to be unconstitutional promotion based on such seniority - in the peculiar circumstance of the case, protected.

The appellant was released from the Air Force on 01.12.1980 after remaining in service for about 15 years. Having obtained necessary qualifications, he applied for one of the 2 posts reserved for ex-servicemen in the H.P. Judicial Service in the year 1983. He was selected and was, on 01.02.1984 appointed as Sub-Judge-Cum-Judicial Magistrate. On his representation in terms of the Ex-servicemen (Reservation of vacancies in the Himachal Pradesh Judicial Service) Rules, 1981 (hereinafter "the Reservation Rules, 1981") for the period spent in approved military service, which was 11 years in the case of the appellant being counted towards the Himachal Pradesh Judicial Service for the purpose of fixing pay and seniority, by an order dated 31.08.89. The High Court fixed the pay of the appellant by giving him credit of 11 years approved military service. Later by its order dated 01.11.1991, the High Court gave him the benefit of the period spent in approved military service being counted for the purpose of seniority in the Himachal Pradesh Judicial Service. He was placed at the bottom of the 1974 batch of judical officers. Thus his seniority was stepped up from Sl. No. 43 to Sl. No. 13. One G, who was then a Senior Sub-Judge-cum-Chief Judicial Magistrate filed a writ petition challenging the constitutional validity of the Rules granting benefit of seniority to the judicial officers recruited in the quota of ex-servicemen as also the legal validity of the order dated 01.11.1991. Other judicial officers who were above the appellant and became below him as a consequence of the order dated 01.11.1991 passed by the High Court were not joined as parties to the petition. A division bench of the High Court dismissed the writ petition. On 26.11.1992 G's SLP was dismissed by a non-speaking order. The appellant"s seniority having been stepped up, he was appointed as Senior Sub-Judge-Cum-Chief Judicial Magistrate on 15.12.1992. On a further representation made by the appellant his seniority was further stepped up by the High Court's order dated 06.08.1993. In August 1993, two writ petitions were filed by two sets of judicial officers challenging both the orders of the High Court dated 01.11.1992 and 06.08.1993. The constitutional validity of the Reservation Rules, 1981 was also challenged on the ground that the Rules had been framed by the State Government without consulting the High Court of Himachal Pradesh as required by Article 234 of the Constitution. A division bench of the High Court allowed the writ petitions and struck down the two impugned orders of the High Courts and the consequent action of stepping up of the seniority of the appellant. The Division Bench, however, left the benefit of apply fixation allowed to the appellant and his appointment in the reserved quota of ex-army personnel undisturbed. Before the Supreme Court the appellant contended that the constitutional validity of the Reservation Rules, 1981 as well as the validity of the order dated 01.11.1991 having been upheld by the H.P. High Court in G's petition and that order having achieved finality, the benefit available to the appellant thereunder could not be denied to him. Dismissing the appeals, held.

G's petition was not filed in a representative capacity. The petitioners in the two writ petitions, the judgment passed wherein is under challenge herein, were not joined as parties in the petition filed by G and, therefore, the judgement in G's case cannot, on any principle of law, bind the private respondents herein (who were the writ petitioners in the two writ petitions filed before the High Court). The two writ petitions were filed in the year 1993 laying challenge to the seniority list of 1990 as modified in the year 1991. The writ petitions were neither belated nor barred by the doctrine of laches. The decision in George case was based on a fallacy going to the root of the matter. A perusal of the judgement in George case shows the Division Bench having proceeded on an erroneous assumption that the constitutional validity of the Reservation rules, 1981 was upheld by the Full Bench of the High Court of Himachal Pradesh in Mohinder Kumar Sood Case. The divison bench of the High Court was therefore, not excluded from now going into the merits of the challenge laid to the constitutional validity of the Reservation Rules, 1981 and testing the same on the touchstone of Article 234 of the Constitution (Para 17).

Recruitment to judicial services in the State of Himachal Pradesh is governed by the H.P. Judicial Service Rules, 1973 framed by the Governor in consultation with the High Court and in exercise of the powers conferred by Article 234 read with Article 309 of the Constitution of India. These rules do not make any provision for reservation in favour of SC, ST, OBC or even ex-army personnel. Since, the period spent by the appellant in approved military service could be counted towards seniority in judicial service only by reference to the Reservation rules of 1981, it becomes necessary to examine the validity of these Rules (Para 8).

The life of the 1975 Rules expired on April 1980. The State Government proposed to extend the life of these Rules and for the purpose sougth the approval of the High Court. In a full court meeting on 06.03.1981, the High Court resovled that it is not in the interest of the Judiciary to agree to any further reservation. The opinion of the High Court was communicated to the State Government. What happened thereafter is something strange. On 01.08.1981 the Government of Himachal Pradesh notified in the Government Gazette a fresh set of rules, entitled the Ex-servicemen (Reservation of Vacancies in the H.P. Judicial Service) Rules, 1981. The publication of the Reservation rules, 1981 was brougth to the notice of the High Court on 28.08.1981 the full court passed a resolution expressing grave concern on enforcement of the proposed amendment which had been disapproved of by the High Court by its resolution dated 06.03.1981. The Government, though informed accordingly, gave no response (Paras 10 to 13 and 16).

The Division Bench of the High Court has, in the impungned judgement, recorded a finding on the basis of material and records that these Reservation Rules, 1981 were never referred by the Governor to the High Court and never had any occasion to consider the Rules (Para 14).

The provision in Article 234 of the Constitution for appointment to the judicial service of the State (excluding District Judges) after consultation with the State Public Service Commission and the High Court of the state is mandatory. Such consultation is not a matter of mere formality; it has to be meaningful and effective. The constitutional scheme aims at securing an independent judiciary which is the bulwark of democracy. The status which the High Court as an institution enjoys in the constitutional scheme and the expertise and the experience which it possesses of judicial services command with justification a place of primacy being assigned to the High Court in the process of consultation (Para 15).

The Reservation Rules, 1981 having been framed by the Governor without consultation with the High Court of Himachal Pradesh are ultra vires the Constitution and hence ineffective and unenforceable in view of Article 234 of the Constitution. The Division Bench of the High Court rightly held that those Rules were void an a nullity. The orders dated

01.11.1991 and 06.08.1993 passed by the High Court of Himachal Pradesh giving benefit of eleven years of approved military service to the appellant have also been righty struck down by the High Court (Para 16 and 18).

However, with a view to balance equities and avoid any hardship to the appellant, it is directed that in spite of these appeals being dismissed and the judgement under appeal being implemented, the appellant shall continue to hold the post presently held by him. He shall be considered by the High Court for appointment by promotion on the post of Senior Sub-Judge-cum-Chief Judicial Magistrate or equivalent post at a point of time when he would become eligible for such consideration pursuant to the judgement under appeal of the High Court. If he is found fit for such promotion, he shall be so promoted and for future his seniority in the cadre of Senior Sub-Judge-cum-Chief Judicial Magistrate shall be reckoned from the date of such promotion. If he may be found not fit for promotion then he may be reverted to the post of sub-judge-cum-judicial magistrate. In any case, till such consideration, he shall continue to hold the post presently held by him as a special case (Para 19). A C Thalwal v. High Court of H.P. (2000) 7 SCC 1: 2000 SCC (L&S) 812: Air 2000 SC 2732: (2000) 5 SLR 129. Bench Strength 3, Coram: Dr. A S Anand, C.J., R C Lahoti and K G Balakrishnan, J.J. (Date of decision: 17.08.2000).

Mohinder Kumar Sood v. H.P. Public Service Commission, AIR 1982 HP 78(FB), explained and distinguished Supreme Court Advocate-on-Record Assn. v. Union of India (1993) 4 SCC 44), Chandramouleshar Prasad v. Patna High Court (1969) 3 SCC 56, Hari Datt Kainthla v. State of H.P. (1980) 3 SCC 189: 1980 SCC (L&S) 335, followed (1995) 2 Simla LC 205, affirmed.

Appendix A
The ex-servicemen (Re-employment in Central Civil Services and post) Rules, 1979.

No. 39016/10/79-Estt-(c)
Government of India,
Ministry of Home Affairs,
Department of Personnel
& Administrative Reforms,
New Delhi-110001
The 15th December, 1979.

In exercise of the powers conferred by the proviso to article 309 of the Constitution, the President hereby makes the following rules for regulating the recruitment of ex-servicemen in the Central Civil Services and Posts, namely:-

1. Short title and commencement:
   (a) These rules may be called the Ex-servicemen (re-employment in the Central Civil Services and Posts) Rules, 1979.
   (b) They shall be deemed to have come into force on the first day of July, 1979.

2. Definitions:

   In these rules, unless the context otherwise requires –
   (a) "Armed Forces of the Union" means the Army, Navy and Air Force of the Union.
   (b) "Disabled ex-servicemen" means the ex servicemen who while serving in the Armed forces of the Union was disabled in operations against the enemy or in disturbed areas.
   (c) "Ex-servicemen" means a person who has served in any rank (whether as a combatant or non-combatant) in the Armed Forces of the Union,

including the armed forces of the former Indian States, but excluding the Assam Rifles, Defence Security Corps, General Reserve Engineering Force, Lok Sahayak Sena and Territorial Army, for a continuous period of not less than six months after attestation, and

(a) has been released, otherwise then at his own request or by way of dismissal or discharge on account of misconduct, inefficiency, or has been transferred to the reserve pending such release or

(b) has to serve for not more than six months for completing the period of service requisite for becoming entitled to be released or transferred to the reserve as aforesaid.

(d) "Para-military forces" means the Border Security Force, Central Reserve Police Force, Indo-Tibetan Border Police, Central Industrial Security Force, Assam Rifles and Railway Protection Force.

(e) "Reserved vacancies" means vacancies reserved under rule 4 for being filled by ex-servicemen.

3. Applications:

These rules shall apply to all the Central Civil Services and posts, Group "C" and Group "D" and to the posts of the level of Assistant Commandant in all Para-military forces.

4. Reservations of vacancies:

(a) Ten per cent of the vacancies in the posts of the Assistant Commandant in all para-military forces: ten per cent of the vacancies in each of the categories of Group "C" posts and of such posts in each "C" service, and twenty per cent of the vacancies in each of the cagtegories of Group "D" posts and of such posts in each Group "D" service, including permanent vacancies filled initially on a temporary basis and temporary vacancies which are likely to be made permanent or are likely to continue for three months and more, to be filled by direct recruitment in any year shall be reserved for being filled by ex-servicemen.

Provided the percentage of reservation so specified for ex-servicemen in category of posts shall be increased or decreased in any one recruitment year to the extent to which the total number of vacancies reserved for ex-servicemen, Scheduled Castes and Schedules Tribes (including the carried forward reservations for Scheduled Castes and Schedules Tribes) and for any other categories taken together falls short or is in excess, as the case may be, of fifty per cent of the vacancies in that category of posts filled in that year.

Provided further that in case of an increase in the reservation for the ex-servicemen under the preceding proviso, the additional vacancies so made available for them shall be utilized first for the appointment of disabled ex-servicemen and if any such vacancies still remain unfilled thereafter the same shall then be made available to other ex-servicemen.

(b) Out of the vacancies reserved for being filled by ex-servicemen, vacancies shall be reserved for candidates belonging to the Scheduled Castes and Scheduled Tribes in accordance with such orders as are issued in this behalf by the Central Government from time to time.

Provided that if any ex-servicemen belonging to the Scheduled Castes or Schedules Tribes is selected, his selection shall be counted against the overall quota of reservation that shall be provided for the Scheduled Castes or Scheduled Tribes in accordance with the orders issued by the Central Government time to time.

(c) No vacancy reserved for ex-servicemen in a post to be filled otherwise, than on the result of an open competitive examination, shall be filled by the appointing authority by any general candidate, until and unless the said authority.

(i) has obtained a "non-availability certificate" from the employment exchange (where a requisition is placed on an employment exchange)

(ii) has verified that non-availability of a suitable candidate by reference to the Director General Resettlement and recorded a certificate to that effect and

(iii) has obtained approval of the Central Government.

5. Special provision regarding age limit:

For appointment to any vacancy in Central Civil Service Group "C" and Group "D", whether reserved or not under these rules, every ex-servicemen who has put in not less than six months continuous service in the Armed Forces of the Union shall be allowed to deduct the period of such service from his actual age and if the resultant age does not exceed the maximum age limit prescribed for the post or service for which he seeks appointment by more than three years, he shall be deemed to satisfy the condition regarding age limit.

6. Special provision regarding educational qualifications:

(a) For appointment to any reserved vacancy in group "D" posts, every ex-servicemen who has put in not less than three years service in the Armed forces of the Union shall be exempted from the minimum educational qualification, if any prescribed in respect of such posts.

(b) For appointment to any reserved vacancy in Group "C" posts, the appointing authority may, at its discretion, relax the minimum educational qualification, where such qualification prescribed is a pass in the Middle school examination or any lower examination, in favour of ex-servicemen who have put in at least three years service in the Armed Forces of the Union and who are otherwise considered fit and suitable for appointment to such posts, in view of their experience and qualification.

(c) For appointment to any reserve vacancy in Group "C" posts, to be filled partly by direct recruitment and partly by promotion or transfer, where the minimum educational or technical qualification prescribed for appointment by direct recruitment is higher than the prescribed for promotees or transferees, and ex-servicemen shall be deemed to satisfy the prescribed educational or technical qualification if he:

   (i) satisfy the educational or technical qualification prescribed for direct recruitment to the post from which promotion or transfer to the post in question is allowed and

   (ii) has identical experience of work in a similar discipline and for the same number of years in the Armed Forces of the Union, as prescribed for promotees or transferees.

Explanation: For the purpose of this rule, in computing the period of three years service, there shall be added any period of service which an ex-servicemen has rendered while serving in a corresponding post or posts in a civil department, or a public sector undertaking or an autonomous organization, whether under the Central Government or any State Government, or in a Nationalised Bank to the period of service rendered in the Armed Forces of the Union.

7. Amendment of recruitment rules:

All rules regulating the recruitment of persons of Group "C" and Group "D" posts and services under the Central Government shall be subjected to the provision of these rules and shall be construed accordingly.

8. Interpretation:

If any question arises as to the interpretation of these rules, the question shall be decided by the Central Government and the decision of the Central Government shall be final.

Sd/_ (R.C. Gupta) Deputy Secretary, to the Government of India.

Amendment (Rules) 1986

No. 36034/5-85Estt (SCT)
Government of India
Ministry of Personnel, P.G.&Pensions
(Department of Personnel&Training)
New Delhi, the 27th October, 1986

Notification

GSR, in exercise of the powers conferred by the proviso to article 309 of the Constitution, the President hereby makes the following rules further to amend the Ex-servicmen (Re-employment in Central Civil Services and posts) Rules, 1979 namely:-

1. (a) These rules may be called the Ex-servicemen (Re-employment in Central Civil Services and Posts) Amendment Rules, 1986.

   (b) They shall come into force on the date of their publication in the official Gazette.

2. In rule 2 of the ex-servicemen (re-employment in Central Civil Services and Posts) Rules, 1979 for clause (c) the following clause shall be substituted, namely:

   (a) 'ex-servicemen' means a person, who has served in any rank (whether as a combatant or as a non-combatant) in the Regular Army, Navy and Air Force of the Indian Union but does not include a person who has served in the Defence Security Corps, the General Reserve Engineering Force, the Lok Sahayak Sena and the Para Military Forces; and

(i) who has retired from such service after earning his/her pension; or

(ii) who has been released from such service on medical grounds attributable to military service or circumstances beyond his control and awarded medical or other disability pension; or

(iii) who has been released, otherwise than on his own request, from such service as a result of reduction in establishment of; or

(iv) who has been released from such service after completing the specific period of engagement otherwise then at his own request or by way of dismissal or discharge on account of misconduct or inefficiency, and has been given a gratuity; and includes personnel of the Territorial Army of the following categories, namely:

(a) pension holders for continuous embodies service

(b) persons with disability attributable to military service and

(c) gallantry award winners

Explanation: The persons serving in the Armed Forces of the Union, who on retirement from service, would come under the Category of ex-servicemen may be permitted to apply for re-employment one year before the completion of the specified terms of engagement and avail themselves of all concessions available to ex-servicemen but shall not be permitted to leave the uniform until they complete the specified term of engagement in the Armed Forces of the Union.

Note: The principal rules were published vide notification No. GSR-1530, dated 29th December, 1979 in the Gazette in India, part-II, section 3, Sub-section (i) at Page 3004-05.

Sd/- (Bata K. Dey)
Director (JCA)

13

Financial and Administrative Benefits and Privileges from the Central Government

The Central Government has provided a number of privileges and concessions to both the serving and the ex-Defence personnel. Amongst others, they include monetary grants for gallantry awards, pension and gratuities, medical, travel and tax concessions. Now let us examine each of them in some detail.

Pensions

Family Pension:

A number of types of pensions are admissible to the member/dependents of the Armed forces. For the purpose of this chapter, only two types of pensions are more important – ordinary family pension and the special family pension. In most cases, for the families of the personnel who have retired, ordinary Family pension would be applicable.

Let us first look at various amounts that are admissible. As at present rate, which are subject to change by the change of rules, the rates of pension are mostly dependent on the reckonable emoluments last drawn by the individual. The present rates are as under:

Ordinary Family Pension:

(a) for emoluments not exceeding Rs. 1500 p.m. 30% of the reckonable emoluments subject to a minimum of Rs. 375 p.m.

(b) Emoluments exceeding Rs. 1500 p.m. but not exceeding Rs. 3000 p.m.: 20% of the reckonable emoluments subject to a minimum of Rs. 450 p.m.

(c) Emoluments exceeding Rs. 3000 p.m.: 15% of reckonable emoluments subject to a minimum of Rs. 600 p.m. and maximum of Rs. 1250 p.m.

In case where the deceased pensioners had rendered a minimum of seven years of service, the amount of family pension is paid as double the rate of 50% of the pay last drawn whichever is less for a period of seven years or till the deceased would have attained 65 years of age, if he had survived, whichever is earlier.

Also in case of retired individuals, the enhanced rate of pension should not exceed the normal amount of pension admissible for the deceased.

Special Family Pension

Families of personnel whose death is accepted as due to or aggravated by Military service are eligible for special family pension irrespective of the fact whether the deceased person had completed seven years or not. In addition, where the widow has a child, children allowance is also taken into account.

The present rates of Special Family Pension are :-

(a) Not exceeding Rs. 1500 p.m. — 50% of the reckonable emoluments

(b)	Exceeding Rs. 1500 but not exceeding Rs. 3000	40% subject to minimum of Rs. 750 p.m.
(c)	Exceeding Rs. 3000	30% subject to minmum of Rs. 1200 and maximum of Rs. 2500 p.m.

If the widow has a child the rate of special family pension would be 60% of the reckonable emoluments subject to minimum of Rs. 750 and maximum of Rs. 2500 p.m.

Special rate for children will cease when the child attains the age of 25 years or starts earning or in case of daughter, when she gets married. As per existing orders, the details of ordinary family pensions due are noted on the pension payment order (PPO) of every retiring service person eligible for pension, where such an endorsement exists on the PPO, the widow can draw family pension by giving a copy of death certificate of her husband to the Pension Disbursing Officer.

In respect of those pensioners in whose case the amount of family pension has not been endorsed on the PPO, the Government, vide Ministry of Defence Office Memorandum No. 6(4)/87/1369/B/D/(Pens) dated 13th Jun, 1988 has laid down the procedure for getting such family pension entitlement endorsed on their PPO. Suffice for such pensioner to know that they should submit the application form duly completed to their Pension Disbursing Authorities (PDA)/Bank. A format of the application form is place as Appendix I at the end of this chapter. The application should be filled in triplicate. After necessary action by the PDA, service HQ, and CDA, the family pension will be notified to the PDAs/Bank.

As a matter of precaution the concerned personnel should keep checking with their respective PDAs/Bank about the progress.

In the event of the death of the pensioner it is likely that the wife may have a problem in establishing her identity. It is, therefore, advisable that an application with the joint photograph should be submitted to the PDAs/Bank during the life time of the pensioner. In the event of the death, a copy of the death certificate alongwith a copy of the PPO and this application duly attested should be given to the Bank.

In the event of the death of the ex-serviceman, an intimation alongwith a copy of the death certificate is also sent to the respective Service HQ or record office as the case may be.

Monetary Awards to the Gallantry Award Winners

Evolution of Indian Gallantry Awards

This world rests on the arms of heroes like a son of those of his sire. He, therefore, that is a hero deserves respect under every circumstance. There is nothing higher in the three worlds than heroism. The hero protects and cherishes all, and all things depend upon the hero.

– Mahabharata, Santi Parva, 99 17-18

Gallantry has always commanded respect and recognition. In primitive societies leadership of the clan or tribe fell upon the bravest. The origin of the state saw the brave elevated to kingship, India, the most distinguished of the braves among the Indo-Aryans, became the King and the Commander.

The evolution of regular armies, however, demanded elaboration of the system of honours and awards. In the Vedic age this was done by granting a share to soldiers in the booty. Gradually some conventions with regard to the disposal of the spoils of war came to be established and the soldiers claimed a share proportionate to their contribution. To illustrate the point, charioteers were entitled to one-fourth of the booty. The Manuscript lays down that spoils such as chariots, elephants, parasols, animals, women and vessels should go to the brave who wins them. On the other hand, the wealth captures by the troops as a result of collective action was to be justly distributed by the ruler among them. A share in the booty continued to be an incentive for the soldiers till a much latter date and in the Agni Purana a ruler is advised to distribute the spoils of war among his servants in an equitable manner.

Epic Age

In the Epic Age, more emphasis came to be laid upon heavenly rewards. This development can be related to the philosophical and religious leanings of the age which was reflected in the attitude of the people. In the Mahabharata, the merit of dying as a martyr in the cause of Dharma is all along appreciated as the easiest way to heaven. On the event of an impending battle, Janaka is reported to have shown his soldiers, through his Yogic powers, the glory of the martyr in heaven and the ignominy of the coward in hell.

Governments of India vide its letter No. 3(6)/93/D (Ceremonial) dated 31st January, 1995 has enhanced the monetary allowance attached to the gallantry awards. For example, PVC, MVC, and VrC carry with them a monthly allowance of Rs. 350. Rs. 275 and Rs.200 per month respectively. It will be of interest to know that on the death of the recipient the allowance is payable to his wife also for her life.

Similarly, Indian Airlines also grants 50% concession on air fare to the recipient of PVC, Ashok Chakra, MVC and Kirti Chakra. Railways has also extended the concession of 50% fare and has included in its list the recipient of PVC, Ashok Chakra, MVC, Kirti Chakra, Vir Chakra and Shaurya Chakra and war widows or those who are disabled whilst in action. In case of gallantry award winners i.e. the recipients of PVC, MVC, VrC etc. the Indian Railways has further liberalized its rules and have granted for the issue of first class/second A.C. sleeper complementary passes to the recipients and widows along with a companion. This pass is valid from any railway station to any railway station in the country and is to be issued by the Divisional Manager of the railway concerned to whom an application on a plain paper given the name, residential address, attested photocopy of gallantry award citation is to be forwarded with the request for a issue of the complementary card (Ministry of Railways No. E(W)96 PS 5-6/22 dated 23rd February, 1996). In modern times, almost all the countries in the world have instituted some rewards mostly monetary to the gallantry award winners. So also almost all the States in India have announced monetary awards for the gallantry award winners of the armed forces.

The question of bringing uniformity in all States regarding the monetary grants to the winners of gallantry and other awards has been repeatedly discussed at the Kendriya Sainik Board meetings. As a matter of fact on 9th April, 1994, the Additional Secretary, Department of Defence vide D.O. Letter No. 2394/AS® 94 have recommended to all the States and the Union Territories Governments to bring uniformity and have suggested the following amounts:

	Cash Grant Total	Cash in lieu of Land	Total	Annuity
Param Vir Chakra	22,500	1,50,000	1,72,500	1,000
Maha Vir Chakra	15,000	1,00,000	1,15,000	400
Vir Chakra	7,000	50,000	57,000	300
Kirti Chakra	12,000	75,000	87,000	350
Shaurya Chakra	5,000	40,000	45,000	250
Sarvottam Yudh Seva Medal	17,000	1,10,000	1,27,000	600

	Cash Grant Total	Cash in lieu of Land	Total	Annuity
Uttam Yudh Seva Medal	10,000	65,000	75,000	350
Yudh Seva Medal	4,000	30,000	34,000	
Sena/Nao Sena/ Vayu Sena Medal	3,000	20,000	23,000	250
Mention in-Despatches	2,000	10,000	12,000	150
PVSM	15,000	1,00,000	1,15,000	400
AVSM	7,000	50,000	57,000	300
VSM	3000	20,000	25000	250

Need for Review

At the first sight, it might appear that the amounts admissible are quite reasonable and decent. However, deeper analyses would reveal that these rates were fixed more than 4 decades back and are far removed from the present day reality. In view of the changing social environments and the erosion of the value of the money. It is necessary that these rates are periodically reviewed remain in consonance with the current realities. It must be said to the credit of Govt. of Himachal Pradesh that recently they have increased for winners of Maha Vir Chakra to Rs. 15 lakhs, Vir Chakra and Shaurya Chakra to Rs. 10 lakhs respectively.

It also must be remembered that the Gallantry Awards are admissible only for those acts which are performed during war or war like situations and an official declaration of a war is a must. It is more than 3 decades, which India fought a declared war and is also unlikely, that in the near future any war will be fought unless it is thrust on us. The rates, therefore, are only a paper exercise. To make it more meaningful, it should be also applicable to the exceptional acts of devotion and gallantry for which awards in VSM series are awarded.

Exemption from House Tax

Most of the State Governments also provide for exemption of House tax to ex-servicemen, gallantry award winners and war widows. For example, the Municipal Corporation of Delhi vide their Public Notification (2000-2001) has exempted the house tax to ex-servicemen etc. as under:

War widows of gallantry award winners are exempted 100% from house tax for the house used for their living and not let out for any other purpose. Similarly, ex-servicemen are given special rebate of 20% or Rs. 1000/-, whichever is less, where the property is self-occupied. It is restricted only to one residential dwelling unit.

Travel Concessions & Telephones

The Gallantry award winners are entitled for free railway complimentary passes along with a companion to any place in India except Metro Railways, Calcutta. Ministry of Railways (Railway Board) Letter No. E(w)2002 PS 5-6/99 dated 25-2-2002 refers. Similarly, the gallantry award winners of Param Vir Chakra, Mahavir Chakara and Vir Chakara are also entitled to travel free in AC 3 Tier of Rajdhani and Chair Cars of Shatabidi and Jan Shatabidi Express Trains. Even war widows of ex-servicemen who died in action are entitled to 75% of the concessions in the railway fare to any place in India.

Indian Airlines also grants 50% concessions on the air fare to the recipients of Param Vir Chakra, Ashok Chakra, Mahavir Chakra and Kirti Chakra.

Exemptions from Income Tax

Pensions payable to the grantee of award winners including Vayu Sena Medal (Gallantry) and their dependents are exempted from Income Tax by the Govt. of India, Ministry of Finance Notificate No. S.O. 1048 (E) dated 24th November, 2000 published vide Gazette of India Extraordinary Part II dated 29th January, 2001.

Gratuity-Under section 10 (10), Income Tax Act, gratuity received by employees is exempt from tax subject to the conditions and to the extent permitted under the Act.

Sub-section (10) provides for tax exemption of gratuities in the following manner. In the case of Government employees, the following payments by way of gratuities are exempted from tax.

Death-cum-retirement gratuities received under the revised pension rules of the Central Government, the Central Civil Services (Pension) Rules, 1972 or any similar scheme applicable to the members of Civil Servies of the Union, or gratuity received under the pension Code or Regulations by holders of posts connected with defence of Civil Posts under the Pension Code or Regulations by holders of posts connected with defence or of civils posts under the Union, or the members of all India Services or the members of Civil Services of a State or holders of Civil Posts under state, or the employees of a local authority.

Medical Concessions

A free medical treatment has been a long outstanding demand of the ex-servicemen and their various institutions for the last few decades. As the existing provisions contained in the Medical Regulations for the Armed Forces restricts such treatment only to the discretion of the Officer Commanding of the Military Hospitals. It is also restricted whereby some ailments of serious nature like heart. Respiratory diseases are not covered for the ex-servicemen.

The ex-servicemen were forced to move a Special Writ Petition in the Supreme Court of India for the issue of necessary direction to grant free medical treatment to ex-servicemen and their families irrespective of the nature of the disease or the availability of best medicines. The case is still pending in the Supreme Court. In reply to the Writ Petition, the Govt. of India has set up an Ex-Servicemen Contributory Health Scheme (ECHS) which came into effect on 1st April, 2003 vide Govt. of India letter No. 22(1)/01/US(WE)/D(Res) dated 30th December, 2002. The scheme is functioning under the integral staff with its Central office located at Army Headquarters and thirteen Regional Centers located at various major cities. It will cater for the Medicare of all ex-servicemen in receipt of pension; including disability and family pension. The scheme will be fully implemented by 31st March, 2008. There will be a total of 227 Polyclinics in the country, Out of these 123 Polyclinics will be at non-military stations. The ECHS is a contributory scheme. Every ex-serviceman retired/retiring after 1st April, 2003 will compulsorily become a member of the ECHS by contributing his/her share. Similarly, those retired prior to 1st April, 2003 can become members by paying the contribution in lump-sum or in 3 equal installments. There will be no restriction of age or medical condition. The scheme will be headed by the Adjutant General of Indian Army and a Managing Director (Major General). The Polyclinics at non-military stations will be set up in a phased manner.

Applications for becoming Members

The application forms for enrolment to ECHS are available free of cost at all the Army stations HQrs, all Air Force stations and Naval establishments. It can also be accessible from the website www.indianarmy.nic.in/arechs.htm. The application forms should be filled up carefully by the person concerned in black ink and submit the same along with an affidavit, the format of which is given in the application form itself.

All ESM are required to make one time contribution based on their monthly pension (excluding DA) Pension means uncommuted pension and the rates of contribution depends upon the rate of pension starting from Rs.1800/- to Rs. 18,000/-. The payment is to be made to the MRO attached to the application form to the Govt.Treasury, RBI or the SBI. After scrutiny of the application and its approval a Smart Card will be issued to the person concerned. The affidavit is to be sworn on a non-judicial stamp paper of Rs. 10/- and attested by a Magistrate or Notary Public. The completed application form should be submitted only to the various collection points after reporting personally to the Station HQrs.

Exemption from Contribution

War widows: War widows or whose spouse had died due to enemy action in international war action in peace keeping missions abroad, borders skirmishes, action against extremist are employed in an aid to civil power or operations, specially notified by the Central Government are exempt from payment of contribution.

Similarly, cases of those who have been disabled during war, was taken up in writ petition number 1812/2005 before the High Court at Delhi in the case disabled war pensioners v/s Union of India and other and the court noted. That the matter has already been forwarded to the relevant ministry and is under the consideration of the government (Ministry of Defence). The court directed that the decision in this matter should be taken within 4 weeks and communicated to the petitioner. It is learnt that the same has been agreed by the ministry of defence and relevant government orders already issued. War disabled pensioners, who were disabled due to the injuries, received during proclaimed wars or any other encounter, which has been specifically accorded such status are also exempted from payment of contribution (ECHS) authority "Government of India ." Department of EX - SMS, well leter no. PC-2/ (24) (2)-05/US (WE)/DC. result dated 24-07-2005.

Treatment

The starting point for medical attendance will be the nearest military/non-military Polyclinic. The available treatment within capabilities of the Polyclinic shall be provided at the first instance. These Polyclinics will be opened for 8 hours during the week days and shall remain closed on Sundays and Gazetted holidays. Patients requiring attention outside working hours will be handled by the Duty MOs of Service Hospitals (in military stations) and on-call civilian doctors in non-military stations. To avail the medical treatment from a Polyclinic empanelled hospital it is mandatory that the pensioner/widows/dependants should first report to the nearest Polyclinic along with their ECHS membership smart card. In case the required treatment is beyond the scope of the Polyclinic, the medical officer then would refer the patient to the local military hospital with facilities available. Should MH not have the desired facility or the specialty, the ECHS patient will have the choice of going to any empanelled hospital at the Station. The empanelled hospital will be his first choice and not of the doctor. The list of empanelled hospitals is given at Annexure 'B' to this chapter. In case of emergency, the ECHS member can either report to the nearest service hospital or the nearest empanelled hospital in which case, the bill should be paid by the ECHS or even non-empanelled can report to any nearest non-empanelled hospital in which case, the ECM or his representative will have to pay the charges to the non-empanelled hospital initially. The bill in original will be forwarded subsequently to the ECHS Central Organization, New Delhi for reimbursement. The onus of informing the Polyclinic or ECHS Regional Centre or proving the emergency shall be that of the ECM patient.

Cathedral of Relief Rehabilitation and Resettlement – DGR

No work for ex-servicemen, problems and solutions is complete, without mention of the work being done by the

Directorate General Rehabilitation and Resettlement, Ministry of Defence. To get a first hand account of the work being done by the Directorate, the author visited the office of the Directorate General himself and spoke to various officers and the following emerged:

Background and Organization

With over eight million ex-soldiers (including Officers, Sailors and Airmen) on the retired list and over fifty thousand service personnel retiring every year at a comparatively young age, their resettlement and rehabilitation is really a gigantic task. But this is a national necessity for the national cause, because they are retired at an early age to keep a young profile of the armed forces for effectively safe-guarding the nation's defence. Further, the professional competence achieved during their service careers also is not much of a relevance in the civil sphere or economic activity. This again is not because of their own volition or fault, but because of the nature of duties they are called to perform, again, for the national interest.

Realising this imperative, the Central Government has for this purpose created the office of the Director General Resettlement in the Ministry of Defence at the centre and is at present located in West Block IV, R.K. Puram, New Delhi-110066. The apex body for this purpose is the Kendriya Sainik Board with 45 members, including a number of Ministers at the centre, Chief Ministers, the Service Chiefs and a number of other concerned dignitaries. Apart from the DGR and four Zonal Resettlement Directorates, there are at present 29 Rajya Sainik Boards and 307 Zila Sainik Boards. As mentioned earlier at the centre, their activities are co-ordinated by the Kendriya Sainik Board which is headed by a secretary who is a serving officer of the rank of Brigadier or equivalent.

The office of the Director General Resettlement is divided into Five Directorates apart from the Kendriya Sainik Board.

They are: Directorate of Re-employment. Directorate of Self-employment, Directorate of Training, Directorate of Publicity and Directorate of Statistics and Records. For the present purpose, the more relevant are the Directorates of Training, Re-employment and Self-employment.

Directorate of Training

Directorate of Training organizes various training programmes or retiring as well as retired officers JCOs and officers of the three services. This is primarily to equip them with the skills, which are required in the civil sector and also to decide the career they would like to adopt after retirement. Service personnel are eligible for these courses during last 18 months of their service or within one year of their retirement up to a maximum age of 55 years under normal circumstances. Those who wish to avail of this facility, should ascertain from this Directorate various training courses available, their duration, location etc.

Directorate of Re-employment

This Directorate assists retiring/retired officers and men in getting re-employment provided they qualify the test of being an ex-servicemen. For obtaining this assistance registration can be obtained from Zilla/Rajya Sainik Board or unit welfare officers or directly from this directorate at the office of the DGR. After registration, this Directorate sponsors individuals for various vacancies; which are notified from the defence establishments, government departments. para-military or similar organizations, public sector undertaking particularly under the Ministry of Defence. This office also sponsors candidates to security agencies, other organizations and nationalized banks. For the senior officers, particularly of the rank of Brigadiers and above, another avenue for employment in the civil sectors is through the Bureau of Public Enterprises, who notifies various available posts in the public sector undertaking to the service headquarters through the Ministry of Defence. In receipt of the requisitions the service headquarters forward the names of suitable officers with their dossiers. BPE after interview, selects suitable officers and forward their names to the concerned Ministry for appointment.

Whilst on the subject of employment it may be recalled that as an aftermath of 1962, 1965 and 1971 wars liberal statutory rules were made and instructions issued for employment of war disabled service personnel, reservation of vacancies for them, relaxation of age limits and other qualifications. They were mostly for government department, government controlled corporations and public sector undertakings. To cite, some of these rules The Ex-Servicemen Reservation of Vacancies in Civil Services and Posts Class III and IV Rules 1971. The Released Emergency Commissioned and Short Service Commissioned Officers (Reservation of Vacancies) Rules, 1971. The Released Emergency Commissioned Officers and Short Service Commissioned Officers (engineering, medical services) Reservation of Vacancies Rules 1971 and various instructions to public sector undertakings in accordance with the "Articles of Associations" of the concerned undertakings are relevant. These rules provided for various concessions like reservations, seniority, age limits, qualifications etc. Some of these rules may have expired with the long passage of time, and some may still be in force. Nevertheless, some of them are reproduced in Chapter 12 for use, if any.

Directorate of Self-employment

This Directorate has formulated many useful schemes in collaboration with Industrial Development Bank, National Bank for Agriculture and Rural Development, Khadi Village Industries Commission, some Nationalized Banks and Public Sector Corporations for self-employment of ex-servicemen in

Industry, Agriculture, Village Industries, Service Establishments, Transportation etc.

At present there are three schemes called SEMFEX I, II and III (Self Employment for Ex-servicemen) in operations. Semfex I, relates to setting up of various industries with a project cost upto 15 lakhs, Semfex II relates to farm sector and non-far sector relating to agriculture upto a project cost of 7.5 lakhs and Semfex III which is operated in conjunction with Khadi & Village Industries Commission relate to setting up of various small and village cottage industries. Under these schemes elaborate provisions have been made for soft seed capital assistance, term loans at concessional rates, prolonged repayment periods and necessary training and support. They are available to ex-servicemen and their widows. Normal upper age limit is 60 years. Details of all these schemes can be obtained from the office of Dte Publicity, DGR and it is well worth to have a look at these schemes immediately before or after retirement, to decide which will suit a particular individual, if he desires to venture into self-employment.

Here a word of caution is necessary. Whilst these schemes on paper look very attractive and the office of the DGR will dish out very impressive figures as to how many hundreds of crores of amount of loans have been disbursed and how many thousands of applications have been approved, but to get through, even the so-called simplified procedures is not so easy. The reasons are no very far to seek. Whilst the officials of the DGR and its subordinate offices may be very enthusiastic, the implementation and sanctions are to be done by the implementing banks, financial institutions and other organizations, who are not so enthusiastic. As a matter of fact, in the heart of many of them frown on the preferential treatment being meted out to ex-servicemen. They cause the delays and put all types of impediments, citing their own rules as a convenient excuse. Therefore, only those ex-servicemen, who are really keen, have the patience, sagacity, sound health, and the capacity to run round and chase, should think of venturing. Nevertheless the sweat and patience is the price one has to pay to achieve any success.

This Directorate also has many other useful schemes, like transportation of coal, petroleum products, allotment of Mother Diary booths, UTI agencies, setting up of service industries like telephone booths, etc. and it is advisable to get the details of these schemes either by paying a personal visit or writing to Directorate of Publicity, office of the DGR to obtain the maximum advantage, of the efforts put in by the DGR.

Kendriya Sainik Board also has a number of welfare funds like the Flag Day Fund, Disabled Army Personnel Widows & Orphan Fund, Lady Linlithgo Fund, Victor Sassoon Fund, Military Nurses Benevolent Fund, Indian Soldiers, Sailors and Airmen Board Fund etc. from which also financial assistance can be had in penury circumstances, by getting in touch with Zilla Sainik Boards or Secretary Kendriya Sainik Board, R.K. Puram (West Block IV) New Delhi.

A list of Rajya Sainik Boards and their addresses are given in Appendix II at the end of this chapter.

List of Rajya Sainik Boards

1. Director
Department of Sainik Welfare
H.No. 11-5-432/1/A, I Floor
Opp. Singareni Collieries Office
Lakdikapool
Hyderabad-4
2. Director
Relief, Rehabilitation & Resettlement
Government of Arunachal Pradesh
New Itanagar-791110
3. Director of Sainik Welfare
Assam Sainik Bhavan
Lachit Nagar
Guwahati-781007

4. Director
   Department of Sainik Kalyan
   Government of Bihar
   Home Department
   Patna-800015
5. Secretary
   Rajya Sainik Board
   Collectorate Building
   Panaji
   Goa-403001
6. Director
   Sainik Welfare & Resettlement
   Barrack No. 3,
   Government Polytechnic Campus
   Ahmedabad-380015
7. Secretary
   Rajya Sainik Board,
   Sainik Bhawan,
   Sector 12, Panchkula,
   District Ambala, Haryana
8. Director
   Sainik Welfare
   Department of Sainik Welfare
   Government of Himachal Pradesh
   Hamirpur-177001
9. Director of Sainik Welfare
   Department of Sainik Welfare
   Ambphalla
   Jammu-180005
10. Director Sainik Welfare
    Department of Sainik Welfare & Resettlement
    Field Marshal K M Cariappa Bhavan
    No. 58 Fd Mshal KM Cariappa
    Bangalore-560025
11. Director
    Department of Sainik Welfare
    Vikas Bhavan
    Thiruvananthapuram-695033

12. Director
    Department of Sainik Welfare, MP
    Southern Shopping Centre,
    GTB Complex, TT Nagar,
    P.B. No.: 364
    Bhopal-462003
13. Director
    Department of Sainik Welfare
    Council Hall
    Pune-411011
14. Secretary
    Rajya Sainik Board,
    Old District Hospital
    BT Road,
    Imphal-795001
15. Director Sainik Welfare
    Dte. of Sainik Welfare
    Public Service Commission Building
    Beyond DC Building,
    Shillong-793001
16. Director Sainik Welfare
    Department of Sainik Welfare
    Treasury Square
    Aizwal, Mizoram-706001
17. Secretary
    Rajya Sainik Board,
    Home Department, Home Branch,
    Kohima-797001
18. Secretary
    Rajya Sainik Board,
    Nageswar Tangi
    Lewis Road,
    Bhubaneshwar-751002
19. Director
    Dte. of Sainik Welfare, Punjab
    SCO No. 1136-37
    Sector-22B, Chandigarh-160022

20. Secretary
Rajya Sainik Board,
Secretariat Building
Jaipur-302005
21. Secretary
Rajya Sainik Board, Sikkim,
Gangtok-737101
22. Director
Ex-servicemen Welfare
22 Sydenhams Road,
Madras-600003
23. Secretary
Rajya Sainik Board, Tripura
Kunjban, Agartala,
Tripura-799006
24. Director
Sainik Kalyan Evam Punarvas
Kariappa Bhavan, Kaiser Bagh
Lucknow-226001
25. Secretary
Rajya Sainik Board,
Department of Social Welfare,
Writer's Building, Block F,
Calcutta-700001
26. Secretary
Rajya Sainik Board,
A & N Administration,
Secretariat,
Port Blair-744101
27. Zila Sainik Welfare Office
UT Chandigarh
Opposite Aroma Hotel
Sector-21D (Sainik Rest House)
Chandigarh-160022
28. Secretary
Rajya Sainik Board,
1, Rajpur Road,
Delhi-110054

29. Secretary
    Rajya Sainik Board,
    No. 51, Montiorser Street,
    Pondicherry-605001

Grants and Funds

Now, let us turn in brief to the Grants and Funds, which are available and are being administered by the Central Government and three Service Head Quarters for benefits of servicemen / Ex-servicemen and their families.

1. **From the Central Government**

   (a) Raksha Mantri's Discretionary Fund:

   Application for assistance from the above fund can be submitted by the ex-servicemen/widows/dependents in connection with expenses on marriage, house repairs, monthly grants, medical grants, children education grant and Penury grants. All various grants ranging from Rs. 8000/- to Rs. 15000/-. Authority DGR News letter 1 of 2005, for assistance from this fund, Secretary, KSB , may be contacted, or respective Rajya Sainik Board and/or District Soldiers/Sailors and Airman Boards.

   (b) Armed Forces Flag Day Fund:

   This fund is utilized for grant of construction/repair of houses, grant of marriage for daughters of widows etc.

   (Authority KSB letter: 105/SB/7/EC/91/KSB dtd. 10.11.1992, for this kindly write to Secretary, KSB, R.K. Puram, New Delhi-66

   (c) KSB also maintains Sainik rest houses and after care of the dependents of ex-servicemen for leprosy and TB and in the Cheshire houses.

2. **Army Head Quarters**

(a) Adjutant General's Welfare Fund:

To provide financial assistance to the retired officers, men of the Indian Army, Army Head Quarters maintains AG welfare fund. To decentralize the administration. The fund is also allocated to command Head Quarters and Regimental Centres. The Fund Caters to all types of genuine needs of ex-servicemen like, financial assistance for rehabilitation, medical expenses, education expenses for children, grant for daughter's marriage and even for accommodation relief. In short, this is a fund for every specific purpose for both officers and men in need. Details and forms, nearest formation Head-Quarters are the concerned record office or even, AG Branch (CW-4), Army Headquarters, New Delhi can be addressed.

(b) Army Wives Welfare Association:

This association profices financial assistance at one time grant to widows of officers, JCO's, and OR's, within 3 years of the death. The rates for officers, JCO's and OR's , at present is Rs. 2000, 1200, 1000 and Rs. 800 respectively. Application should be forwarded to the Secretary, AWWA, DHQ, P.O. New Delhi-110001 with a copy of death certificate.

(c) Army Scholarship Welfare Fund and Grants:

A number of schemes for the grant of scholarship to the children of army personnel, is either married or unmarried are in operation under the Army Wives Welfare Association and Army Scholarship schemes for the Army. Details may be had by writing to Staff Officer, AWWA, C/o AG Branch, Army Head quarters, New Delhi-01 or Secretary, ESSA, Welfare directorate (CW-4), AG Branch, West Blcok-3, R.K. Puram, New Delhi-66.

3. **Navy**

Indian Navy operates its welfare and rehabilitation schemes for the naval pensioners primarily through the Indian Naval Benevolent Association, some of the various grants available are a lump sum amount on death of naval personnel on attaining the age of 80 years or above.

(a) Specialized medical treatment for self and spouse and schemes for needy and meritorious children of Naval pensioners, for school, college and vocational training.

(b) Financial assistance for Self-employment and rehabilitation

(c) Additional assistance by Local Branches to Naval Wives Welfare Association which are operating at various naval establishments.

Needy persons should write to the Secretary, of all these associations at Naval Head-Quarters, or should contact the nearest Naval establishment.

4. **Air Force**

Air Force Welfare Fund provides for financial needs to the retired Air Force Personnel, for medical treatment, house repairs, marriage grants. It also operates death grants and family assistance schemes at various rates to the Ex-Airforce Personnel. For details reference may be made to the Secretary, Air Force Welfare Benevolent fund, Air Head Quarters, New Delhi or the concerned commander or Station Head-Quarters.

Air Force also maintains Subroto Memorial Schemes, Indian Air Force and HAL scholarship or schemes.

Air Force Wives Welfare Association

Rehabilitation grants, scholarships and a lot of other assistance is also provided by the Air force wives welfare association to the families of the Indian Air force personnel.

Marshal of the Air Force and Mrs. Arjun Singh trust fund has also been established since 2005 for welfare activities and particularly, the educational needs of needy Ex-Air Force personnel. The person interested to know the details may write to The manager of the above trust C/O Air Force Association, Race Corse, New Delhi.

Having seen, some of the various funds and schemes, which are available to the families of ex-servicemen, from the Army, Navy and the Air Force. It is necessary to remember that details of the schemes and amounts are likely to change (more often for improvement) are vary (out of experience). It is therefore, advisable to refer to the authorities concerned at the time of occurrence and obtain a booklet containing the latest details of the schemes in force.

It is equally necessary to note that such benefits are exempted from Income Tax under section 10 of the Income Tax Act, 1961.

14

Benefits by Various State Governments

No reference to the welfare of Ex-servicemen is complete, unless it also refers in however brief, to the various benefits and schemes formulated by the respective State Governments for the welfare and welfare of their families. It will be recalled that most of these schemes were formulated, revived or liberalized as an aftermath of 1962, 1965 and 1971 wars. It is but natural that some of the concessions and schemes would have lapsed with the expiry of time and some are still in force. Most of these measures, relate to reward for gallantry awards, cash grants for those killed or disabled in action, grant of war Jagirs, land grants, educational concessions, reservation of vacancies, priority in employment, protection in matters of houses and lands for resumption and the like. It is therefore advisable that for the latest schemes in operation, reference is made to the Rajya Sainik Boards of the State concerned. Nevertheless, a brief glimpse of the various concessions known to be still in vogue to war widows, Dependents of those killed or disabled in war including casualties of operation Pawan and Meghdoot would be in order.

Jammu & Kashmir

J&K Houses and Shops Rent Control Act, 1966
II-A Restoration of Possession to Defence personnel

Notwithstanding anything to the contrary contained in this Act, possession of a residential building shall be restored within one month from the date of application, if:

(a) the landlord is member of the Defence Force and requires it for occupation of his family and produces a certificate from his Commanding Officer showing that he is serving under special conditions within the meaning of Section 3 of the Indian Soldiers (Litigation) Act, 1925.

(b) the landlord is a member of the Defence Forces and requires it for his own occupation on retirement, release or discharge from the Defence services and produces a certificate from the Commanding Officer evidence of his release, retirement or discharge; and

(c) if the landlord is the wife of a deceased member of Defence Forces, who requires it for her own occupation and produces certificate from the Commanding Officer of his deceased husband to the effect that her husband died while serving under special conditions within the meaning of Section 3 of the Indian Soldiers (Litigation) Act, 1925.

Amendment to Section 13 Act XXXIV of 1966

In Section 13 of the Principal Act

(i) For the brackets and letter "(b) wherever occurring the brackets and letter"(h)"
Shall be and shall always be deemed to have been substituted:

(ii) in sub-section (i), for the words and figures section or because of section 11A" substituted.

Amendment under SRO 396 Dt. 8th September, 1981

Rule 6 provides that the Rent Controller will get the premises physically vacated within 7 days of passing the orders, after he has made the brief enquiries to satisfy himself.

Union Territory of Chandigarh

The East Punjab Urban Rent Restriction Act (Extension to Chandigarh) Act, 1974. (Act No. 54 of 1974)

An Act to extend the East Punjab Urban Rent Restriction Act, 1949, to the Union Territory of Chandigarh. (See AIR March, 1975).

Uttar Pradesh

The State of Uttar Pradesh has provided three fold safeguards in its rent control laws in favour of the Armed Forces.

One in relation to a landlord who is a member of the Armed Forces, two in relation to such a tenant and third in relation to heirs of the member of the Armed Forces who have died whilst serving under special conditions.

In relation to such a landlord Section 14(3) (iii) of the UP Urban Buildings (Regulation of Letting & Eviction) Act, 1972 provides that a landlord may apply to the controller for order directing the tenant to put the landlord in possession of the residential building if the landlord is a member of the Armed Forces of the Union of India and requires it for the occupation of his family and if he produces a certificate of his prescribed authority referred to in Section 7 of the Indian Soldiers Litigation Act, 1925 that he is serving under special conditions within the meaning of Section 3 of that Act or is posted in a non-family station.

The explanation to the sub-section provides that the certificate of the prescribed authority shall be conclusive evidence that the landlord is serving under special conditions or is posted in a non-family station. The word 'Family' means parents and such relation of the landlord as ordinarily live with him and are dependent upon him.

For a member who is a tenant, Section 21 of the same Act provides that no application for eviction shall be entertained in case of a residential building against any tenant, who is a member of the Armed Forces of the Union and in whose favour the prescribed authority under the Soldiers Litigation Act, 1925 has issued a certificate that he is serving under special conditions within the meaning of Section 3 of that Act or where he has died by enemy action whilst so serving there against his heirs.

So also Section 20 which deals with bar of suits for eviction of tenant except on specified ground for the arrears of rent the period of four months has been increased to six months in relation to person serving under special conditions or where he has died whilst so serving there in relation to his heirs.

Section 21 of the said Act after its amendment in the explanation provides yet another valuable provision.

It states that where the landlord of any building is a serving or retired Indian soldier as defined in the Indian Soldiers Litigation Act, 1925 and such building was let out at any time before retirement or a widow of such soldier and such building was let out at any time before the retirement or death of her husband, whichever occurs earlier:

And such landlord needs such building for occupation by himself or member of his family for residential purposes, his representation that he needs the building for residential purposes for himself or the member of his family shall be deemed sufficient for the purpose of clause (a) and where such landlord own more than one building this provision shall apply in respect of one building only.

For the Ex-servicemen and their families in the state of UP there is a very valuable judgement in the case of Mohinder

Pal Singh v. Additional District Judge, Dehradun Civil Miscellaneous Writ Petition No. 2791 of 1989 dated 03-11-92 (AIR 1993 Allahabad 176). In the said landmark judgement the Hon'ble High Court has held that vide section 21(1) proviso 4 explanation clause (3) (As amended by UP Act, 31 of 1985) that the said provisions for soldiers contained in the amendment applies to all types of buildings and to retired soldiers or their widows. They noted the fact that the explanation as originally enacted was confined to a "Residential Building" and to the members of the family of a Indian soldier serving under special conditions, whereas after its amendment by UP Act 31 of 1985 Clause (III) of the explanation has made it applicable to "all buildings" and to any soldier that is serving or retired and his widow, it does not effect any of the vested rights of the tenant of such building.

It also held that under section 21 (IA) application by the specified landlord – landlord in occupation of public building which he is to vacate on cessation of employment – prescribed authority has no option but to order eviction provision of sub-section (IA) are mandatoray – non-obsinate clause in section 21(IA) giving it over-riding effect of section (2) further established its mandatory nature.

In the facts of these cases the respondent was serving as a Colonel in the Indian Army and was occupying a public building at 27, The Mall, Delhi Cantonment. He stood superannuated with effects from 21st July, 1982 and vacated his official residence on 30th September, 1982. Whilst examining the relevant provision, the learned High Court said that the authority has not been given any option with regard to an order of eviction in case covered by sub-section (IA).

Madhya Pradesh

Section 20-A has been inserted in the Madhya Pradesh Accommodation Control Act, 1961, to provide for special provision for recovery of possession of the premises by the members of family of landlord, who is killed whilst in active service in Army, Navy or the Air Force.

It provides that where the landlord in respect of any accommodation being a member of the Naval, Military, Air or other Armed Forces of the Union dies on active duty and the said accommodation or a part thereof is required for the bonafide residence of a member of his family, the Court may on an application by such member of the family, place him in vacant possession of such accommodation or part thereof, as the case may be, by evicting the tenant or every other person who may be in occupation thereof if the Court is satisfied:

(a) That the landlord was the owner of such accommodation and,

(b) That the member of the family is in need of the accommodation or a part thereof for his residence and no other suitable alternative accommodation is possessed by him.

It is pertinent to note that in this provision not only members of the Army, Navy or the Air Force are covered but also members of other armed forces of the Union such as BSF, Coast Guards or the CRPF.

Rajasthan

On 22nd May, 1987 the Governor of Rajasthan promulgated the Rajasthan Premises (Control of Rent and Eviction) (Amendment) Ordinance amending Section 13 of the Rajasthan Premises (Control of Rent and Eviction) Act, 1950.

It now enables the retired members of the armed forces of the Union as also a war widow or other legal representative of a deceased member, to seek eviction of their tenants in a summary manner by moving an application to the District Magistrate on the ground that the premises are required for the use and occupation of such member. A bill to this effect will be tabled before the Rajasthan State Assembly shortly.

Tamil Nadu

Tamil Nadu Building (Lease and Rent Control) Act, 1960 stipulates the grounds and procedure for evicting a tenant from the premises.

Section 10 sub-section 3-A (a) Tamil Nadu Building (Lease & Rent Control) Act, 1960 stipulates that:

(a) A landlord who has been or is a member of the Armed Forces can obtain

The possession of the premises if he,

(i) is released or has retired from service and the building is bonafidely required for his residence; or

(ii) is stationed at a place where on account of Military exigencies, he cannot live with his family or dies or is on active duty and the building is bonafidely required for the residence of his family.

The Controller shall, on application made by the landlord who is a member of the Armed Forces or the member of his family, as the case may be, if he is satisfied that the claim of the landlord or the member of his family is bonafide, pass an order directing the tenant to put the landlord or the members of his family in possession of the building and if the controller is not so satisfied he shall make an order rejecting the application.

Notwithstanding anything contained in clause (a) of Section 10(3A) where the landlord who is a member of the armed forces or the member of his family produces a certificate from the prescribed authority under the Indian Soldiers (Litigation) Act, 1925 (Central Act IV of 1925) that the landlord is serving under special conditions with in the meaning of Section 3 of that Act, the application referred to in clause (a) shall be disposed if, as far as may be within a period of one month and if the claim of the landlord of the members of his family is accepted, the controller shall pass an order directing the tenant to put the landlord or the member of his family in possession of the building on such date as may be specified in the order which shall not be later than one month from the date of such order.

Explanation: For the purpose of this sub-section "Member of the Armed Forces" means a person in the service of the Air Force, Army or Navy of the Union of India and includes a seaman and "seaman" includes a master, pilot or apprentice employed or engaged as a member of the crew of a ship or a sailing vessel to which the Merchant Shipping Act, 1958 (Central Act 44 of 1958) applies.

Provided that if a question arises whether any person is a member of the Armed Forces, such question shall be decided by the controller and his decision shall be final.

Mysore (Karnataka)

Mysore (Karnataka) Rent Control Act, 1961 stipulates the grounds and procedure for evicting a tenant from the premises.

Section 21(b) contains special provisions for recovery of premises by members of Armed Forces or a member of a deceased member of such Forces. It provides that notwithstanding anything contained in the Act:

(a) A landlord, who is a member of the Armed Forces of the Union, or who was such a member and is duly retired which term shall include premature retirement shall be entitled to recover possession of any premises on the ground that the premises is bonafidely required by him for occupation by himself or any member of his family and the court shall pass a decree for eviction on such ground, if the landlord, at the hearing of the suit, produces a certificate given by the head of his service or his Commanding Officer, to the effect that:

(i) he is presently a member of the Armed Forces of the Union or he was such a member and is now retired, and

(iii) he does not possess any other suitable accommodation in the local area where he or the members of his family can resides.

(b) Where a member of the Armed Force of the Union dies while in service or such member is duly retired as stated above and dies within five years of his retirement, his widow who is or becomes a landlady or any premises shall be entitled to recover possession of such premises on the ground that the accommodation is bonafidely required by her for occupation by herself, or for any member of her family and the Court shall pass a decree for eviction on such ground, if such widow at the hearing of the suit, produces a certificate signed by the area or sub-area Commander within whose jurisdiction the accommodation is situated to the effect that:

(i) She is the widow of a deceased member of the Armed Forces as aforesaid, and

(ii) She does not possess any other suitable accommodation in the local Area where she or the members of her family can reside.

Explanation: For the purposes of clause (a) of this section, the expression 'the head of his service' in the case members retired from the Indian Army includes the Area Commander, in the case of members retired from the Indian Navy includes the Flag Officer Commanding-in-Chief and in the case of the members retired from the Indian Air Force includes the Station Commander.

For the purpose of this section, any certificate referred to in sub-section (i) shall be conclusive evidence of facts stated therein.

Kerala

Kerala Building (Lease and Rent Control) Act, 1965 specified the grounds and procedure for evicting a tenant from the premises. Extract of Section 11A of the Kerala Building (Lease & Rent) Act, 1965.

Notwithstanding anything contained in Section 11, in the case of a residential building where the landlord is a member of the Armed Forces of the Union of India, and the building is required for the occupation of himself on his release from services, and he makes an application for eviction of the tenant to the Rent Control Court, or where on the occurrence of death in action of a member of the Armed Forces, a member of his family requires recovery of possession of the building for his own residence or where on the posting of a member of the Armed Forces to serve under special conditions, a member of his family requires recovery of possession of the Building for his own residence and an application is made to the Rent Control court for eviction of the tenant, the Rent Control Court shall dispose of the same, as far as may be within one month, and if the claim of the landlord or member of his family is accepted, the Court shall make an order directing the tenant to put the landlord or the member of his family as the case may be in possession of the building on a date to be specified in the order, and such date shall not be later than fifteen days from the date of the order.

Provided that an application under this section for recovery of the possession of a building on the ground that the landlord is serving under special conditions of service shall not be entertained by the Rent Control Court unless the same is accompanied by a certificate of the prescribed authority referred to in Section 7 of the Indian Soldiers (Litigation) Act, 1925 that the landlord is serving under special conditions within the meaning of Section 3 of the said Act.

Explanation: For the purpose of this section "Family" shall mean such relations of the landlord as ordinarily live with him and are dependent on him.

West Bengal

Extract of Section 298 (ii) of West Bengal Tenancy Act, 1956 (1979 Amendment)

Provision to Section 29 (b) (ii):

(a) Where the landlord has retired, or will retire within a period of less than one year, as member of the Naval, Military or Air Force of the Union of India, a certificate by the Area or Sub-Area Commander within whose jurisdiction the premises are situated or by the Head of his service or his Commanding Officer that he has retired, or will retire, as such member and that he requires the premises for his own occupation and for the occupation of his family after retirement, or

(b) Where the landlord is the parent or the wife of such member of the naval, military or air force of the Union of India, as aforesaid, a certificate by the Area or Sub-Area Commander within whose jurisdiction the premises are situated that he or she is the parent or the wife, as the case may be, of such member of the naval, military or air force of the Union of India and that he or she requires the premises for his or her own occupation and for the occupation of his or her family after the retirement of such member, or

(c) Where the landlord is a relation (other than a minor child or the widow) and a dependent of a member of the naval, military or air force of the Union of India, and ordinarily resides with him or a minor child or the widow or such member who dies while in service or within five years of retirement, a certificate by the Area or Sub-Area Commander within whose jurisdiction the premises are situated that he or the relation and dependent as aforesaid or the minor child of the widow, as the case may be of the deceased member of the naval, military or air force, and requires the premises for his or her own occupation of his or her family, shall be produced before the Controller while filing the application, and such certificate shall be conclusive evidence of the fact stated therein.

No civil Court shall entertain any application by a landlord being a government employee, and who being in occupation of any residential premises allotted to him by his employer to vacate such residential accommodation, or in default to incur certain obligations on the ground that he owns a residential accommodation either in his own name or in the name of his wife or dependent child at or near the place where he is posted for the time being or by a landlord who has retired or will retired or will retire within a period of less than one year as a member of the Naval, Military or Air Force of the Union of India, or by a landlord who is a relation (other than a minor child or widow) and a dependent of a member of the naval, military or air force of the Union of India and ordinarily resides within or a minor child or the widow of such member who dies while in service or within five years of retirement for the recovery of possession of any premises. Section 13(h) of the same Act also provides that where a landlord is a member of the Armed Forces of the Union of India and requires it for occupation of his family and produces a certificate of the prescribed authority of Indian soldiers (Litigation) Act, 1925 that he is serving under special conditions, that certificate shall be conclusive evidence that the landlord is serving under special conditions or is posted in a non-family area.

The family for this purpose means parents and such relations of the landlord as ordinarily reside with him and are dependent on him.

Pension regulations for the Army 1961 Part I Rule 173. Grant of Disability pension whether Chief Controller of Defence Account (Pension) can override the opinion of the Medical Board. Relying on the judgment of the Supreme

Court and various High Courts, it was held – ability assessed by the Medical Board must be accepted by the CDA(Pension)

(Delhi High Court 2001 Military Law Journal 2002, Delhi-16)

Jammu & Kashmir

1. Cash awards to winners of Gallantry and Other awards

Jammu & Kashmir

	Cash Grant	*Cash in lieu of Land*	*Annuity*
Param Vir Chakra	22,500	1,50,000	1,000
Maha Vir Chakra	15,000	1,00,000	400
Vir Chakra	7,000	50,000	300
Ashok Chakra	20,000	1,25,000	-
Kirti Chakra	12,000	75,000	-
Shauarya Chakra	5,000	40,000	-
Sarvottam Yudh Seva Medal	17,000	-	-
Uttam Yudh Seva Medal	10,000	-	-
Yudh Seva Medal	4,000	-	-
Sena/Nao Sena/ Vayu Sena Medal	3,000	20,000	-
Mention-in-Despatches	2,000	10,000	-
PVSM	15,000	-	-
AVSM	7,000	-	-

2. Govt. of Jammu & Kashmir has reserved for serving Defence personnel, ex-servicemen and war widows, 2%, 2% and 1% respectively of the plots and flats available in each housing colony developed by the Govt. agencies vide Annexure to Govt. of J&K Order No. 192-HUD/CR of 1991. These are out of 5% of plots/flats available in each housing colony developed by the Govt. agencies under the discretionary quota of the Govt.

3. For restoration of possession to Defence personnel, vide J&K Houses and Shops Control Act, 1966, provisions have

been made for the restoration of possession to the Defence personnel. It provides "notwithstanding anything to the contrary in the Act, possession of the residential building shall be restored within one month from the date of the application if – (a) the landlord is a member of the Defence forces and requires it for occupation of his family and produces the certificate from his Commanding Officer showing that he is serving under special conditions within the meaning Section 3 of the Indian Soldiers' Litigation Act, 1925, (b) the landlord is a member of Defence forces and requires it for his owns occupation on retirement released or discharged from the Defence forces and produces a certificate from his Commanding Officer evidence of his release, retirement or discharge and (c) if the landlord is the wife of a deceased member of the Defence forces who requires it for her own occupation and produces a certificate from the Commanding Officer of her deceased husband to the effect that her husband died whilst serving under special conditions within the meaning of Section 3 of the Indian Soldiers' Litigation Act, 1925.

4. Jammu & Kashmir Agrarian Reforms Act, 1976 provides for the resumption of land. It provides:-

   Resumption of land permitted by sub-section (i) shall be subject to the following conditions, namely, (a) the application for the resumption shall be made in the prescribed manner within 6 months of the commencement of this Act; (b) the applicant for resumption shall, within 6 months of the commencement of this Act take up normal residence for the purpose of cultivating such land personally in the village in which the land sought to be resumed is situated or in an adjoining village except in the case of a person serving in Defence forces who shall take up such normal residence for personal cultivation within 6 months of the date on which he ceases to serve in the Defence forces.

The extent of land that may be resumed shall, subject to the provisions of sub-section (ii) be determined in the following manner, namely: (i), (ii), (iii) a person serving in Defence forces on or after the 1st day of April, 1965 or a widow or an orphan who is minor or a lunatic or an imbecile of an insane person or a person who is crippled or incapacitated by old age or infirmity shall be permitted to resume land 20% in excess of the land otherwise presumable under sub-clauses (i) or (ii).

5. Reservation of 5% and 10% vacancies in Group 'C' and Gp 'D' posts. Age relaxation upto 48 years.
6. Exemption from Sales Tax in CSD (D) canteens for ex-servicemen.
7. 5% reservation in house sites/houses.
8. Exemption of tuition fee for children of ex-servicemen upto post-graduate level.
9. Ex-gratia grant to killed/disabled over 50%:

   Officers – Rs. 50,000

   JCOs – Rs. 30,000

   Ors – Rs. 20,000

1. Grant of Rs. 750 for daughter's marriage to war widows/ disabled killed in war.

Himachal Pradesh

Ex-servicemen are exempted from the payment of examination/application fees in respect of applications for recruitment to State services vide Government of Himachal Pradesh letter No. 11/85/72-GA dated 15th March, 1974.

2. Ex-servicemen and serving soldiers are exempt from payment of municipal taxes like house-tax, property tax etc. in respect of the properties owned by them in urban area as vide Govt. of Himachal Pradesh, Deptt. of Urban Development Letter No. LSG-D(i)-9/94-3 dated 22nd June 2002.

3. **Eviction of tenants**

   Members of the armed forces may apply to the Controller for orders directing the tenants to put the landlord in possession if the landlord is a member of the armed forces and requires it for occupation for his family and he produces a certificate of the prescribed authority referred to in Section 7 of the Indian Soldiers' Litigation Act that he is serving in the special conditions within the meaning of Section 3 of that Act or is posted to a non-family station. A certificate of the prescribed authority shall be conclusive evidence that the landlord is serving under special conditions or is posted to a non-family station.

4. **War Jagirs**

   Vide Himachal Pradesh War Awards Act, Himachal Pradesh Government is empowered to award jagirs to parents whose children have served in the armed forces during the Emergency or serving or has served in the armed forces during the Emergency at the prescribed rates which vary according to the number of children serving under the armed forces. Such war jagirs are not liable for seizure or attachment by processes of any court at the instance of the creditors or in satisfaction of a decree or order of any court. Such war awards have been enhanced by the Himacahal Pradesh War Awards (Amendment Act, 1983).

5. 10 per cent reservation exists for allotment of house sites and houses. Similarly, 15 per cent of the Group 'A', 'B', 'C' & 'D' posts are reserved for ex-servicemen.

6. State Government also awards grant of Rs. 5000 on the marriage of the daughter, financial assistance to the widows of ex-servicemen at the time of death and lump-sum grant to the war widows for marriage of their daughters.

7. Cash awards for winners of gallantry awards and other awards are as under:-

	Cash Grant	*Cash in lieu of Land*	*Annuity*
Param Vir Chakra	22,500	1,50,000	1,000
Maha Vir Chakra	15,000	1,00,000	400
Vir Chakra	7,000	50,000	300
Ashok Chakra	-	-	600
Kirti Chakra	-	-	350
Shaurya Chakra	-	-	250
Sarvottam Yudh Seva Medal	18,000	-	600
Uttam Yudh Seva Medal	11,000	-	350
Yudh Seva Medal Sena/Nao Sena/ Vayu Sena Medal	3,000	20,000	250
Mention-in-Despatches	2,000	10,000	150
PVSM PSM	-	-	600
AVSM	-	-	350
VSM	-	-	250

Punjab

1. Cash awards to winners of Gallantry and other Awards:

	Cash Grant	*Cash in lieu of Land*	*Annuity*
Parama Vir Chakra	22,500	1,50,000	2,000
Maha Vir Chakra	15,000	1,00,000	800
Vir Chakra	7,000	50,000	600
Ashok Chakra	20,000	1,25,000	800
Kirti Chakra	12,000	75,000	350
Shauraya Chakra	5,000	40,000	250

(Contd.)

	Cash Grant	Cash in lieu of Land	Annuity
Sarvottam Yudh Seva Medal	17,000	-	800
Uttam Yudh Seva Medal	10,000	-	300
Yudh Seva Medal	4,000	-	250
Sena/Nao Sena/ Vayu Sena Medal	3,000	-	250
Mention-in-Despatches	3,000	-	150
PVSM	-	-	600
AVSM	-	-	350
VSM	-	-	250

2. Ex-servicemen are exempted from payment of examination fee, court fee, stamp duty and registration fee.
3. 12.5% National Route Permits are reserved for ex-servicemen.
4. Grant of exemption to ex-servicemen from payment of Municipal Taxes.
5. 10% reservation for allotment of house sites and houses.
6. War Jagir allowance of Rs. 300 per annum.
7. 15% reservation in each of the groups 'A', 'B', 'C' and 'D' posts.
8. Grant of Rs. 5,000 on the marriage of the daughter of a non-pensioner widow by State Govt.
9. Financial assistance to widows of ex-servicemen at the time of death of their husband – Rs. 500.
10. Lump sum grant of Rs. 15,000 to war widows for marriage of their daughter.

East Punjab Urban Rent Restriction Act, 1949 lays down grounds and procedure for eviction of tenants. Section 13(3)(1-a) of the said Act provides that, "In the case of a residential building, if the landlord is a member of the Armed Forces of the Union of India and requires it for the occupation of his family and if he produces a certificate of the prescribed authority referred to in Section 7 of the Indian Soldiers (Litigation) Act, 1925, that he is serving under special conditions within the meaning of Section 3 of that Act.

Explanation: The certificate of the prescribed authority shall be conclusive evidence that the landlord is serving under special conditions. Family means such relations of the landlord as ordinarily live with him and are dependent upon him.

Where an application made by member of Armed Forces, it shall be disposed of, as far as may be, within a period of one month and if the claim of the landlord is accepted the controller, shall make an order directing the tenant to put the landlord in possession of the building on a date to be specified in the order and such date shall not be later than fifteen days from the date of the order.

It would be seen from the above provision that it only extends to those members of the Armed Forces who are serving under special conditions within the meaning of Section 3 of Indian Soldiers (Litigation) Act, 1925. Hence the extent of effect of this provision is quite minimal.

Haryana

1. Cash awards to winners of Gallantry and other Awards.

	Cash Grant	*Cash in lieu of Land*	*Annuity*
Parama Vir Chakra	22,500	1,50,000	1 ,500
Maha Vir Chakra	15,000	1,00,000	600
Vir Chakra	7,000	50,000	450
Ashok Chakra	20,000	1,00,000	600
Kirti Chakra	12,000	50,000	450
Shaurya Chakra	5,000	30,000	300
Sena/Nao Sena/ Vayu Sena Medal	3,000	20,000	300
Mention-in-Despatches	3,000	10,000	150

2. Soldiers are exempted from the levy of Entertainment Duty.
3. War Jagir allowance @ 1,000 per annum enhanced by State govt. to the parents of only son or two more sons who served in Armed Forces during 1962 or 1971 emergencies.
4. Reservation of 5% posts in Gropup. 'A' and 'B' and 17% in Group 'C' and Gp 'D' posts for ex-servicemen.
5. Reservation of seats in professional institutions.
6. Financial assistance to widows of ex-servicemen at the time of death of their husband – Rs. 2,000.
7. Reservation of 5-20% house sites and industrial plots.
8. Wasteland of armed force personnel will not be taken over under utilization of Lands Act.
9. 10% reservation of houses, national permits and residential plots.
10. Exemption from levy of Sales Tax.
11. Stipend to children of ex-servicemen from Rs. 25 to Rs. 170.
12. Ex-gratia grant to war widows/disabled soldiers (above 50% disability).

    Officers - Rs. 50,000

    JCOs - Rs. 30,000

    Ors - Rs. 20,000
13. Free education upto 3 children upto degree class.
14. Daughter's, marriage of war widows/war disabled/orphans grant Rs. 6000/-.
15. Government of Haryana vide local govt. Directorate Notification No. 21/23/89-CER dated 5th June, 1993 have exempted house-tax on buildings and lands owned by ex-servicemen or their families under sub-section (2) of section 72 of the Haryana Municipal Act, 1973 occupied by self.

The relevant notification states..........In pursuance of the provisions of sub-section(2) of section 72 of the State Act, the governor of Haryana is pleased......to direct that the following properties shall be exempt from the payment of tax, namely.....

(9)......of buildings and lands owned by ex-servicemen or families of deceased soldiers ex-servicemen provided that they have no other residential house in Haryana State and residing in it themselves and have not let out any portion of the houses....

Provided further that the condition of letting out of the houses shall not apply to those who are in receipt of pension amounting to Rs. 375 per month or less.

Haryana Urban (Control of Rent and Eviction) Act 1973 lays down the grounds and procedure by which a tenant can be evicted by the landlord.

Grounds for Eviction for Members of the Armed Forces

Haryana Urban (Control of Rent and Eviction) Act 1973 Section 13(3)(a)(v) stipulates that, "a landlord may apply to the Controller for an order directing the tenant to put the landlord in possession in the case of residential building if he is a member of the armed forces and requires it for the occupation of his family and produces a certificate from the prescribed authority (authority competent to sanction leave of absence) that he is serving under special conditions within the meaning of Section 3 of Indian Soldiers Litigation Act, 1925 (as per Section 3 of ISL Act and Indian Soldier shall be deemed to be serving under special conditions when he is or has been serving under war conditions, or overseas or at any place beyond India or at any such place within India as may be specified by the Central Government by notification in the official Gazette".

For Non-residential Building

As per Section 13 (3a) of Haryana Urban (Control of Rent and Eviction) Act, 1973, "landlord who stands retired or discharged as a NCO from the Armed Forces or who was a minor son at the time of death of the deceased landlord, and requires it for his personal use, may within period of 3 years from the date of retirement or discharge or attaining the age of eighteen years apply to the Controller for an order directing the tenant to put the landlord in possession.

Time Limit for Eviction

A landlord who seeks to evict his tenant shall apply to the Controller for direction to that effect. If the Controller, after giving the tenant a reasonable opportunity of showing cause is satisfied, the Controller may make an order directing the tenant to put the landlord in possession of the building within such period as stipulated or extended.

If the application is made by a member of the Armed Forces, it shall be disposed of, as far as may be within a period of one month and if the claim of the landlord is accepted, the controller shall make an order directing the tenant to put the landlord in possession of the building or land on a date to be specified in the order and such date shall not be later than 15 days from the days of the order.

Delhi

1. Cash awards to winners of Gallantry and other Awards.

	Cash Grant	*Cash in lieu of Land*	*Annuity*
Parama Vir Chakra	1,00,000	-	-
Maha Vir Chakra	50,000	-	-
Vir Chakra	25,000	-	-
Ashok Chakra	50,000	-	-
Kirti Chakra	25,000	-	-
Shaurya Chakra	15,000	-	-
Sena/Nao Sena/ Vayu Sena Medal	5,000	-	-
Mention-in-Despatches	3,000	-	-

2. 10% reservation in Group 'C' posts and 20% in Group 'D' posts.
3. Reservation of houses – 1% (DDA).
4. Reservation of shops by DDA – 2%, Industrial Plots – 5%, ST Permits – 10%.
5. Grant for marriage of daughters of widows – Rs. 3,000.
6. Employment in Group 'C' and 'D' posts to war widows/ dependents of those killed/disabled in war.
7. 5% seats reserved in Medical and Engineering colleges to war widows/dependents of those killed/disabled in war.

For the benefit of members of the Armed Forces, Delhi Rent Control Act was amended in 1988 by insertion of Section 14B, vide Delhi Rent Control (Amendment) Act, 1988 (576 of 1988), Section 14B provides right to recover immediate possession of premises to accrue to members of the Armed Forces, etc.:

(1) Where the landlord:-
   (a) is a released or retired person from any armed forces and the premises let out by him are required for his own residence or
   (b) is a dependent of a member of any armed forces who had been killed in action and the premises let out by such members are required for the residence of the the family of such member, such person or as the case may be the dependent may, within one year from the date of his release or retirement from such armed forces or, as the case may be, the date of death of such member, or within a period of one year from the date of commencement of the Delhi Rent Control (Amendment) Act, 1988, whichever is later, apply to the Controller for recovering the immediate possession of such premises.

(2) Where the landlord is a member of any of the armed forces and has a period of less than one year preceding the date of his retirement and the premises let out by

him are required for his own residence after his retirement, he may, at any time, within a period of one year before the date of his retirement, apply to the Controller for recovering the immediate possession of such premises.

(3) Where the landlord referred to in sub-section (1) or (2) has let out more than one premises, it shall be open to him to make an application under that sub-section in respect of only one of the premises chosen by him.

Explanation: For the purpose of this section, "armed forces" means an armed force of the Union constituted under an Act of Parliament and includes a member of the police force constituted under Section 3 of the Delhi Police Act, 1978 (34 of 1978).

For the term "armed forces" in this context reference may be made to Sarasati Devi v. Distt. Magistrate of Deoria decided where it was held:

Armed Forces: The expression "armed forces" has also not being defined anywhere in the Act. However, ;the explanation to Section 14B states that for the purpose of Section 14B, "armed forces' mean an armed force of the Union constituted under an Act of Parliament and includes a member of the police force constituted under Section 3 of the Delhi Police Act, 1978. The explanation enlarges the scope of the expression "armed forces" by including a member of the police force constituted under Section 3 of the Delhi Police Act, 1978.

Armed Forces of the Union means the regular Army, Navy and Air Forces or any part of any one or more of them as defined in the Army Act, and it could never have meant the members of the National Cadet Corps who are not part of the regular Armed Forces of the Union.

Saraswati Devi v. District Magistrate of Deoria
AIR 1936 All 236

Madhya Pradesh

1. Cash awards to winners of Gallantry and other Awards:

	Cash Grant	Cash in lieu of Land	Annuity
Param Vir Chakra	25,000	75,000	-
Maha Vir Chakra	15,000	50,000	-
Vir Chakra	10,000	25,000	-
Ashok Chakra	25,000	50,000	-
Kirti Chakra	15,000	40,000	-
Shaurya Chakra	5,000	20,000	-
Sarvottam Yudh Seva Medal	15,000	-	-
Uttam Yudh Seva Medal	10,000	-	-
Yudh Seva Medal	5,000		
Sena/Nao Sena/ Vayu Sena Medal	5,000	-	-

2. Exemption of Excise Duty on Canteen items.
3. Reservation in Group 'B' posts – 2% Group 'C' – 3% and Group 'D' – 5%.
4. Reservation of house sites – 5%.
5. Reservation of seats in professional colleges.

Vide Rule 136(3) of Madhya Pradesh Municipal Corporation, a house owned by servicemen and ex-servicemen and their widows which is built by them during the life time for self-occupation, the house-tax is exempt vide Madhya Pradesh Municipal Corporation Amendment Rules, 1997.

Madhya Pradesh Accommodation Control Act has been amended vide Amendment Act of 1983 whereby under Section 23D (3) in respect of "an application by a landlord who is retired servant of any Government including a retired member of the Defence Services or a widow or physically handicapped person, it shall be presumed unless the contrary is proved that the requirement by the landlord with reference to clause (a) or clause (b), as the case may be, of Section 23A is bonafide."

Rajasthan

1. Cash awards to winners of Gallantry and other Awards.

	Cash Grant	*Land*	*Annuity*
Param Vir Chakra	15,000	25 Bigas	-
Maha Vir Chakra	7,000	25 Bigas	-
Vir Chakra	2,500	25 Bigas	-
Ashok Chakra	15,000	25 Bigas	-
Kirti Chakra	7,500	25 Bigas	-
Shaurya Chakara	2,500	-	-
Mention-in-Despatches	2,000	2,000	-

2. Reservation of seats in Group 'C' posts – 12.5% and Group 'D' posts – 15%.
3. Reservation in allotment of Industrial plots/sheds – 2%.
4. Exemption of Rent Tax to the war widows who own houses in any Municipality/Municipal Corporation of the State and are themselves residing therein or have sublet their houses from payment of Rent Tax, under Section 104 of the Rajasthan Municipality Act of 1959.
5. Marriage grant to daughters of ex-servicemen/widows – Rs. 4000.
6. Cash grant of Rs. 2,000 to war widows/dependants to those killed/disabled in war.
7. Irrigated land 25 bigas in canal area to the families of those killed or disabled in war.
8. Allotment of house-sites and constructed houses priority given. 10% reservation of plots and 2% of flats for widows and ex-servicemen.

9. Daughter's marriage grants Rs. 4,000 per daughter.
10. Exemption from payment of House Tax to the ex-servicemen, widows of ex-servicemen and their minor children who are not income-tax payers vide Notification No. Tax.F3L.SB, 72-78 dated 12-11-1975.
11. Vide Rajasthan Premises (Control of Act and Eviction) (Amendment) Ordinance, 1987, a new Section 16 in Rajasthan Act 17 of 1950 has been added which states, namely, Section 16 i.e. right of landlord to recover immediate possession in certain cases.

    (i) Notwithstanding anything to the contrary contained in this Act or any other law for the time being in force or in any contrast or usage, a landlord who was a member of the armed forces of the Union, his war widow, or his other legal representative shall on application being made in this behalf, be entitled to obtain an immediate order of abetment of the tenant from premises let out by such members thereof on any of the following grounds:-

    (a) that he has retired from service which will include compulsory or voluntary retirement, within a period of one year prior to the date of commencement of the Rajasthan Premises Ordinance 1987 or the date of making such application or

    (b) at any time prior to the commencement of the said ordinance subject to there being no agreement or lease in writing concerning such premises subsisting at the time of making such application and such premises having not being let out to the present tenant, on the allotment of the date of such retirement and that such premises are required for the use and occupation of himself or his family members or that she is war widow of a member of the armed forces of the Union and such premises are required for use and occupation of such war widows..................

(ii) a certificate issued by the Head of the Service in which the member of the armed forces is employed for the time being or his Commanding Officer to the effect that such member or his war widow or his other legal representative requires the premises for the use and occupation of himself or herself or the family members of such members on any of the grounds specified in clause (a), clause (b) and clause (c) of sub-section 1 shall conclusive evidence to the effects stated therein.

Uttar Pradesh

1. Cash awards to winners of Gallantry and other Awards:

	Cash Grant	*Cash in lieu of Land*	*Annuity*
Param Vir Chakra	2,00,000	-	1.000
Maha Vir Chakra	1,25,000	-	400
Vir Chakra	57,000	-	300
Ashok Chakra	20,000	-	200
Kirti Chakra	17,000	-	-
Shaurya Chakra	5,000	-	100
Sarvottam Yudh Seva Medal	1,25,000	-	150
Uttam Yudh Seva Medal	75,000	-	100
Yudh Seva Medal	35,000	-	100
Sena/Nao Sena/ Vayu Sena Medal	3,000	-	100
Mention-in-Despatches	2,000		
PVSM	15,000	-	400
AVSM	7,000	-	300
VSM	3,000	-	200

2. Reservation of 8% posts in Group 'A', Group 'B' (ECOs) and 3% in Group 'C' and 'D' posts.
3. Reservation of seats in professional colleges.
4. War Jagir allowance of Rs. 100 p.a. for 5 years.
5. Priority in allotment of Gram Sabha Land by Land Management Committee to service personnel killed/ disabled in war, landless ex-servicemen.
6. 5% reservation in allotment of house plots and shops.
7. Reservation in Medical/Eng/Polytechnic and Agricultural colleges.
8. Ex-gratia grant of Rs. 15,000 to families of service personnel killed and Rs. 10,000 to those disabled in action and boarded out in Operation Pawan and other operations.
9. Full exemption from tuition fee, hostel charges, costs of book stationery and uniform to the wards of widows/ those killed in action.
10. Daughter's marriage grant as per financial condition.
11. Rent Control Act and Land Tenancy Act have been amended to facilitate ex-servicemen in resumption of house/land.
12. 3% reservation in allotment of houses/plots and shops to the serving personnel, ex-servicemen and dependents of those killed in action built by UP Vikas Parishad and Vikas Pradhikaran of State.

Bihar

1. Cash awards to winners of Gallantry and Other Awards:

	Cash Grant	*Cash in lieu of Land*	*Annuity*
Param Vir Chakra	22,500	1,50,000	1000
Maha Vir Chakra	15,000	1,00,000	400
Vir Chakra	7,000	50,000	300
Ashok Chakra	20,000	1,25,000	800
Kirti Chakra	12,000	75,000	350
Shaurya Chakra	5,000	40,000	250
Sena/Nao Sena/ Vayu Sena Medal	17,000	1,10,000	600
Mention-in-Despatches	2,000	-	-

2. Reservation of Industrial plots/sheds – 50%.
3. Reservation of 10% house sites/houses.
4. Grant for one daughter's marriage amounting to Rs. 2,000.
5. 10% reservation for houses/house sites.
6. Allotment of surplus land to Armed Forces personnel and widows of service personnel killed in war.
7. Allotment of agricultural land 5 acres and 12-1/2 Dismal land housing to the dependents of those killed/disabled in war.
8. Rs. 10,000 financial assistance for house/flats repairs.
9. Daughters marriage grant of Rs. 2,000.
10. Special educational concessions to the wards of service personnel killed/disabled.
11. Favourable provisions in Rent Control Act for ex-servicemen to get their houses vacated from tenants.
12. Reservation of 10% in allotment of houses of Housing Boards.

Assam

1. Cash awards to winners of Gallantry and other Awards.

	Cash Grant	*Cash in lieu of Land*	*Annuity*
Param Vir Chakra	22,500	1,50,000	1000
Maha Vir Chakra	15,000	1,00,000	400
Vir Chakra	7,000	50,000	300
Ashok Chakra	20,000	1,25,000	800
Kirti Chakra	12,000	75,000	350
Shaurya Chakra	5,000	40,000	250
Sarvottam Yudh Seva Medal	17,000	1,10.000	600
Uttam Yudh Seva Medal	10,000	65,000	350
Yudh Seva Medal	4,000	30,000	250
Sena/Nao Sena/ Vayu Sena Medal	3,000	20,000	250
Mention-in-Despatches	2,000	10,000	150
PVSM	15,000	1.00.000	400
AVSM	7,000	50,000	300
VSM	3,000	2,000	250

2. Reservation of seats in professional colleges/technical institutions for the children of serving and ex-servicemen.
3. 5% reservation of industrial plots/sheds for ex-servicemen.
4. 2% reservation of vacancies for ex-servicemen in Group 'C', Group 'D' and posts in the State Government Depts.
5. Financial assistance of Rs. 500/- for funeral expenses at the death of ex-servicemen.
6. Preference in reservation of house sites/houses for ex-servicemen.
7. Daughter's marriage grant of Rs. 1000 to the widows of ex-servicemen.

8. Reservation of industrial plots/sheds – 50%.
9. Educational grant to the children of war widows/ dependents of those killed/disabled in war.
10. Interest subsidy on loan given to ex-servicemen for their self-employment ventures.
11. Favourable provisions in Rent Control Act for ex-servicemen to get their houses vacated from tenants.
12. Reservation of 10% in allotment of houses of Housing Boards.
13. 5% reservation of industrial plots/shops for ex-servicemen.

Tripura

1. Cash awards to winners of Gallantry and other awards:

	Cash Grant	*Cash in lieu of Land*	*Annuity*
Param Vir Chakra	22,500	-	-
Maha Vir Chakra	15,000	-	-
Vir Chakra	7,000	-	-
Ashok Chakra	20,000	-	-
Kirti Chakra	12,000	-	-
Shaurya Chakra	5,000	-	-
Sarvottam Yudh Seva Medal	17,000	-	-
Uttam Yudh Seva Medal	10,000	-	-
Yudh Seva Medal	4,000	-	-
Sena/Nao Sena/ Vayu Sena Medal	3,000	-	-
Mention-in-Despatches	2,000	-	-
PVSM	15,000	-	-
AVSM	7,000	-	-
VSM	3,000	-	-

2. 2% reservation in Group 'C' and Group 'D' posts.
3. Reservation of seats for children of defence personnel/ ex-servicemen in Engs/Technical College/Polytechnic etc.
4. Reservation for national permit for ex-servicemen.
5. 10% reservation of house sites/houses.
6. Ex-gratia grant of Rs. 2500 to war widows/dependants of those killed/disabled in war.
7. Exemption of house tax to war widows/dependents of those killed/disabled in war.
8. Allotment of agricultural land to war widows/dependents of those killed/disabled in action.
9. Ex-servicemen irrespective of their level of income are exempted from payment of house tax vide letter No. 110/EV/Ad.III dated 27th June, 1983. However, they are to pay water, light and conservancy charges.
10. Vide Tripura Buildings(Lease) Rent Control (Amendment) Act, 1982, members of the armed forces or such a member and is duly retired which will include premature retirement shall be entitled to recover possession of any premises on the ground that the premises are bonafidely required by him for occupation for himself or any member of his family and Rent Controller can pass a decree for eviction on such grounds if the landlord at the hearing of the suit produces a certificate signed by the Head of the Service or a Commanding Officer to the effect that he is presently a member of the armed forces or was such member and he does not possess any other suitable residence in the local area where he or the members of his family wish to reside. For the purpose of this Section, the term Head of Service means in case of Indian Army, the Area Commander and in the case of the officer who retired from Navy, include the Flag Officer of the Commanding in Chief and in case of an officer retires from Air Force include the Station Commander.

11. For the purpose of this Section, any certificate granted therein shall be inclusive evidence stated therein.
12. In addition, an ex-gratia assistance in the event of death due to insurgency/violence is payable to the members of the armed forces and para-military forces etc. to the extent of Rs. 1,50,000. This is in addition to any other benefit they are entitled from the Central Government (Govt. of Tripura Memorandum No. F.11(1)-FIN(G)/94 dated 4th June, 1998).

Mizoram

1. Cash awards to winners of Gallantry and other awards:

	Cash Grant	*Cash in lieu of Land*	*Annuity*
Param Vir Chakra	22,500	-	-
Maha Vir Chakra	15,000	-	-
Vir Chakra	7,000	-	-
Ashok Chakra	20,000	-	-
Kirti Chakra	12,000	-	-
Shaurya Chakra	5,000	-	-
Sarvottam Yudh Seva Medal	17,000	-	-
Uttam Yudh Seva Medal	10,000	-	-
Yudh Seva Medal	4,000	-	-
Sena/Nao Sena/ Vayu Sena Medal	3,000	-	-
Mention-in-Despatches	2,000	-	-
PVSM	15,000	-	-
AVSM	7,000	-	-
	3,000	-	-

2. Old age pension of Rs. 100 p.m. to ex-servicemen above 60 years.

3. Exemption from payment of House Tax when occupied by self. (Notification dated 16.9.92).
4. Reservation in Group 'C' posts – 10% and Group 'D' posts – 20%.
5. Ex-gratia grant of Rs. 10,000 for all ranks.
6. Remission of house and land revenue for ex-servicemen and during the life time of widow only. (Notification No. IRR/A-96-88 of 16.9.92).
7. Exemption from house tax to war widows/dependents of those killed/disabled in war.

Sikkim

1. Cash awards to winners of Gallantry and other awards:

	Cash Grant	*Cash in lieu of Land*	*Annuity*
Parama Vir Chakra	22,500	1,50,000	1000
Maha Vir Chakra	15,000	1,00,000	400
Vir Chakra	7,000	50,000	300
Ashok Chakra	20,000	1,25,000	800
Kirti Chakra	12,000	75,000	350
Shaurya Chakra	5,000	40,000	250
Sarvottam Yudh Seva Medal	17,000	-	600
Uttam Yudh Seva Medal	10,000	-	350
Yudh Seva Medal	4,000	-	250
Sena/Nao Sena/ Vayu Sena Medal	3,000	-	250
Mention-in-Despatches	3,000	-	150
PVSM	-	-	400
AVSM	-	-	300
VSM	-	-	250

2. Reservation in both Group 'C' and 'D' posts.
3. Reservation in allotment of houses – 5%.
4. Exemption from payment of house tax and entertainment tax.
5. War Jagair allowance of Rs. 1000 p.a. and Jangi Inam @ Rs. 5 per month.
6. Financial assistance of Rs. 1000 to widow on death of her husband.
7. Daughter's marriage grant – Rs. 1000 each upto two daughters.
8. Ex-gratia grant of Rs. 10,000 all ranks for those killed or disabled in war.
9. Vide Govt. of Sikkim Gazette Extraordinary dated 2nd August 2002, electricity upto 100 units is exempt, For units 101 and above, the electricity charges is on concessional rates.
10. Ex-servicemen and widows of ex-servicemen of the age of 50 years and above are entitled to travel free of charge throughout the State in all buses operated by the Transport Department, Govt. of Sikkim vide Notification dated 2nd March, 2002.

Meghalaya

1. Reservation of house sites – 10% for ex-servicemen.
2. Funeral expenses for the ex-servicemen/their families/ widows Rs. 1000.
3. Financial assistance to widows at the time of death of their families/widows Rs. 1000.
4. Ex-gratia grants of Rs. 5000 to each war widows/dependents as and when such casualty occurs.

Pondicherry

1. Cash awards to winners of Gallantry and other awards:

	Cash Grant	*Cash in lieu of Land*	*Annuity*
Parama Vir Chakra	1,50,000	-	500
Maha Vir Chakra	15,000	-	-
Vir Chakra	7,000	-	-
Ashok Chakra	20,000	-	-
Kirti Chakra	12,000	-	-
Shaurya Chakra	5,000	-	-
Sarvottam Yudh Seva Medal	17,000	-	-

2. Reservation in Group 'C' posts – 10% and Group 'D' posts – 20%. Provision for carry forward, unfilled vacancies for one year.
3. 2% reservation for house sites and houses.
4. 3% reservation for children of serving/retired defence personnel in professional colleges. Death relief grant/funeral allowance – Rs. 1000. Grant for any one daughter of ex-servicemen/widow – Rs. 3,000.

West Bengal

1. Cash awards to winners of Gallantry and other awards:

	Cash Grant	*Cash in lieu of Land*	*Annuity*
Parama Vir Chakra	22,500	1,50,000	1000
Maha Vir Chakra	15,000	1,00,000	400
Vir Chakra	7,000	50,000	300
Ashok Chakra	20,000	1,25,000	800

(Contd.)

	Cash Grant	*Cash in lieu of Land*	*Annuity*
Kirti Chakra	12,000	75,000	350
Shaurya Chakra	5,000	40,000	250
Sarvottam Yudh Seva Medal	17,000	-	600
Uttam Yudh Seva Medal	10,000	-	350
Yudh Seva Medal	4,000	-	250
Sena/Nao Sena/ Vayu Sena Medal	3,000	-	250
Mention-in-Despatches	3,000	-	150
PVSM	-	-	400
AVSM	-	-	300
VSM	-	-	250

2. 5-10% reservation in Group 'C' and Group 'D' posts.
3. 5% reservation each in allotment of house site and houses constructed by WBHB.
4. Marriage grant given for the daughters of ex-servicemen – Rs. 2,000.
5. Ex-gratia grants: Officers – Rs. 5,000, JCO – Rs. 3,000 and Ors – Rs. 2,000.
6. Education stipends for children upto Rs. 100 p.m.
7. Free travel by State Govt. buses and trams.
8. Stipend @ Rs. 200 p.m. plus Rs. 315 as book grant for student of Engg./Medical/Professional courses of war widows/those killed disabled in action.
9. Vide West Bengal (Amendment) Act, 1977 Section 12, the property tax in respect of any property belonging to ex-servicemen, family of the deceased soldiers who has no other land or building in any part of the State and property owned in Calcutta is exempt from the property tax.

Arunachal Pradesh

1. Cash awards to winners of Gallantry and other awards:

	Cash Grant	*Cash in lieu of Land*	*Annuity*
Parama Vir Chakra	22,500	1,50,000	1000
Maha Vir Chakra	15,000	1,00,000	400
Vir Chakra	7,000	50,000	300
Ashok Chakra	20,000	1,25,000	800
Kirti Chakra	12,000	75,000	350
Shaurya Chakra	5,000	40,000	250
Sarvottam Yudh Seva Medal	17,000	-	600
Uttam Yudh Seva Medal	10,000	-	350
Yudh Seva Medal	4,000	-	250
Sena/Nao Sena/ Vayu Sena Medal	3,000	-	250
Mention-in-Despatches	3,000	-	150
PVSM	-	-	400
AVSM	-	-	300
VSM	-	-	250

2. 5%, 10% and 20% reservation in Group 'B', Group 'C' and Group 'D' posts respectively.
3. Exemption from tuition fees for dependents of ex-servicemen.
4. Financial assistance of Rs. 50 p.m. to widow of ex-servicemen not entitled to family pension.
5. Special schemes for employment to war widows/ dependents of those killed/disabled in war.
6. Reservation/preferential allotment of plot/flat from State Housing Board/Development Authority to the war widows.

Maharashtra

1. Cash awards to winners of Gallantry and other awards:

	Cash Grant	*Cash in lieu of Land*	*Annuity*
Parama Vir Chakra	22,500	1,50,000	-
Maha Vir Chakra	15,000	1,00,000	-
Vir Chakra	7,000	50,000	-
Ashok Chakra	20,000	1,25,000	-
Kirti Chakra	12,000	75,000	-
Shaurya Chakra	5,000	40,000	-
Yudh Seva Medal	17,000	1,10,000	-

2. Reservation in Group 'C' and Group 'D. posts – 15%.
3. 5% reservation of seats in Medical College, Eng, Agriculture College etc.
4. Rs. 5,000 and Rs. 1000 respectively to widows or parents of those killed or disabled in war.
5. Allotment of flats on preferential basis – 5%.
6. Daughter's marriage grant – Rs. 2000 upto three daughters.
7. House construction grant of Rs. 40,000 for war widows.
8. Allotment of land for cultivation and house to the dependents of those killed in action.
9. Rent Control Act and Rent Tenancy Act have been amended to facilitate resumption of household/land by ex-servicemen. (See Houses, Rent and Evictions Section).
10. Rs. 2 lakh as financial assistance for dependents of those killed in any operation w.e.f. May, 1995.
11. Rs. 50,000 as financial assistance for disabled persons having more than 50% and 25,000 and Rs. 25,000 financial disability between 20-50% in any action or operation.

12. World War II veterans are given Rs. 600 p.m. as financial assistance.

Goa

1. Cash awards to winners of Gallantry and other awards:

	Cash Grant	*Cash in lieu of Land*	*Annuity*
Param Vir Chakra	22,500	1,50,000	-
Maha Vir Chakra	15,000	1,00,000	-
Vir Chakra	7,000	50,000	-
Ashok Chakra	20,000	1,25,000	-
Kirti Chakra	12,000	75,000	-
Shaurya Chakra	5,000	40,000	-
Sarvottam Yudh Seva Medal	17,000	1,10,000	-

2. Reservation of 10% and 20% posts in Group 'C' and Group 'D' posts.
3. 2% reservation for house sites and houses for ex-servicemen.
4. Rent Control Act amended to enable ex-servicemen to get rented houses back for their bonafide use.
5. Grant of Rs. 2,000 for marriage of daughter of war widows/ ex-servicemen.
6. Financial assistance of Rs. 500 to the widow at the time of death of her husband.
7. Necessary provision exists in the land revenue code giving preference to ex-servicemen in allotment of Govt. land.
8. War Jagir allowance to the parents whose child/children has joined the defence forces at the time of grant w.e.f. 1st April, 2000.
9. Rs. 5000 as travel and incidental expenses to ex-servicemen.

10. Rs. 5,000 as lump-sum grant on the death of a pensioner.

Karnataka

1. Cash awards to winners of Gallantry and other Awards:

	Cash Grant	*Cash in lieu of Land*	*Annuity*
Param Vir Chakra	22,500	1,50,000	1000
Maha Vir Chakra	15,000	1,00,000	400
Vir Chakra	7,000	50,000	300
Ashok Chakra	20,000	1,25,000	800
Kirti Chakra	12,000	75,000	350
Shaurya Chakra	5,000	40,000	250
Sarvottam Yudh Seva Medal	17,000	1,10,000	800
Uttam Yudh Seva Medal	10,000	65,000	350
Yudh Seva Medal	4,000	30,000	250
Sena/Nao Sena/ Vayu Sena Medal	3,000	20,000	250
Mention-in-Despatches	2,000	10,000	150

2. 5-9% reservation for house sites/houses for service personnel and ex-servicemen.
3. 10% reservation in each of the Groups 'A', 'B', 'C' and 'D' posts.
4. Ex-gratia grant of Rs. 10,000 to war widows/dependents of those killed/disabled in war.
5. Marriage grant for daughter Rs. 4,000.
6. Two acres of wet or four acres of rainfed or eight acres of dry land are given to the families of service personnel killed in action free of cost. If land is not available for allotment, a cash grant of Rs. 25,000 is given to the war widows.

7. House of 550 sq. ft. For officers, 350 sq. ft. for other ranks built on site, allotted by the State Govt.
8. Under Karnataka Land Reforms (Amendment) Act, 2003, Section 77 of the main Act has been amended to include the landless persons or other persons residing in villages in same panchayat area whose gross annual income does not exceed Rs. 20,000 and ex-military personnel has been added.
9. Similarly, Kartnataka Act, 1999 as vide Section 29 laid down that where the landlord is a released or retired person from any of the armed forces of the Union and the premises let out by him is used or his dependents/ sons or daughters are required for his own use or where such member having been killed in action, the premises let out by such members are required for the use of the family of such members, such persons, his spouse or the dependents as the case may be, may within one year from the date of his release/retirement or the date of his death or date of death of such member or within one year from the date of the amendment of this Act, whichever is later, apply to the court for recovery of the immediate possession of such person and such court will pass order accordingly.

   For the purpose of this Section, immediate possession shall mean possession recoverable on the expiry of 60 days from the date of order of eviction.
10. Provisions have been made vide Karnataka State War Awards (Amendment) Rule, 1996 to provide for War Jagir allowance @ Rs. 450 per annum where his only son or only child has joined the armed forces of the Union.
11. Children of defence personnel killed or disabled in action and studying in educational institutions under the Department of Education are entitled to complete exemption and other fees levied by such educational institutions vide AG's Branch Army HQ letter No. 56368/ Policy/AG/CW-3(b) dated 17th August, 1990.

12. Similarly, admissions to professional colleges like medical and engineering (around 20 seats in MBBS, 1 seat in BDS and 2 seats in engineering college – Annamalai University) are available to KSB for widows and war widows and those killed/disabled in action or died while in service or disabled in service due to military service.

Tamil Nadu

1. Cash awards to winners of Gallantry and other Awards:

	Cash Grant	*Cash in lieu of Land*	*Annuity*
Param Vir Chakra	22,500	-	500
Maha Vir Chakra	15,000	-	-
Vir Chakra	7,000	-	-
Ashok Chakra	20,000	-	-
Kirti Chakra	12,000	-	-
Shaurya Chakra	5,000	-	-
Sarvottam Yudh Seva Medal	17,000	-	-
Uttam Yudh Seva Medal	10,000	-	-
Yudh Seva Medal	4,000	-	-
Sena/Nao Sena/ Vayu Sena Medal	3,000	-	-
Mention-in-Despatches	2,000	-	-
PVSM	15,000	-	-
AVSM	7,000	-	-
	3,000	-	

2. Reservation in allotment of plots/industrial sheds – 10% to ex-servicemen.
3. 7% reservation in allotment of house sites and houses for ex-servicemen/widows.
4. Reservation of seats in professional colleges.

5. Grant of Rs. 2500 is paid for marriage of one daughter of an ex-servicemen.
6. Subsidy of Rs. 25,000 for construction of industrial sheds/ purchase of plots to ex-servicemen.
7. Daughter's marriage grant – Rs. 25,000.
8. Free education to the children of war widow/dependents of those killed/disabled in war.
9. Ex-gratia grant of Rs. 15,000 for other ranks only.
10. 7% houses constructed by State Housing Board reserved for serving and retired person and widows.
11. Financial grant of Rs. 1000 p.a. for war widows for 10 years and thereafter Rs. 750 p.a. for life time.
12. Daughter's marriage grant – Rs. 5000 to war widows/ those killed/disabled in action.
13. Exemption from House Tax to the widows/those killed/ disabled in action and gallantry award winners.
14. Land Tenancy Act and Rent Control Act have been amended for exemption of land and houses for ex-servicemen.
15. Property in assignment in land, 3 acres of dry land and 1.5 acres of wet land for war widows and dependents of those killed in action.
16. Allotment of HSG houses/flats free of cost to the ex-servicemen for operation 'Vijay'.

Gujarat

1. Cash awards to winners of Gallantry and other Awards:

	Cash Grant	*Cash in lieu of Land*	*Annuity*
Param Vir Chakra	22,500	-	
Maha Vir Chakra	15,000	-	-
Vir Chakra	7,000	-	-
Ashok Chakra	20,000	-	-

(Contd.)

	Cash Grant	Cash in lieu of Land	Annuity
Kirti Chakra	12,000	-	-
Shaurya Chakra	5,000	-	-
Sarvottam Yudh Seva Medal	17,000	-	-
Uttam Yudh Seva Medal	10,000	-	-
Yudh Seva Medal	4,000	-	-
Sena/Nao Sena/ Vayu Sena Medal	3,000	-	-
Mention-in-Despatches	2,000	-	-
PVSM	15,000	-	-
AVSM	7,000	-	-
	3,000	-	

2. Grant of surplus land upto 16 acres to war widows.
3. 10% reservation of seats in different educational institutions for the children/dependents of defence personnel.
4. Reservation of seats in different educational institutions for the children/dependents of defence personnel.
5. 10% and 20% reservation in Group 'C' and 'D' posts respectively.
6. Lump sum grant of Rs. 4,000 to 6,000 for two daughter's marriage of indigent ex-servicemen/widow.
7. 25% reservation of vacancies in veterinary service.
8. Emergency and short service commission officers – fixation of pay in the civil posts on appointment to unreserved vacancies – provision of.
9. Funeral expenses upto Rs. 1,000 are given to indigent widows of ex-servicemen.

10. Rent Control Act and Land Tenancy Act amended in favour of ex-servicemen/widows/dependents.
11. Land for agricultural activities upto 16 acres to next of kin of martyrs of operation 'Vijay' irrespective of rank and tenure of service.
12. Two acres of land for construction of houses for next of kin of operation 'Vijay' of martyrs in urban areas.

Kerala

1. Cash awards to winners of Gallantry and other Awards:

	Cash Grant	*Cash in lieu of Land*	*Annuity*
Param Vir Chakra	22,500	1,50,000	1000
Maha Vir Chakra	15,000	1,00,000	500
Vir Chakra	7,000	50,000	300
Ashok Chakra	20,000	1,25,000	600
Kirti Chakra	12,000	75,000	350
Shaurya Chakra	5,000	50,000	250
Sarvottam Yudh Seva Medal	17,000	1,10,000	800
Uttam Yudh Seva Medal	10,000	65,000	350
Yudh Seva Medal	4,000	30,000	250
Sena/Nao Sena/ Vayu Sena Medal	3,000	20,000	250
Mention-in-Despatches	2,000	10,000	150

2. Financial assistance of Rs. 1000 as marriage grant for daughter's marriage of poor ex-servicemen, annual income less than Rs. 9,000 p.a.
3. Rs. 500 ex-gratia grant on death to widow of ex-servicemen, whose annual income is below Rs. 9.000 p.a.

4. 3% reservation each for allotment of house sites and houses for ex-servicemen.
5. Reservation of 10% of surplus land for ex-servicemen in each village.
6. 4.5% reservation of industrial plots/sheds.
7. Grant to ex-servicemen for marriage of their daughters – Rs. 1,000
8. Immediate grant of Rs. 5 lakh to each dependent of those killed in action disabled in war, Rs. 1 lakh to serious wounded persons. In case of other injuries, such amount will be decided depending upon the gravity of each case.
9. Reservation in all professional courses.
10. Widows are exempted from payment of house tax.
11. Rent Control Act has been amended for the benefit of ex-servicemen.
12. 3% reservation each for allotment of house sites and houses for ex-servicemen.

Chandigarh

1. Cash awards to winners of Gallantry and other Awards:

	Cash Grant	*Cash in lieu of Land*	*Annuity*
Param Vir Chakra	22,500	1,50,000	4200
Maha Vir Chakra	15,000	1,00,000	3000
Vir Chakra	7,000	50,000	2400
Ashok Chakra	20,000	1,25,000	600
Kirti Chakra	12,000	75,000	3000
Shaurya Chakra	5,000	40,000	2100
Sarvottam Yudh Seva Medal	17,000	1,10,000	1200

(Contd.)

	Cash Grant	*Cash in lieu of Land*	*Annuity*
Uttam Yudh Seva Medal	10,000	65,000	1200
Yudh Seva Medal	4,000	30,000	250
Sena/Nao Sena/ Vayu Sena Medal	3,000	20,000	250
Mention-in-Despatches	2,000	10,000	150
PVSM	15,000	1,00,000	400
AVSM	7,000	50,000	300
VSM	3,000	20,000	250

2. 10% reservation in Group 'C' posts and 20% in Group 'D' posts.
3. Reservation in allotment of houses 6% for ex-servicemen.
4. Rs. 300 p.a. War Jagir allowance to parents of children who have served in the Armed Forces in 1962 and 1971 Operations.
5. 5% reservation in ITI and Govt. Crafts Institute for Women.
6. Grant of Rail travel concession to war widows/dependents of those killed/disabled in war.
7. 50% fare concession in CTU buses in U.T. to war widows/ dependents of those killed/disabled in war.
8. Daughters marriage grant to ex-servicemen/widow Rs. 5,000.
9. Rent Control and Land Tenancy Act have been amended to facilitate ex-servicemen in resumption of their houses/ lands.
10. East Punjab Urban Land Restriction (Amendment) Act, 1985 has been extended to Union Territory of Chandigarh on 15th December, 1996 by Notification GSR 1287(E).

Orissa

1. Cash awards to winners of Gallantry and other Awards:

	Cash Grant	*Cash in lieu of Land*	*Annuity*
Param Vir Chakra	22,500	-	
Maha Vir Chakra	15,000	-	-
Vir Chakra	7,000	-	-
Ashok Chakra	20,000	-	-
Kirti Chakra	12,000	-	-
Shaurya Chakra	5,000	-	-
Sarvottam Yudh Seva Medal	17,000	-	-
Uttam Yudh Seva Medal	10,000	-	-
Yudh Seva Medal	4,000	-	-
Sena/Nao Sena/ Vayu Sena Medal	3,000	-	-
Mention-in-Despatches	2,000	-	-
PVSM	15,000	-	-
AVSM	7,000	-	-
	3,000	-	

2. Reservation of 3% seats in each of the Group 'B' 'C' and 'D' posts.
3. 5% reservation in allotment of houses. Priority allotment of house sites.
4. Reservation of seats in professional colleges for children of serving/retired defence personnel.
5. Exemption of Municipal Holding tax.
6. Ex-gratia grant to next of kin of casualties of IPKF killed, wounded and missing is Rs. 10,000, Rs. 5,000 and Rs. 4,000 respectively to war widows/dependents to those killed/disabled in war.

7. Chief Minister has announced Rs. 2 lakh to next of kin of those killed in Operation Vijay, Kargil Sector.
8. One plot 40′ × 60′ to be allotted at Bhubaneswar to next of kin of martyrs of Operation Vijay.

Andaman & Nicobar Islands

1. Reservation of Group 'C' posts – 10% and Gp. 'D' posts – 20%.
2. Old age grant of Rs. 100/- p.m.
3. Free medical treatment in Government hospitals.
4. Stipend to ex-servicemen trainees in agriculture and other trades.

15

Extracts from Some Rare Rules and Notifications

More often than not, when a particular legal provision is sought to be cited in support of a particular proposition it becomes necessary to see the provision in the entire context and then place it before the court or the authority, where such proposition is being made. To locate the authority, at times, becomes a daunting task. This is particularly true when the provision is contained in a special law, which is not easily traceable.

To overcome this problem, it was considered necessary to reproduce some of the Rules and Notifications which are not readily available.

Rules which were issued to meet the special problems/ situations arising out of 1962, 1965 and 1971 wars have not been included since it was felt that cases relating thereto have long been settled.

Therefore, an effort has been made to include only those provisions which are useful but are not readily and easily available. This, it is hoped, will be of great help to those who need them for practical use.

The Indian Soldiers (Litigation) Rules, 1938

Contents

No. 455 dated the 14th May, 1938. In exercise of the powers conferred by Section 13 of the Indian Soldiers (Litigation) Act, 1925 (4 of 1925), the Central Government, after consulting the High Courts concerned, is pleased to make the following rules, namely:-

1. These rules may be called the Indian Soldiers (Litigation) Rules, 1938.
2. Ommitted.

   2 (i) In these rules "the Act" means the Indian Soldiers (Litigation) Act, 1925 (4 of 1925)

   All words used herein and defined in the Act shall be deemed to have the meaning respectively attributed to them by the Act.
3. The prescribed authority for the purposes of sub-clause (iv) if clause (b) of Section 3 and Section 6, 7 and 8 of the Act shall be the authority competent to sanction leave of absence to an Indian Soldier.

Authority – The Indian Soldiers (Litigation) (Amendment) Rules, 1971

4. The certificate given by a Collector under Section of the Act shall be in Form A of the Schedule.

5. (1) The notice given by the Court under Section 6 of the Act shall be in Form B of the Schedule and shall be sent:-

   (a) In the case of persons subject to the Army Act, 1950, to the prescribed authority, care of the General Officer Commanding-in-Chief of the Command in which the Court is situated and

   (b) In the case of persons subjects to the Air Force Act, 1950, to the prescribed authority care of the Assistant Chief of the Air Staff (Personnel), Air Headquarters, New Delhi.

   (2) The certificate of the prescribed authority under Section 7 of the Act shall be in form C9 of the Schedule.

   Authority – The Indian Soldiers (Litigation) (Amendment) Rules 1971

6. If at any time it appears to the prescribed authority that the circumstances in which he certified to the Court under Section 7 of the Act that a postponement of the proceedings was necessary in the interests of justice, no longer exists, he shall forthwith certify to the Court to that effect of Form D of the Schedule.

7. On receipt of a certificate from the prescribed authority under Section 7 of the Act that a postponement of the proceedings is necessary in the interests of justice, the Court shall postpone the proceedings until the receipt of a certificate in Form D from the prescribed authority or until the soldier is represented in

the proceedings by some person duly authorized to appear, plead or act in his behalf.

8. The prescribed authority for the purposes of Section 12 of the Act shall be:-

   (a) in the case of persons subjects to the Army Act, 1950, the General Officer Commanding-in-Chief of the Command in which the Court is situated and

   (b) In the case of persons subject to the Air Force Act, 1950, to the Assistant Chief of the Air Staff (Personnel), Air Headquarters, New Delhi.

Authority – The Indian Soldiers (Litigation) (Amendment) Rules, 1971.

Schedule

Form A

Collector's certificate under Section 5 of the Indian Soldiers (Litigation) Act, 1925.

From

The Collector,

District..................

To

....

....

In ref...........................No....................of 19.............

....

No. dated

Sir,

I have the honour to certify under Section 5 of the Indian Soldiers(Litigation) Act, 1925 (4 of 1925), that I have reason to believe that.......son of........who is an Indian soldier ordinarily residing/having property in my district and who is a party in the above-mentioned (enter name of Court), is unable to appear therein.

Yours faithfully

Collector

Notes:-

(1) This certificate should be sent by post in a registered cover or by hand and an acknowledgement should be obtained for it.

(2) It should be addressed in the case of a High Court, to the Registrar of the Court, or in the case of a Board of Revenue, to The Secretary of such Board or in the case of a Financial Commissioner, to the Clerk of the Court, or in other cases, To the Presiding Officer of the Court

Form B.

Notice under Section 6 of the Indian Soldiers (Litigation) Act, 1925.

In ref...

No...of.......................................

Versus

To

The Officer Commanding (enter name of unit/depot of unit)

Care of the General Officer Commanding-in-Chief

....Command

Please take notice that upon the certificate of the Collector of........under Section 5 of the Indian Soldiers (Litigation) Act,

1925 (4 of 1925) having had reason to believe that ....son of..........an Indian soldier who is a party in the above-mentioned proceeding now pending in this Court and is not represented by any person duly authorized to appear, plead or act on his behalf, is unable to appear therein, this Court has, under Section 6 of the said Act, suspended the proceedings. If, within the period prescribed in Section 8 of the said Act, no certificate is received from you under Section 7 thereof, the Court will, if it thinks fit, continue the proceeding.

Given under my hand and the seal of the Court, this the ......day of....19... The Presiding Officer of the Court/Registrar

(i) For the words and brackets "The Officer Commanding (enter name of Unit/depot of unit)" the expression "The prescribed Authority" shall be substituted.

(ii) For the words "Care of the General Officer Commanding-in-Chief..............Command" the following shall be substituted, namely; "Care of the General Officer Commanding-in-Chief ....Command", the Assistant Chief of the Air Staff (Personnel), Air Headquarters, New Delhi.

(iii) In the text of the form in line 4, for the word "that" the expression "that" shall be substituted.

The Prescribed Authority is the authority competent to sanction leave of absence to an Indian soldier. On receipt of the notice from the Court, the General Officer Commanding-in-Chief/Assistant Chief of the Air Staff (Personnel) (as the case may be) shall cause the notice to be forwarded, as soon as possible to the authority competent to sanction leave of absence to the Indian soldier concerned. The time limit within which the prescribed authority's certificate should reach the Court is two months in the case of a soldier resident in the district in which the Court is situated, and three months in other cases. Section 8 of the Indian Soldiers (Litigation) Act, 1925, refers

Authority – The Indian Soldiers
(Litigation) (Amendment) Rule, 1971

Note:

This notice should be sent by post in a registered cover or by hand and an acknowledgement should be obtained for it.

Form C

Certificate under Section 7 of the Indian Soldiers (Litigation) Act. 1925.

From

The Officer Commanding (enter name of Unit/depot of unit).

To

No.........................of........................19......

Versus

No............................dated............................

Sir,

I have the honour to acknowledge receipt of your notice dated.......under Section 6 of the Indian Soldiers (Litigation) Act, 1925 (4 of 1925) in the above-mentioned proceeding, and to certify under Section 7 of the said Act that........son of.........in respect of whom the above-mentioned notice has been given, is serving under special conditions and that a postponement of the proceeding in respect of that soldier is necessary in the interests of justice.

(i) For the words and brackets "The Officer Commanding (enter name of unit/depot of unit.)" the following shall be substituted namely:-

....

(ii) For the words "Officer Commanding", below the words "Yours faithfully", the words "Prescribed Authority" shall be substituted.

Authority – The Indian Soldiers (Litigation) (Amendment) Rules, 1971

Yours faithfully

Prescribed Authority

Notes:-

(1) This certificate should be sent by post in a registered cover, or by hand and an acknowledgement should be obtained for it.

(2) It should be addressed in the case of a High Court, to the Registrar of the Court, or in the case of a Board of Revenue to the Secretary of such Board, or in the case of a Financial Commissioner, to the Clerk of the Court, or in other cases to the Presiding Officer of the Court.

Form D

Certificate under Rule 6 of the Indian Soldiers (Litigation) Rules, 1938

From..

To ....

In ref..............................No................of......................19

Versus

No.......................dated..

Sir,

I have the honour to invite a reference to my letter No...........Dated..........and to certify under Rule 6 of the Indian Soldiers (Litigation) Rules, 1938 that circumstances no longer exist for the postponement of the above-mentioned (enter name of Court) wherein ....son of.....as Indian soldier, is a party.

(Yours faithfully)

Prescribed Authority

Notes:-

(1) This certificate should be sent by post in a registered cover, or by hand and an acknowledgement should be obtained for it.

(2) It should be addressed, in the case of High Court, to the Registrar of the Court, or in the case of a Board of Revenue to the Secretary of such Board, or in the case of Financial Commissioner, to the Clerk of the Court, or in other cases to the Presiding Officer of the Court.

Extracts from Government Letters Regarding arrest of Soldiers

Subjects – Report of the Arrest of Soldiers Charged with the Commission of Criminal Offences Copy of the letter No.31/49-Judl dated the 27th January, 1949 from the Ministry of Home Affairs to all Provincial Governments.

I am directed to request that, if the State Government/you have no objection, necessary instructions may be issued to the District Magistrates requesting that when a person subject to the Military, Naval or Air force law is arrested by police and charged with the commission of any offence as early intimation as possible of his arrest is sent to the Officer Commanding the Unit of Regiment to which the man arrested belongs. The District Magistrate should also be instructed to forward to the Officer Commanding, if asked for, prompt reports of the result of trials and copies of judgments.

Subject – Report of the Arrest of Soldiers charged for the Commission of Criminal Offences.

1. Home Departament Circular letter Nos. 11-1001 to 11-1009 dated the 6th August, 1974.
2. Home Department Circular letter No. F.709/29-Judl. dated 13th August, 1929.

I am directed to invite attention to the following circular letters of the late Home department (copies enclosed) and to say that some instances have occurred in which the instructions contained therein were not followed. It is, therefore, requested that if the Provincial government see no objection/ be asked to send the report of the arrest by the police of any Indian Military personnel to the Officer Commanding of the regiment to which the person belongs, immediately after arrest and to maintain close cooperation in such matters between the Military and Civil authorities.

Subject – Report of the Arrest of Soldiers charged with the Commission of Criminal offences. Copy of Ministry of Home Affairs Letter No. F.9/7/60-Judl.II dated.

Index